BANDWIDTH RECOVERY FOR SCHOOLS

BANDWIDTH RECOVERY FOR SCHOOLS

Helping Pre-K–12 Students Regain Cognitive Resources Lost to Poverty, Trauma, Racism, and Social Marginalization

Cia Verschelden

Foreword by Kofi Lomotey

STERLING, VIRGINIA

Published by Stylus Publishing, LLC.
22883 Quicksilver Drive
Sterling, Virginia 20166-2019

Library of Congress Cataloging-in-Publication Data
Names: Verschelden, Cia, 1955- author.
Title: Bandwidth recovery for schools : helping Pre-K-12 students regain
   cognitive resources lost to poverty, trauma, racism, and social
   marginalization / Cia Verschelden ; Foreword by Kofi Lomotey.
Description: First edition. | Sterling, Virginia : Stylus, [2020] |
   Includes bibliographical references and index. |
Identifiers: LCCN 2020043519 | ISBN 9781642670776
   (paperback) | ISBN
   9781642670769 (hardback) | ISBN 9781642670783 (pdf) |
   ISBN 9781642670790 (epub)
Subjects: LCSH: Education--Aims and objectives--United States. |
   Educational equalization--United States. | Racism in education-
   -United States. | Poor--Education--United States. | Marginality,
   Social--United States.
Classification: LCC LA217.2 .V47 2020 | DDC 370.1--dc23
LC record available at https://lccn.loc.gov/2020043519

13-digit ISBN: 978-1-64267-076-9 (cloth)
13-digit ISBN: 978-1-64267-077-6 (paperback)
13-digit ISBN: 978-1-64267-078-3 (library networkable e-edition)
13-digit ISBN: 978-1-64267-079-0 (consumer e-edition)

Printed in the United States of America

All first editions printed on acid-free paper
that meets the American National Standards Institute
Z39-48 Standard.

Bulk Purchases

Quantity discounts are available for use in workshops and for staff development.

Call 1-800-232-0223

First Edition, 2021

For all schoolchildren and youth, who ask so little of us—
just to be safe and loved so they can learn, grow, and realize
the promise of a life well lived.

CONTENTS

FOREWORD

I have been concerned for some time with the quality of education in U.S. public (and private) schools. More specifically, I have explored, through many routes, the overwhelmingly negative experiences of Black children in these schools (Lomotey, 1990). This quagmire is so complex that fingers can legitimately be pointed in several directions and at numerous constituency groups. School administrators have a role to play in the creation and perpetuation of this crisis; teachers certainly share some responsibility; parents could also do a better job; and students, themselves, are not always at their best. Indeed, society at large plays a role in the disenfranchisement of millions of children of Black, Latinx, Asian American, and Indigenous heritage in U.S. schools. Certainly, the federal government, state and local governments, and the local communities from which these children come share in bringing about the limited success of many students in these groups.

This is not, of course, a new phenomenon; indeed, it has been a challenge since students in these groups were first enrolled in U.S. schools. Much has been written focusing on the responsibility of each of these constituencies in bringing about and in remedying this educational crisis (Gay, in press; Milner, 2015; Noguera & Alicea, in press). It is a truism that the most important relationship in this situation is that which occurs between the student and the teacher; this is where the "rubber meets the road." However, my focus over the years has been on the importance of principals in bringing about student success in school (Lomotey, 1987, 2019). In particular, I have talked about principals (a) having confidence in the ability of all children to be successful; (b) having compassion for all children, their families, and their communities; and (c) being committed to the success of all children (Lomotey, 1993). Others, of course, have looked at the importance of other constituency groups in providing quality education for children of Black, Latinx, Asian American, and Indigenous backgrounds (Foster, 1997; Winn, 2018).

Often book titles do not direct the reader to the content of the book. That is, the reader cannot always determine from a book's title what the book is really about; this is not the case with Cia Verschelden's book. This book is about recovering the bandwidth of parents; teachers; administrators; and, most importantly, students in pre-K–12 schools. *Bandwidth* is the capacity for individuals to capitalize on their cognitive resources to think, learn, act, and develop. In other words, it is the wherewithal to full intellectual development and the ability to navigate life. Verschelden—in a profound, articulate, clear, and resolute manner—has provided a description of the challenges we face in U.S. education, and she offers valuable insights into how we can address these challenges. She discusses the role of parents, teachers, administrators, and students.

The bandwidth of many youths is stifled, Verschelden contends, as a result of the impact of poverty, trauma, racism, and social marginalization. She refers to these factors as *bandwidth stealers*. Additional examples are other forms of oppression, including those based on mental and physical illnesses. Full access to one's bandwidth is necessary, Verschelden says, in order to achieve one's full potential. Extending this notion of bandwidth, a bandwidth tax is imposed by these factors—such as racism and poverty—limiting the ability of portions of the brain to function and facilitate intellectual growth; they limit the development of the brain.

Verschelden highlights the impact of bandwidth constraints, particularly for poorer children, illustrating that poorer children are more likely to experience exposure to toxins, substandard housing, mental illness, and food insecurity. All of these factors, she argues, contribute to a bandwidth tax. She emphasizes that there is much research documenting the impact of poverty on children. She contends that other factors contribute to a reduction in bandwidth including class consciousness; racial desegregation; feelings of not belonging; immigrant status (and the uncertainty associated with it); lesbian, bisexual, gay, transgender, queer, and questioning (LBGTQQ) status; and stereotype threat (fearing success because of what people think of your group). Verschelden also discusses the impact of bullying and microaggressions on one's bandwidth.

Although Verschelden's focus is on the success of marginalized[1] children, she acknowledges the reduced bandwidth of teachers, administrators, and parents, arguing that in order to aid children—in order to help them recover their lost bandwidth—we must first recover the lost bandwidth of parents, teachers, and administrators.

Verschelden tells us why marginalized students have heretofore been unsuccessful in schools. She then discusses the significance of parents and teachers in this dilemma. She moves to a discussion of what, in fact, can bring about the success of these children, before sharing an instructive case study of the city of Rochester, New York, and selected schools therein. Finally, she offers advice for principals and superintendents before summarizing and contextualizing her discussion right smack in the middle of the COVID-19 pandemic.

An underlying theme running through this book relates to the historical and contemporary impact of race and racism in U.S. society. Verschelden says at one point, "We (humans) have made a mess of things, holding on to racism for centuries, so that we find ourselves, in 2020, living in a country where millions of children are denied a chance to truly thrive at school" (p. 50, this volume).

In discussing bandwidth shrinkage for parents, Verschelden provides a clear discussion of challenges that many parents face, emphasizing that their bandwidth loss contributes directly to the bandwidth loss that their children experience. Relatedly, she points out that teachers suffer bandwidth loss largely as a result of insufficiently funded schools, low teacher salaries, and a focus on high-stakes testing—again, negatively impacting the bandwidth loss of children.

Verschelden clearly illustrates the importance of several factors that can positively impact the potential for success for all children; these include (a) assets-based versus deficit-based attitudes, (b) acknowledgment of their funds of knowledge (every child brings something to the table), (c) the ungendering of schools and classrooms, (d) a culturally responsive education, (e) respect, (f) acknowledgment of the legitimacy of dialects, (g) a feeling of belonging, and (h) a sense of certainty in their lives.

U.S. schools are not currently designed to work for many marginalized students; to be blunt, they only work for a few students. Indeed, this book is about the future of U.S. public schools, our children, and our nation. It is about creating educational environs wherein all children can be successful. And Verschelden reminds us that —as currently constructed— schools are not capable of doing this. Verschelden's message is one of extreme optimism—a critical need given our current circumstances. All of our children have such tremendous qualities and strengths; we just need to acknowledge them and (enable students to) take advantage of them.

Cia Verschelden has prepared a volume that is pregnant with relevance for parents, students, teachers, school leaders, political leaders, and community persons. We can help families, communities, schools, and the larger society and ultimately improve the life chances of all children—by creating an environment wherein they can utilize all of their bandwidth; Verschelden has provided a roadmap in order for us to do that.

Kofi Lomotey
Western Carolina University

Note

1. In her use of the term *marginalized,* Verschelden is referring to not only people from Black, Latinx, Asian American, and Indigenous communities but also differently abled and LBGTQQ students.

References

Foster, M. (1997). *Black teachers on teaching*. The New Press.

Gay, G. (in press). Culturally responsive teaching: Ideas, actions, and effects. In H. R. Milner & K. Lomotey (Eds.) *Handbook of urban education* (2nd ed.). Routledge.

Lomotey, K. (1987). Black principals for Black students: Some preliminary observations. *Urban Education, 22*(2), 173–181. https://doi.org/10.1177/004208598702200203

Lomotey, K. (Ed.) (1990). *Going to school: The African-American experience*. State University of New York Press.

Lomotey, K. (1993). African American principals: Bureaucrat/administrators and ethno-humanists. *Urban Education, 27*(4), 395–412. https://doi.org/10.1177%2F0042085993027004005

Lomotey, K. (2019). Research on the leadership of Black women principals: Implications for Black students. *Educational Researcher, 48*(6), 336–348. https://doi.org/10.3102/0013189X19858619

Milner, H. R. IV. (2015). *Rac(e)ing to class: Confronting poverty and race in schools and classrooms*. Harvard Education Press.

Noguera., P. A., & Alicea, J. A. (in press). The role of education in reducing racial inequality: Possibilities for change. In H. R. Milner & K. Lomotey (Eds.) *Handbook of urban education* (2nd ed.). Routledge.

Winn, M. T. (2018). *Justice on both sides: Transforming education through restorative justice*. Harvard Education Press.

ACKNOWLEDGMENTS

John von Knorring, at Stylus Publishing, and Emma Mercier, an early childhood educator, read the manuscript at least twice through and offered invaluable insights on its development. Thanks to Stylus Publishing for permission to reprint images in the introduction from *Bandwidth Recovery: Helping Students Reclaim Cognitive Resources Lost to Poverty, Racism, and Social Marginalization* (Verschelden, 2017). Mercier also provided several practice ideas from her work with young children in New Zealand. Margaret Martelle and Mary Anne Martin, long-time elementary school teachers, also read the manuscript and gave me affirmation and ideas. Emma Forbes-Jones and Steve Damarjian advised me on some vocabulary and technical issues. I was inspired by the work Shaun Nelms and his colleagues are doing in Rochester, New York, and that work became the focus of the case study in chapter 17. John Strazzabosco met with me to discuss his writing about students living in poverty in the Rochester area. Several people also generously contributed wisdom from their practice as teachers and school leaders: Karen Sáenz, Chuck Pearson, Julie Landsman, Sandy Kent, Sonya Hernandez, Jim Edminster, Jennifer Bronski, and Christopher Alas. Thanks to all of you for your engagement in this vital conversation about creating learning environments where all students can thrive.

This book is about the future of public schools and the children whose lives are so significantly shaped by the experiences they have there. If you are a teacher or school leader or parent, please read it. This is not about blaming or shaming, but about understanding the urgent need to reframe our practices so that all children and youth (and their teachers and parents) can learn and thrive.

Here is the basic premise: Each of us has a finite amount of mental bandwidth, the cognitive resources that are available for learning, growing, working, taking care of our families, relating to friends, and so on. Some people call these *attentional resources*; this is not about how smart we are but about how much of our brain power is available to us for the tasks at hand. When our bandwidth is taken up by the stress of persistent economic insecurity or if we often experience the negativity that comes with racism, classism, homophobia, religious intolerance, ableism, and other "differentisms," there is less available for learning and developing. This is true for not only young children and youth but also their parents and teachers.

My mom says I cried every morning for the first week of kindergarten. I grew up in a very small Kansas town and went to Catholic school for first through eighth grades. The kindergarten was at the small public school on the hill. I suppose I was just afraid of the new environment as my siblings and I had never been to preschool or any other type of group learning before. We were home with my parents, upstairs from the family-owned funeral business, with both parents around to take care of us. After the first week of kindergarten, I was apparently fine. For first grade, I had Sister Catherine Marie, a lovely, gentle nun, barely taller than her young charges. Grade school was mostly good for me—a time of recess and friends and learning. I can still remember the plump, warm hand of Mrs. Perry, our fourth-grade teacher, who cared for us like her own children, and the lessons we learned from the nuns and the Jesuit priests who had a seminary in our little town. Even as a child, I realized how privileged I was to have loving parents, to be growing up in a safe and secure home, and to have inherited what seemed to be natural school-smarts. I knew that some of my friends did not have the advantages I had and that this would impact them throughout their lives. So much of a child's foundation is set in their preschool and elementary school years;

when those years are fraught with stress and struggle, life chances are often seriously diminished.

There is much concern today about the decreasing ability of public pre-K–12 schools to educate all children and youth effectively for college and career. Although economically secure White students often go to excellent schools that are well resourced, low-income, poor, and Black and Brown children, in increasing numbers, are going to high-poverty, underresourced, poor-performing, majority-minority schools (Boschma & Brownstein, 2016; EdBuild, n.d.; National Center for Education Statistics, 2019a, 2019b) thus increasing a still-growing and historically high inequality (Kochhar & Cilluffo, 2017). Among nonmajority and poor and near-poor children, educational outcomes are disappointing and, whereas more of these students are going to college, fewer are graduating (Shapiro et al., 2017).

There is no shortage of ideas about who is to blame for this situation—unmotivated kids, uninvolved parents, and ineffective teachers—however blaming each other does not seem to be particularly useful, and it might even keep us from getting together and addressing the challenges that really matter. In my view, kids, parents, and teachers want what all of us want—to have their basic needs met and live happy and fulfilling lives. We all need food and shelter; to feel safe and loved; to be appreciated and affirmed for our knowledge and skills; to be given honest feedback and guidance so we can learn and grow; and to be able to bring our true selves—including all our identities—to school, work, and life.

In the United States today, thankfully, there are millions of kids, parents, and teachers who have most of these basic needs because they have access to and work in well-resourced private and public early-learning centers and schools where there is respect and acceptance for all the stakeholders in the education and positive development of the young minds of children and adolescents. Unfortunately, there are more millions of kids, parents, and teachers who, because of poverty and economic insecurity, racism, xenophobia, classism, homophobia and transphobia, and other kinds of "differentisms," live and work in poor neighborhoods that have severely underresourced early-learning centers (if any) and schools where everyone and everything is stressed out and stretched to the limit. Parents work many hours a week to meet the basic needs of their families and, therefore, sometimes have very little time to devote to supporting their children's schoolwork.

Schools are inadequately staffed and facilities and materials are scarce, pushing teachers to spend their inadequate pay on school supplies for their classrooms and food for their hungry students. Kids attend school in buildings that are crumbling and use outdated materials and hand-me-down textbooks salvaged from schools that have the funds to buy new ones. Classrooms have many more students per teacher than is recommended, resulting in individual children not receiving the attention they need for learning and development.

Under these circumstances, children are being deprived of the opportunity to use their hearts and minds to grow and develop and apply their knowledge and skills to build a better life for themselves and a better society. In fact, we are squandering the brain power of millions of children every year through the neglect of foundational care and education of our infants, toddlers, children, and adolescents.

How is this? The idea is related to *mental bandwidth*. Let me explain. As you sit reading this book, your brain is busy with about 11 million bits of activity per second. Of those 11 million bits, you have conscious control over fewer than 100 (Chaiken & Trope, 1999). It is this conscious mental activity that I am calling *bandwidth*. Bandwidth can also be described as the cognitive resources you have available to listen, learn, make choices, manage relationships, and everything else. We might call them *attentional resources* because they represent the part of your brain that you can use to pay attention, learn, and respond. If all of your cognitive resources were available to you, you would have full bandwidth (represented by the graphic of the brain in Figure I.1), and all of your cognitive resources could be completely focused on reading. Your mind would be open to the words and ideas and you would be thinking about, analyzing, categorizing, and storing the information for later recall.

Figure I.1. Full bandwidth.

However, imagine you are reading this book but you are also wondering if your child is fitting in at school or about what your father found out from the doctor today or about how you are going to get done all the things you have to do before the week is out. Not all of your bandwidth is available for processing what you are reading. The concept I will talk about in the first part of the book is that bandwidth is depleted every day for people who are living in poverty or persistent economic insecurity or who are dealing with other people's behavior related to racism, classism, homophobia, xenophobia, and other social phenomena that marginalize people based on someone's idea of "different." When people have depleted bandwidth, they lack enough cognitive resources to learn well, work efficiently and competently, make good choices, form and maintain healthy relationships, and so on. This happens to babies and toddlers, young children, adolescents, parents, and teachers and school leaders and threatens the learning and growth of all of them.

Let us start with poverty and economic insecurity. In their book *Scarcity*, Mullainathan and Shafir (2013) argued that scarcity steals mental capacity. They write about how cognitive resources are taken up by worrying about money and the necessities money buys. They point out that, at least in the United States, we usually blame people for being poor. We say they are poor because they make bad decisions. However, from a bandwidth perspective, Mullainathan and Shafir explain that the condition of being poor *causes* people to make bad decisions (especially in environments that encourage bad decisions, like payday loans and subprime mortgage deals). When you are poor, money is always on your mind, causing you to worry that your car will break down, your child will get sick, you will not have a safe place to live, or you won't be able to provide nutritious food for yourself and your family. So, instead of all your bandwidth being available, like in Figure I.1, your brain looks more like the one in Figure I.2. (These are not anatomical or proportional representations. They are used to show the effects of bandwidth taxes.)

Figure I.2. Depleted bandwidth.

Note. This figures showcases bandwidth deleted by poverty or consistent economic security.

Even very young children can understand money stress. They pick up on the fact that they do not have clothes or shoes as nice as the other kids or that their school lunches from home are sandwiches made of butter and sugar on white bread when the other kids bring meat on whole grain bread. They are certainly aware that their neighborhood is not safe or that they have lost their apartment and are staying with friends. Their understanding gets more sophisticated as they mature, and this worry about money increases throughout childhood. If part of their mind always focuses on those worries, they will have less bandwidth available for learning in school.

Other major bandwidth stealers are what I call *social-psychological underminers* that are related to racism, classism, xenophobia, homophobia, transphobia, ableism, ageism, and other phenomena that result in people who are members of certain groups (or appear to be) being discriminated against, treated unkindly, ignored, left out, and made to suffer frequent indignities due to nothing other than a group identity (real or perceived group). These underminers deplete bandwidth so that the people who experience them operate with limited available cognitive resources (as illustrated in Figure I.3).

Figure I.3. Further bandwidth depletion.

Note. This figures showcases further bandwidth deletion by underminers.

Chronic or frequent mental or physical illness are other conditions that deplete bandwidth. Children and adults who have physical, mental, or cognitive disabilities expend some of their cognitive resources dealing with it. Although the acceptance of people who are differently abled has increased over the years, there is still significant misunderstanding and negative judgment about people with these conditions. Even if a person is in a supportive social environment, the challenges posed by a disability of any kind must, by definition, take up some bandwidth. So, instead of the full complement of

Figure I.4. Greatly diminished, compounded bandwidth.

Note. This figures showcases limited bandwidth as a result of compounding physical, mental, or cognitive disabling conditions in addition to those demands previously discussed.

available cognitive resources, people are operating with limited bandwidth (as illustrated in Figure I.4)

Due to the historical realities of discrimination and economic inequality based on group membership in the United States, people who are non-White; non-U.S.-born; disabled (Semega et al., 2019); or lesbian, gay, bisexual, transgender, or queer (LGBTQ; Jagannathan, 2019) are more likely to live in poverty or in persistent economic insecurity. Thus, we have *intersectionality*, a situation in which people experience multiple underminers that result in exponential bandwidth depletion. We can have the best teachers and the most well-intentioned school leaders, but if students are coming to school with only a small fraction of their mental bandwidth available for learning, they will not be able to learn and thrive.

In order for children and their parents to learn and meet their full potential, they need to have access to all of their bandwidth. This is not about how "smart" someone is, it is about what part of those "smarts" are available to apply to the situation, in school, at work, in a family, and so on. I think we can all agree that we have serious problems to solve in this country and around the world related to the physical environment, international relations, health and health care, well-being for humans and other living things, and many other challenges. We need the collective brain power of all our growing children, who will be our leaders, scientists, teachers, organizers—the problem-solvers of our collective future.

This book is for teachers, parents, school leaders, and members of communities who are interested in the well-being of children and youth and the education of all our children. All of us have a stake in a public school system from which children, from pre-K through high school, emerge as fully formed learners and thinkers and who believe in their ability to affect what happens to them and their communities.

In Parts One and Two, I explain how the mental bandwidth of students, and of their parents and teachers, is depleted by persistent economic insecurity and social-psychological underminers that are the consequences of racism, classism, homophobia, and other "differentisms." In Parts Three and Four, I present ideas on the ways students, parents, and teachers can recover bandwidth, focusing on public pre-K–12 schools. All the interventions and concepts are sure to be equally applicable in privately funded school settings. I focus on public schools because they are what the majority of students attend; in fall 2016, 50.6 million elementary and high school students went to public school in the United States, whereas the comparable figure for private schools was 5.8 million in 2015 (U.S. Department of Education, 2019).

What is important about what goes on in public pre-K–12 education? First, what happens in public education reflects the priorities and choices of state and local governmental bodies, which in turn reflect—or should in a democratic system—the wishes of the people. Thus, the quality of education of our children directly affects future decisions about education and many other social and economic issues going forward. The sustainability of our systems of governance, law, and society rests on our ability to provide educational environments within which children can learn and develop, preparing them to be workers and leaders when they are adults.

PART ONE

BANDWIDTH
STEALERS—STUDENTS

I

POVERTY

Child poverty is associated with lifelong hardship.

—*Pascoe et al. (2016, p. 2)*

Poverty and consistent economic insecurity rob children of mental bandwidth. Mullainathan and Shafir (2013) wrote about the "bandwidth tax" (p. 14) of poverty. Reflecting on their work, Ryan Bell (2017) talked about how poverty kills wonder. He asserted, "Wonder is the fire beneath curiosity, driving humanity to discovery" (p. 16); if poor children do not experience wonder, what will happen to their learning? Shafir, in a conversation with Bell (2017), "emphasized that nothing in his findings suggests that the poor are any less emotionally awake or that there is anything mentally different or fundamentally deficient about them" (p. 18). Bell pointed out, "Wonder . . . is an experience that happens to an available mind" (p. 19). That is a perfect description of the problem with the bandwidth depletion that results from poverty. Parts of children's minds are not available for wonder and for learning.

Mathewson's (2017) research tells us that people in poverty "are constantly struggling to make ends meet and often bracing themselves against class bias that adds extra strain or even trauma to their daily lives" (para. 3). Mathewson continues, saying, "The science is clear—when brain capacity is used up on these worries and fears, there simply is not as much bandwidth for other things" (para. 4). Fortunately, these damaged parts of the brain are ones that are "particularly plastic" (para. 9) and can be strengthened and improved well into adulthood, which is why it is critical to nurture children in school (Mathewson, 2017). That is the hope for educators of children and youth.

What is the extent of child poverty in the United States? According to the National Center for Children in Poverty (Koball & Jiang, 2018), in 2016, of the 72.4 million children under the age of 18, 41% lived in low-income families. Of those, 22% were near-poor, considered between 100% and 200% of the Federal Poverty Threshold (FPT) and 19% were poor (under 100% of the FPT). Research indicates that an income of 200% of the FPT is necessary to meet basic human needs (Cauthen & Fass, 2008). According to the NCCP (2018), a Columbia University research center, "Poverty is the single biggest threat to children's healthy development" (para. 1). Children are much more likely to be poor than people in other age groups. Compared to the 41% of children who are poor or near-poor, 29% of people between 19 and 64 and 28% of people 65 or over are in these categories (Koball & Jiang, 2018). Except for Asians as a group, non-White children are far more likely to live in low-income families than White children; the rate for White and Asian children was 28% in 2016, whereas the comparable rates for Black, American Indian, and Hispanic children were 61%, 60%, and 59%, respectively (Koball & Jiang, 2018). (The data on poverty among Asian groups can be very misleading; 12.3% of Asians live below the FPT, with wide variation among different national origin groups. At the low end, fewer than 7% of Filipino Americans live in poverty, whereas 39% of Burmese Americans live in poverty; see Tran, 2018). Parent educational level is highly correlated with family low-income status; of families in which the parents have not completed high school 82% of the children are low-income and 50% are poor. These rates are 65% and 32% when parents have a high school diploma, and 28% and 11% when they have some college (Koball & Jiang, 2018). The undereducation of children maintains the cycle of poverty and near-poverty when those children become parents. This leads us to ask about the barriers that keep children from succeeding in school.

There is ample research that demonstrates the cost of poverty on children's brain development. Babcock (2018) asserted that brain science

> tells us that poverty affects human behavior and decision-making in profound and predictable ways that often make it harder for those trapped at the bottom of the income scale to get ahead. Stress caused by poverty, trauma, and oppression fundamentally changes how our brains develop and work throughout our lives. The two brain areas most measurably affected by poverty are the prefrontal cortex, which governs executive functioning, including the ability to focus, resist temptations, analyze problems, and achieve goals, and the limbic brain, which assesses environmental threats and governs "fight or flight" responses. Exposed to enough stress, the prefrontal cortex finds fewer opportunities to practice and therefore build executive function skills, and the limbic brain becomes hypervigilant, constantly ready to respond to perceived threats. (p. 1)

The limbic system controls the process of sending fear and stress signals to the prefrontal cortex, so when a person lives in persistent economic insecurity, those messages can overwhelm the capacity of the prefrontal cortex to solve problems, set goals, complete tasks, and make sound decisions. These tasks come under the rubric of "executive function," which includes the abilities to plan, focus attention, remember, and control impulses. To do these things well and consistently, three brain functions are involved—"working memory, mental flexibility, and self-control" (Harvard University Center on the Developing Child, n.d., para. 3). According to the Center on the Developing Child at Harvard University,

> Children aren't born with these skills—they are born with the potential to develop them. If children do not get what they need from their relationships with adults and the conditions in their environments—or (worse) if those influences are sources of toxic stress—their skill development can be seriously delayed or impaired. Adverse environments resulting from neglect, abuse, and/or violence may expose children to toxic stress, which disrupts brain architecture and impairs the development of executive function. (para. 5)

The many and persistent stresses of being poor rob children of the bandwidth they need to learn in school and in life. Among the causes of stress are physical and mental illness, both of which occur disproportionately among people who live in low-income and poor households. In the United States, there is a consistent and strong correlation between socioeconomic status and health, both physical and mental.

> The single strongest predictor of our health is our position on the class pyramid. Whether measured by income, schooling, or occupation, those at the top have the most power and resources and on average live longer and healthier lives. Those at the bottom are most disempowered and get sicker and die younger. (California Newsreel, 2008b, para. 2)

There are ample data to illustrate this statement. In this chapter, I will give a few examples that focus on children and youth and how illness of a parent or grandparent may mean significant stress for the entire family. Poor health in children is an even greater threat than in adults because health is cumulative; ill health in childhood can affect health over the lifespan. According to a study by the Council on Community Pediatrics (Pascoe et al., 2016),

Poverty and related social determinants of health can lead to adverse health outcomes in childhood and across the life course, negatively affecting physical health, socioemotional development, and educational achievement. Poverty has a profound effect on specific circumstances, such as birth weight, infant mortality, language development, chronic illness, environmental exposure, nutrition, and injury. (p. 1)

In the United States, poor children are "more likely to experience conditions that limit their health and ultimately their life chances: injuries, inadequate or delayed health care, physical inactivity, poor nutrition, insecure or substandard housing, and exposure to toxins, high lead levels and violence" (California Newsreel, 2008a, para. 6). Poor children are three times more likely than other children to have unmet health needs (United Health Foundation, 2016). Toxic stress, called "a biology of misfortune" (Boyce, 2012, p. 6), causes serious and cumulative health problems for children that affect lifetime health and quality of life (Pascoe et al., 2016). The inequities that children who grow up in low-income and poor families experience are too numerous to list comprehensively. Compared to their peers in economically secure families, these children are exposed to more violence; experience more separation from family, housing instability, and multiple moves; are more likely to live with divorced or separated parents; have a higher death rate from unintentional injury; and live in families that experience more intimate partner violence, maternal depression, and parental substance abuse (Pascoe et al., 2016), just to name a few.

In regard to correlation with persistent economic insecurity, the story of mental illness is the same. Poorer people are more likely to suffer from mental illness than people who are economically secure. "Mental health problems in childhood can lead to reduced life chances by disrupting education and limiting attainment, impacting social participation and reducing the ability to find and sustain employment—particularly work that provides for an adequate standard of living" (Elliott, 2016, p. 23). We need to pay attention to the mental health of children as half of mental health problems start by age 14 and three quarters by age 24 (National Alliance on Mental Illness, n.d.).

According to the 2011–2012 National Survey of Children's Health (Bitsko et al., 2016), 14% of children aged 2 years to 8 years "were reported to have a diagnosed mental, behavioral, or developmental disorder" (p. 1). Poverty was an important factor, along with other demographic and social factors (Figure 1.1). According to Zero to Three (2017),

Young children who live in families dealing with parental loss, substance abuse, mental illness, or exposure to trauma are at heightened risk of

developing IECMH [Infant and Early Childhood Mental Health] disorders (Felitti et al., 1998). And the stressors of poverty can multiply these
risks. If untreated, IECMH disorders can have detrimental effects on every
aspect of a child's development (i.e., physical, cognitive, communication,
sensory, emotional, social, and motor skills) and the child's ability to succeed in school and in life. (p. 2)

As depicted in Figure 1.1, child gender, age, income level, and primary language are key indicators of mental illness diagnoses. It is interesting that race
and ethnicity do not strongly predict mental health diagnoses. This may be due
to factors other than the actual occurrence of mental health issues in non-White
children. According to McGuire and Miranda (2008), research on the prevalence of mental illness indicates that non-White people have about the same or
lower incidence of mental illness as White people. However, disparities appear in
the access to, use of, and quality of mental health care. A variety of studies have
shown that, compared to Whites, non-White people have less access to care, are
less likely to use services, are more likely to delay use, receive lower quality care
when they do engage, and are more likely to terminate treatment prematurely.
So there may be a situation of underreporting of mental health challenges in
non-White children. Whatever the case, the incidences of mental health struggles among our youngest children suggest that the effective recognition and
treatment of these disorders is critical to overall positive child development.

Figure 1.1.   Factors in disorders among young children.

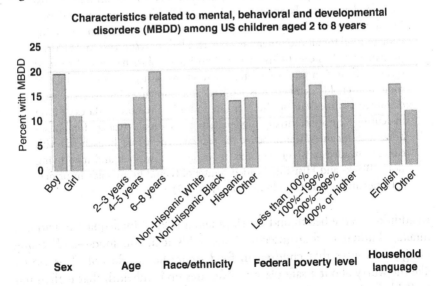

Note: From Bitsko et al., 2016.

Two major stresses that may affect children living in low-income and poor families are housing and food insecurity. "The Department of Health and Human Services has defined *housing insecurity* as high housing costs in proportion to income, poor housing quality, unstable neighborhoods, overcrowding, or homelessness" (Cutts et al., 2011, p. 1508, emphasis added). According to a study by Cutts et al. (2011) of over 22,000 low-income caregivers of children younger than 3 years old, housing insecurity was associated with poor health, lower weight, and developmental risk in the children. Their data showed that crowding was associated with both food insecurity and multiple moves, which were in turn associated with poor child health, developmental risk, and lower child weights. Housing insecurity, a problem for many low-income people, disproportionately affects Black and Hispanic households. For instance, in 2005, close to 11% of Black people in the United States, 9% of Hispanics, and only 4.4% of White people lived in severely or moderately substandard housing (Jacobs, 2011). In 2010, seven times the number of Black family members as White family members used homeless shelters (Nunez, 2012). In addition to physical health risks, the worry about not being sure of a safe place to live takes up significant mental bandwidth for children and adolescents in low-income and poor families. Housing insecurity often comes hand-in-hand with food insecurity, where we also see disparities across racial and ethnic groups.

According to a United States Department of Agriculture report (Coleman-Jensen et al., 2017),

In 2016 . . . 12.3 percent of U. S. households (15.6 million households) were food insecure. Food-insecure households (those with low and very low food security) had difficulty at some time during the year providing enough food for all their members due to a lack of resources. In 2016, 4.9 percent of U.S. households (6.1 million households) had very low food security. In this more severe range of food insecurity, the food intake of some household members was reduced and normal eating patterns were disrupted at times during the year due to limited resources. Rates of food insecurity were substantially higher than the national average for households with incomes near or below the federal poverty line, households with children headed by single women or single men, women and men living alone, Black- and Hispanic-headed households, and households in principal cities and nonmetropolitan areas. (pp. 1–2)

In addition to the health and developmental risks of inadequate nutritional intake, children in food-insecure households focus on food—and feeling hungry—in ways that children in food-secure homes do not. This worry, like the worry about a safe place to live, uses up bandwidth that is then not available for learning. You begin to see how the bandwidth stealers related to economic insecurity pile up for a child or young person trying to succeed in school. In addition, the disparities in the distribution of housing and food insecurity result in a far greater burden on non-White children (who also experience the negative effects of racism and classism).

Another set of factors that negatively and disproportionately affect low-income and non-White families is related to the physical environment in which families live. The following studies illustrate the consistent pattern of disparity. One study (Katz, 2012) found,

> Tiny particles of air pollution contain more hazardous ingredients in non-white and low-income communities than in affluent white ones. . . .

> The greater the concentration of Hispanics, Asians, African Americans or poor residents in an area, the more likely that potentially dangerous compounds such as vanadium, nitrates and zinc are in the mix of fine particles they breathe.

> Latinos had the highest exposures to the largest number of these ingredients, while whites generally had the lowest. (para. 1–3)

How does this make sense? Katz went on to explain:

> It's a common scenario in cities nationwide: Due to high housing costs and historical discrimination, low-income and minority neighborhoods are clustered around industrial sites, truck routes, ports and other air pollution hotspots. (para. 19)

Many of these pollutants in the air have been shown to be significantly related to incidents of asthma, cancer, and cardiovascular problems (Katz, 2012). Disparities in exposure to pollution-related health risk is an outcome of environmental racism; "hazardous industries are routinely located closer to minority neighborhoods than white ones" (Witt, 2007, para. 7). Witt went on to explain the pattern:

> The presence of such industrial sites in a neighborhood sharply depresses residential property values, which attracts families earning the lowest incomes. And the presence of low-income families, many of them minorities who often lack political clout, in turn makes it easier for hazardous industries to locate or expand nearby without opposition. (para. 14)

It is easy to understand how this level of disparity happens and how, like racism and economic inequality, the patterns are not easy to interrupt without strong legislation and the political and economic will of a majority of citizens in cities, states, and at the federal level.

The consequences for the lived experiences of people in these polluted neighborhoods go beyond increases in physical illness. If air pollution keeps people in their homes to decrease exposure, they do not get the physical and mental benefits of exercise; they may experience greater degrees of social isolation; and there is less chance for people to congregate in public, outdoor spaces where they might form coalitions for collective action and mutual support. To quote from "Unnatural Causes," related to individual behaviors that do not support good health, "The choices we make are shaped by the choices we have" (California Newsreel, 2008b, para. 4).

The realities of racial segregation exacerbate social, educational, and health challenges, especially for Blacks in the United States. Black people in the United States are the most likely of any group to live in segregated neighborhoods. Although there is nothing inherently damaging about Black people living with mostly other Black people, it is the conditions within those concentrations that can be debilitating to the health and development of Black children. In trying to understand the relationship between segregation and disadvantage, Boustan (2013) suggested that "the association between segregated environments and minority disadvantage is driven in part by physical isolation of black neighborhoods from employment opportunities and in part by harmful social interactions within black neighborhoods, especially due to concentrated poverty" (p. 1).

How has racial segregation in neighborhoods played out in segregation in K–12 schools in the United States? More than 60 years after the Supreme Court declared in *Brown v. Board of Education* (1954) that separate was inherently not equal, do our schools reflect the implications of the decision that children are better off in integrated schools? Unfortunately for Black and Hispanic students, schools are still very segregated. Indeed, some areas have been resegregated since 1990, undoing post-*Brown* progress. The population of schoolchildren is more diverse than ever. In 2016, only 52% of K–12 5- to 17-year-olds were White (Musu-Gillette et al., 2017), but schools are segregated, especially for Black and Hispanic students. Even though Hispanic people are less likely than Blacks to experience neighborhood segregation, their children are more likely to go to segregated schools (Lewis & Cantor, 2016; see Table 1.1).

Schools in which 1% or fewer of the students are White, also termed *apartheid schools*, are most prevalent in certain cities: 50% of Black students in Chicago and 33% in New York attend apartheid schools whereas 30% of the Hispanic students in the Los Angeles metro area attend such schools

TABLE 1.1
Hispanic and Black School Attendance: Race and Income

	50% or More Non-White (2009)[a]	*Fewer Than 10% White (2009)[a]*	*At Least 75% of Students Qualified for Free and Reduced-Price Lunch (Fall 2016)[b]*	*1% or Fewer White (2009)[a]*
Hispanic	80%	43%	45%	15%
Black	74%	38%	44% (8% White)	14%

[a]Orfield et al. (2012).
[b]National Center for Education Statistics. (2019a).

(Orfield et al., 2012). In their Civil Rights Project report, Orfield et al. (2012) concluded:

> The consensus of nearly sixty years of social science research on the harms of school segregation is clear: separate remains extremely unequal. Schools of concentrated poverty and segregated minority schools are strongly related to an array of factors that limit educational opportunities and outcomes. These include less experienced and less qualified teachers, high levels of teacher turnover, less successful peer groups and inadequate facilities and learning materials. There is also a mounting body of evidence indicating that desegregated schools are linked to important benefits for all children, including prejudice reduction, heightened civic engagement, more complex thinking and better learning outcomes in general. (para. 5)

In my research on the deleterious effects of poverty on children and youth, I realized that, sadly, the findings could fill an entire book; for example, see Strazzabosco's (2018) *Ninety Feet Under* and Jensen's (2009) *Teaching With Poverty in Mind.* Because persistent economic insecurity is correlated with so many negative health and social factors, it is unsurprising that children who experience this kind of scarcity are at a distinct disadvantage in terms of available mental bandwidth to succeed in school. Other dynamics that affect the lived experience of poor and low-income children and youth include being left alone at home while parents work (sometimes two or three jobs); being responsible at an early age for the care of younger children or other family members; inadequate supervision; lack of access to school supplies, books, and other learning resources; fear of losing a parent or parents to "the system" (judicial, social services, immigration, medical, mental health, etc.); and lack of a sense of control over what happens to them. (See chapter 12 for how to address the issues of current and historic harm done to children by society and schools through restorative practices.)

Last, I want to touch on another potential underminer, what we might term *class consciousness* (or subconsciousness). Poor children experience something like what Du Bois termed *double-consciousness*, a concept that suggests that Black people have to maintain two identities: their true one and the one that takes into account how White people see them. Du Bois's (1903) description in *The Souls of Black Folks* is, tragically, still relevant today about Blacks and, I suggest, about poor people and others who are considered different by someone's standards:

> It is a peculiar sensation, this double-consciousness, this sense of always looking at one's self through the eyes of others, of measuring one's soul by the tape of a world that looks on in amused contempt and pity. (p. 9)

As Barratt (2011) described so eloquently about college students, poor and low-income children spend some of their bandwidth trying to "pass" as not poor. Even at very young ages, children know if their clothes are not adequate or stylish compared to what their peers are wearing. They realize there are kids who get free breakfast and lunch and that some kids wear clothes they got from the free clothes closet at school. There is significant pressure on kids (and their parents' financial resources) to dress in a way that does not immediately *out* them as poor. Children realize that what is acceptable and normal at home for them is different than it is for the families of other kids. Think about the bandwidth it takes to be constantly on the alert that teachers and classmates might find out how poor you are and make fun of you, judge you, or treat you as "less than." That reflection leads us to the next chapter, which focuses on belonging.

2

BELONGING UNCERTAINTY

All humans have a need to belong. If you have ever been in a place where you were unsure if you would be accepted and affirmed, you have an idea of the importance of belonging. Without that sense, part of you is always on the alert, wondering, "Will I be safe? Will I be loved? How will I manage?" The lack of a sense of belonging can be a major bandwidth stealer. According to Kids Matter (n.d.), belonging is critical for kids in school:

> All children need to feel that school is a safe place where people will care about them, where their needs for support, respect and friendship will be met, and where they will be able to get help to work out problems. When these needs are met children develop a sense of belonging at school. Belonging is very important for children's mental health and wellbeing.
>
> Children who feel that they belong at school are happier, more relaxed and have fewer behavioural problems than other students. They are also more motivated to learn and be more successful with their school work. Research into children's mental health has found that a sense of belonging and connectedness at school helps to protect children against mental health difficulties and improves their learning. (paras. 1–2)

Way back in 1943, Abraham Maslow wrote that humans have several levels of needs, and, ideally, the most basic needs are satisfied so that the more advanced ones are possible (Figure 2.1). Related to children and adolescents in school, if they do not have the basics in their home environment—clean water and air, food, shelter, sleep—we know that their ability to succeed in school is diminished. That is why we have breakfast and lunch programs in schools for children whose nutritional needs are not met at home. The next level is freedom from fear, an environment characterized by consistency and some reasonable sense of

Figure 2.1.   Maslow's hierarchy of needs.

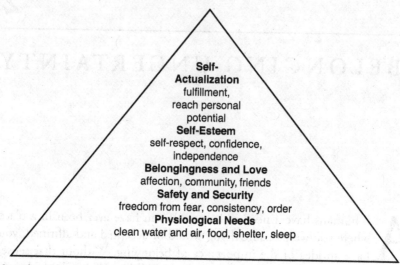

Note. Adapted from Maslow (1943).

order. Research on the effects of poverty on children (chapter 1) indicates that these are things often missing in the day-to-day lives of poor and low-income children, thus the term *economic insecurity*. Other sources of uncertainty that cut across social class are parental physical and mental illness; drug and alcohol addictions; and family, neighborhood, and school violence, resulting in unpredictable, even chaotic, children's lives. Extended families and communities can provide stability and care for children and youth in partnership with schools, which are often places where children can be free of fear, count on things being in order, and have predictability.

Maslow would suggest that only when children are free of fear can they even be open to affection and love, connecting with other kids in friend relationships, and feeling like they are part of a mutually supportive community. It seems to me that it is only when a child feels safe and loved can they be their full self, bringing their heart and mind to the task of learning. A child has to have some reasonable degree of self-confidence and independence before they can think for themself, accept and analyze new information, and learn.

Given the importance of belonging for children and adolescents, we need to carefully examine our school environments and the ways these environments support or hinder a sense of belonging for all students, specifically for certain vulnerable groups of students. There are groups of students who, because of messages from within our schools and from the larger society, might be more likely to feel insecure about belonging. I will briefly discuss four of these groups to illustrate the concept of the belonging challenge: out-of-school suspension students; students living in immigrant families; students with physical or intellectual disabilities, developmental disorders, and/or mental health challenges; and students who fall outside a strict gender binary.

Out-of-School Suspension

The suspension or expulsion of a student can send the message that "kids like you don't belong here." This message is communicated to not only those who are excluded but also their classmates. It is made clear to everyone "that belonging to the classroom community is conditional, not absolute, contingent upon their willingness and ability to be a certain kind of person" (Shalaby, 2017, p. 162).

In the United States, non-White students are much more likely than their White classmates to experience punishment, suspension, and expulsion in schools. I think this speaks volumes about the relative value placed on students of color and the marginalizing effect of "zero tolerance" policies that require schools to inflict harsh punishments, often suspension or expulsion, for certain behaviors. In the service of creating safe school climates, the concept of zero tolerance has resulted in the increased use of consequences that disproportionately remove some groups of children from opportunities to learn (Skiba & Rausch, 2006). This starts early; "black children are 3.6 times more likely to be suspended from preschool than white children," according to the U.S. Department of Education (Gilliam et al., 2016). A 2015 study of California schools (Loveless, 2017) found that for every 1,000 Black students, 178 received out-of-school suspension, compared to just 52 Hispanic students, 44 White students, 12 Asian students, and 54 students overall. A U.S. Department of Education (2016) study of students receiving special education services in over 17,000 school districts showed that from 2011 to 2014, the percentage of students who received out-of-school suspension (10 days or less) varied widely by race/ethnicity: 5% of Black students versus 0.3% Hispanic, 0.2% Native American/Alaska Natives, 0.09% White, and 0.02% Asian students. Skiba et al. (2014) conducted a meta-analysis of data on out-of-school suspensions and expulsions and concluded that race is a significant predictive factor. However, the effect of race disappeared when they took into account school characteristics, such as percentage of Black student enrollment (consistent with data that relate the percentage of non-White school enrollment with other quality measures) and principals' attitudes toward discipline.

They concluded that, to address the disproportionate punishment of Black students, it would be more productive to focus on school variables rather than on the students and their family characteristics.

I relate these statistics about out-of-school suspension to make the case that exclusion—in this case real, physical separation, naturally communicates to students that they do not belong. Landers (2018) asserted that "exclusion damages our students' futures" (p. 22). In addition to being taken away from the opportunity to learn, the social isolation of out-of-school suspension must exacerbate feelings of marginalization and belonging uncertainty in children and adolescents. I further suggest that even for the majority of Black children who are not suspended, the effects of vicarious racism may negatively affect the bandwidth of Black students in general. They empathize with their Black classmates who are suspended and realize that, within this school climate, they may be next, decreasing their "freedom from fear," which is so important to their sense of belonging.

Students Living in Immigrant Families

Immigrant children may experience persistent fear in their lives. Especially in the current political climate in the United States, security has become very tenuous for immigrant children, whether or not they themselves are undocumented. The number of affected children is significant. There were 44 million immigrants (not U.S.-born) living in the United States in 2016, which was 13.5% of the total population (Zong et al., 2018). In the same year, 26% of children (nearly 18 million) in the United States lived in families that included at least one parent who was an immigrant. Most of those children (88%) were themselves born in the United States; among children ages 0 years old to 5 years old, 93.5% were born in the United States (Migration Policy Institute, n.d.). In 2013, India and China surpassed Mexico in numbers of immigrants entering the United States (Chrishti & Hipsman, 2015); however, those from Mexico are still the largest group of immigrants in the United States at 26%, compared to 6% from India; 5% from China; 4% from the Phillipines; 3% each from El Salvador, Vietnam, and Cuba; and 2% to 2.5% each from South Korea and Guatemala (Zong et al., 2018).

Menjívar and Cervantes (2016) describe some of the negative "spillover" effects on children when immigration policy goes beyond the person who is targeted for enforcement. A significant spillover effect is related to work, as parents are likely to be in low-wage jobs that have little long-term security and in which labor violations cannot be challenged for fear of discovery of illegal status, making these workers vulnerable to exploitation and dangerous work conditions. Low-wage jobs come with persistent financial insecurity, and stresses about paying bills and rent can result in families living in sub-standard housing, experiencing frequent moves, and living in overcrowded conditions. Children of undocumented workers have lower educational attainment than other children, and young children in these families are less likely to be in early learning environments. In families in which a member is undocumented, the adults avoid contact with government agencies for fear of detection, so children do not have access to some of the social and health services that might be helpful to them. All of this can have very negative effects on children.

> The possibility of losing a parent to deportation, having to hide a family member's legal status, and living in fear of authority and in social marginal-ity has consequences on children's mental wellbeing including high rates of anxiety, depression, fear, attention problems and rule-breaking behaviors (Delva et al., 2013). (Menjívar & Cervantes, 2016, para. 8)

As I discussed in chapter 1 with reference to children who live with the stress of poverty or persistent economic insecurity, it is clear that given the conditions listed here, the bandwidth of immigrant children is severely depleted, leaving them less able to learn and to succeed in school. In *Forgotten Citizens*, Zayas (2015) reported on his studies of U.S.-born children of undocumented immigrants. He asserted that stress "affects the child's education performance, their developmental trajectories, how they achieve things. It affects the entire neurobiology of a child" (quoted in Edwards, 2018, p. 38).

Students With Physical or Intellectual Disabilities, Developmental Disorders, and/or Mental Health Challenges

Feeling a sense of belonging is a struggle for many of us, including normally developing children and youth. For those who have intellectual, developmental, and physical disabilities, the need to fit in and be part of the group may be especially challenging, adding even more uncertainty to an already stressful school experience.

Three of my four children received special education services for various things from learning disabilities to gifted enhancements, so I know the system from the parent side. I remember lots of documents and meetings and receiving many copies of "Parents' Rights." However, I was a college professor mom in a college town with an excellent public school system, so I suspect my experience does not reflect that of many parents and students in the United States who are in less well-resourced situations. I focused my research on trying to understand what it is like for children and youth who have disabilities related to their sense of belonging in school, which is so critical for all students, academically and socially.

In the 2017–2018 school year, 7 million students ages 3 years to 21 years (14% of all students) in U.S. public schools received special education services. The distribution by type was 34% specific learning disability, 19% speech or language impairment, 14% other health impairment, 10% autism, 7% developmental delay, 6% intellectual disability, 5% emotional disturbance, 2% multiple disabilities, 1% hearing impairment, and 1% orthopedic impairment (McFarland et al., 2019). Among students ages 6 to 21 years, 63% spent 80% or more of the school day in regular general education classrooms (up from 47% in 2000) (McFarland et al., 2019). This inclusion model conforms to the "least restrictive environment" directive in the Individuals with Disabilities Act (IDEA). IDEA is the most recent version of the 1975 law that guaranteed a free appropriate public education for every child with a disability (U.S. Department of Education, n.d.) and is generally accepted as best for students (Kimbrough & Mellen, 2012; Robinson & Truscott, 2014). Inclusion presents bandwidth challenges and opportunities for everyone in the school community.

In my reading about students with disabilities and differently developing students, I found several overarching messages from and about these students and their parents.

- *For many students, the actual "dis-ability" is primarily a result of social and cultural factors in the school and in society.* (See the definition of *disability* from the New Zealand Ministry of Social Development in chapter 18, this volume.)
- *Belonging is not a "special need"* (Turner, 2019, para. 1). All humans need a sense of belonging in order to survive and thrive. Students with disabilities are no different than other students in this way. "Everyone is diminished by a narrow focus on inclusion, which leaves some members of the school community feeling like they don't belong" (Robinson & Truscott, 2014, para. 2).
- *Not belonging is often more disabling than the disability itself* (Daley et al., 2018; Foley et al., 2012). Exclusion or outright rejection deplete bandwidth for students with disabilities, adding to the depletion that results from the social and learning challenges related to their disabling condition.
- *Belonging and having even one friend can act as protective factors against bullying and discrimination for students with disabilities* (Daley et al., 2018; Robinson & Truscott, 2014).

- *Inclusion is not just about sharing space.* There is a large gulf between accepting the presence of "special" students and valuing them as part of the school community (Robinson & Truscott, 2014). "Inclusion is built on the premise that all students should be valued for their unique abilities and included as essential members of a school community. Inclusion is not a place; it is a way of thinking" (Causton-Theoharis & Theoharis, 2008, p. 25).
- *Authentic inclusion is a school system issue, not an individual student issue* (Robinson & Truscott, 2014). We need to be student-ready schools rather than putting the onus entirely on students and their families to be school-ready (White, 2019).
- *This is a whole-school issue in which everyone needs to be "all-in."* A commitment to inclusion is best done full on; if not, exclusion is a too-easy default (Causton-Theoharis & Theoharis, 2008). The transition to full inclusion takes individual and organizational bandwidth and requires a resource commitment to professional development, collaboration, leader support, and open and authentic communication with students and parents.

Students Who Fall Outside a Strict Gender Binary

Last, before we leave the conversation about belonging, I want to address this crucial need for children and adolescents who are transgender or *gender-expansive*, a term that is defined by the Human Rights Campaign as "an adjective used to describe people that identify or express themselves in ways that broaden the culturally defined behavior or expression associated with one gender" (Welcoming Schools, n.d., p. 2). Partially because there are many new terms to describe gender identity and gender-expansiveness, it can sometimes seem like the issues are unendingly complex. As teachers, education professionals, and leaders, we may feel that we should spend more time researching and trying to understand the issues before we make significant changes in our schools and the way we treat students. Chaz Bono, in an interview in the *New York Times*, simplified things regarding transgender people: "There's a gender in your brain and a gender in your body. For 99 percent of people, those things are in alignment. For transgender people, they're mismatched. That's all it is. It's not complicated, it's not a neurosis. It's a mix-up" (quoted in Wilson, 2011, para. 19). My sense is that we have to act now to transform our schools into gender-safe places for everyone. We may make some mistakes because we do not fully understand some of the more nuanced issues about the life experiences of our students. But if we are genuine in our intentions and honest in our actions and communications, I feel confident that the environments we create will be better for all students and the adults in their lives.

Although gender identity is not a new issue, there are conversations happening, especially in elementary schools, which have not occurred in the past. There is a developing awareness that some children feel like they do not fit in the gender role they were assigned at birth and some young children and adolescents just want to *be*, without having to fit into someone else's idea of "girl" or "boy." Parents are realizing that they need to pay attention to the statements of even their very young children about their gender identity. For most of us, this is new territory, so we need to be patient with each other and try to do the best we can to nurture and value all students. Students themselves may be very hesitant to talk about their feelings or to "come out" to teachers and classmates for fear of rejection, or even abuse or violence from classmates or others. They may want to keep a low profile and hope no one notices, leaving them in a situation of survival and unable to thrive (Orr & Baum, n.d.).

According to Martin and Ruble (2010), children between the ages of 18 months and 24 months understand the concept of gender, are able to label people by gender, and use gendered words in speech. By 18 months, most children have a sense of themselves, and begin to look around and observe what that means and how they should behave (Baldwin & Moses, 1996). They quickly figure out what are girl toys and boy toys and what are girl things to do and what are boy things to do. At the same time, gender seems to be a fluid concept; for instance, children believe they can change their gender by wearing different clothes or participating in a different activity. By the time they are 6 or 7 years old, they know that gender is something that stays the same for life (Bem, 1989). And although most children settle into the gender that matches their physical sex characteristics, some children seem to know early on that there was a "mix-up."

Young children are often very insistent and consistent in their ideas about their gender. I once heard a girl, at about age 4 years, watching a male friend sew on a button say, "Men can't sew." A father of a 4-year-old told me that his biologically male child, at an early age, told his mom, "I'm like you, not like Daddy." As it has become clear that their child is a girl, these parents worked with her kindergarten teacher and school to make sure both the classroom and the playground were environments where she could be her true self.

If a family refuses to acknowledge their child's gender identity, that child may experience serious psychological damages and problems developing healthy interpersonal relationships. The child can become withdrawn at home and at school and have an inability to concentrate and learn in school.

"The longer a transgender youth is not affirmed, the more significant and long-lasting the negative consequences can become, including loss of interest in school, heightened risk for alcohol and drug use, poor mental health and suicide" (Orr & Baum, n.d., p. 8).

In the National Transgender Discrimination Survey (Grant et al., 2011), data was gathered from 6,450 transgender and gender-nonconforming people. Of those who had expressed their transgender or nonconforming identity in their K–12 school years, most reported experiencing one or more negative incidents at school, including harassment (78%) and physical assault (35%), and 15% said they had left school because of the mistreatment. Attempted suicide was reported by 41% of respondents, compared to a rate of 1.6% for the general population. For those who reported that they had been harassed or bullied in school, the rate of attempted suicide was 51%. According to the survey report,

> Respondents who have been harassed and abused by teachers in K–12 settings showed dramatically worse health and other outcomes than those who did not experience such abuse. Peer harassment and abuse also had highly damaging effects. (p. 3)

Transgender adults are becoming more "out" in media and culture, and we are seeing that children are realizing and claiming their transgender status when they are quite young. Parents and teachers and extended families are having to learn how to support these young people who are trying to make sense out of life and figuring out how to live as their authentic selves. We are finding out that the attitudes of "He's just going through a phase" and "She's just confused" have been devastating to children and young people, and that we need to figure out how to love and support them.

Transgender and gender-expansive children need special kinds of supports that require the establishment of classroom environments in which all children feel accepted and safe being fully who they are. According to Orr and Baum (n.d.) and their colleagues in *Schools in Transition: A Guide for Supporting Transgender Students in K–12 Schools*:

> The expression of transgender identity, or any other form of gender-expansive behavior, is a healthy, appropriate and typical aspect of human development. A gender-expansive student should never be asked, encouraged or required to affirm a gender identity or to express their gender in a manner that is not consistent with their self-identification or expression. Any such attempts or requests are unethical and will likely cause significant emotional harm. It is irrelevant whether a person's objection to a student's identity or expression is based on sincerely held religious beliefs or the

belief that the student lacks capacity or ability to assert their gender identity or expression (e.g., due to age, developmental disability or intellectual disability). (p. 3)

The authors also point out that there are often trust issues based on the past experiences of students and families with educational institutions. Care needs to be taken to establish—or reestablish—confidence in the teacher and the school related to both their intentions and their actions that demonstrate their trustworthiness and competence to create an environment in which these young students can thrive. Teachers and schools can create learning environments that are not only critical to gender-expansive students but also positive, enriching places for everyone, including classmates, parents, teachers, and the greater school community.

3

STEREOTYPE THREAT
AND IDENTITY THREAT

In the mid-1990s, Claude Steele and Josh Aronson, teaching at Stanford University, gave groups of Black and White students difficult verbal tests under two different conditions. Under the first condition, the students were given a very neutral message about laboratory problem-solving ability. In the second condition, students were told that the test was a measure of intellectual ability. The results of the experiment showed that, under the first condition, Black and White students scored very high on the test and there was no difference between the scores of the two groups. However, under the second condition, Black students scored significantly lower than did White students and significantly lower than what would have been expected given their previous academic performance. The researchers were very interested in the cause of this outcome (Steele & Aronson, 1995).

Even at Stanford University, where all of the students had demonstrated considerable intellectual abilities to qualify for admission, there was still a stereotype that Black students were not as smart as White students. Steele and Aronson reasoned that it was the conscious or subconscious worry about confirming the negative stereotype that distracted the Black students and caused them to score lower on the test. They termed this phenomenon *stereotype threat* (Steele & Aronson, 1995). Since that time, this effect has been found in dozens of studies in many settings with various groups—for instance, women (Spencer et al., 1999) and girls (Ambady et al., 2001) in math, White male students in math (Aronson et al., 1998), women in science and engineering (Steele, 1997), men in measures of social sensitivity (Koenig & Eagly, 2005), and White people in natural athletic ability (Stone, 2002).

Stereotype threat is contextual. It can happen to anyone when they are in a situation in which (a) their membership in a specific group is important to them, (b) they care about whether or not they do well on the specific performance task, and (c) there is a negative stereotype about their group relative to their ability to do well (Steele, 1997). When this happens to students in just one specific instance, there is probably no lasting negative effect. However, children and youth who are members of racial/ethnic groups about whom there are negative stereotypes regarding academic ability encounter daily messages from society—and often from teachers and school administrators— that carry low expectations for their success in school. Stereotype threat for children in school, according to Steele (2010), "constantly unsettles one's sense of competence and belonging" (p. 173).

In *Whistling Vivaldi*, Steele (2010) referred to stereotype threat as "the threat in the air" (p. 9), because the effects are real even without the presence of a blatantly racist, sexist, or homophobic person on the scene. This pervasive threat causes underperformance due to the bandwidth tax of being hypervigilant about confirming a negative stereotype concerning your group. This underperformance has real consequences for children, starting early in elementary school. If stereotype threat affects performance on standardized tests, for example, students can be identified as so-called low performers as early as the third grade. Once that label gets attached, it can have negative consequences for children throughout their K–12 years. If low expectations result in less focus on learning and academic achievement, students can begin to do poorly and, eventually, not qualify to take college preparatory classes in high school and not be encouraged to take college entrance exams. Because education level is one of the strongest predictors of quality of life (Barr, 2014; Lutz & Endale, 2018), the result of stereotype threat can negatively affect a person's entire life by limiting access to education and opportunity.

Because stereotype threat can have such a devastating effect on student success, some students learn to disidentify with the part of themselves that relates to academic achievement in an effort to protect their self-esteem. We form our concept of ourselves from the feedback we get from our environment, including from people in our family, school, neighborhood, church, community, and the media. If the messages children get about their intellectual ability—which may stem from racism, classism, or other "differentisms"—are consistently negative, they might begin to distance themselves from those judgments and expectations. In order to maintain positive self-esteem, children may decide to base their self-esteem on domains in which they can be successful, like family, friends, art, sports, music, community, or a part-time job, and disidentify from the domains in which they have failed or in which they are expected to fail (Aronson et al., 2001). Because a healthy self-esteem is very important to our mental well-being, the strategy to base it on areas where success is likely is very functional from a survival perspective. Unfortunately, the long-term outcome is a child who has given up on the development of their academic potential, sometimes from a very young age. That is the real cost of stereotype threat to real children.

In *Whistling Vivaldi*, Steele (2010) related the many studies over 15 years that grew out of that first Stanford experiment (Steele & Aronson, 1995). Over the course of the research, he began to refer to *identity threat*, which is a broader term that refers to the set of contingencies that each of us live with related to various aspects of our identity, like our race and ethnicity, social class, sexual orientation, gender identity, age, and home language. He talked about the costs of being in an *identity-threat* environment, where we are always on the watch for fear that we will be negatively judged or that people will have low expectations of our ability.

One area of identity threat is related to gender identity. The early years of schooling, including pre-K, can be especially difficult because of the very "gendered" nature of the school environment. Although early childhood education best practice does not label activity "centers" as boy centers and girl centers anymore, I suspect that it is still common that teachers, parents, and children see the "home" center (with the minikitchen, the vacuum, and the pots and pans) as a girl space and the "woodworking and tool" center (with wood blocks, hammers, pliers, and rulers) as a boy space. Even without labels, written or verbal, there are still girl and boy games, girl and boy lines, girl and boy dress-up clothes, girl and boy activities. And, of course, there are girl and boy restrooms in elementary and high schools. Although there has been progress in some locations in the availability of all-gender restrooms, there are still many schools in which they are not available and in which students are forced to use the restroom that matches their assigned sex at birth. In 2015, the U.S. Department of Justice (Ennis, 2017) ruled,

> Under Title IX, discrimination based on a person's gender identity, a person's transgender status, or a person's nonconformity to sex stereotypes constitutes discrimination based on sex. The term "sex" as it is used in Title IX is broad and encompasses gender identity, including transgender status. . . .
>
> Prohibiting a student from accessing the restrooms that match his gender identity is prohibited sex discrimination under Title IX. There is a public interest in ensuring that all students, including transgender students, have the opportunity to learn in an environment free of sex discrimination. (paras. 7–8)

Even in schools in which transgender students are encouraged to use the restroom of their choice, they may not be safe doing so. Anne Ternus-Bellamy (2017) pointed out that restrooms are one of the few places in schools where there are no adults around to monitor student behavior. Trans students may be teased, harassed, or worse by other students inside restrooms. There is still much work to be done in this area so that all children and adolescents are freely able to perform basic biological functions without fear.

Even young children, especially those who already feel vulnerable in some ways, are sensitive to messages, voiced and not, about what is acceptable and valued and what is not. It is a learning process for all of us—students, parents, teachers, school administrators, and leaders—to rethink our classrooms and schools to make them gender-safe, including for trans and gender-expansive students (and teachers and parents, for that matter). Interestingly, the principles of universal design, a concept developed to create learning environments accessible to children with varying abilities, includes consideration of gender as a relevant user characteristic. In making toys, for instance, that appeal to children at various ages, genders, and developmental levels, Universal Design Principle 2 emphasizes the idea of multiple uses. For instance, a jar might be a bug jar for one child and a purse or a tool box to another child (Centre for Excellence in Universal Design & National Disability Authority, n. d) . The idea of universal design is that arrangements that are meaningful and flexible for people with various learning styles and abilities probably work well for everyone and do not exclude certain groups from the opportunity to learn.

Students from pre-K through high school come to school with not just their brains and intellect, but with their spirits and their self-esteem and all of their various identities, including race/ethnicity, culture, family background, social and economic status, language, and so on. Until recently, gender identity would not have made the list, but that time has changed. Even though there have always been "tomboys"—girls who reject "girly" dress and behavior—for at least the pre-K and elementary grades, this was still within the realm of "normal." Some of these girls were also good in sports, which provided them the higher status of an athlete and somewhat mitigated the negative effects of being different in terms of gender roles. Little boys who prefer "girly" things and activities may garner more negative attention.

For children and youth in school, several factors can result in an identity threat environment, including images in classrooms and public areas that do not reflect the race or ethnicity of certain groups; the lack of teachers and other school leaders who share race or ethnicity with the students; low expectations of students by teachers; the necessity for English language learners to constantly translate in their head; racist or anti-immigrant messages; negative attitudes toward students who have physical, cognitive, or mental disabilities; restrooms and other facilities that are strictly gendered; and the lack of safety and affirmation to be your true self at school. Identity threat takes up serious mental bandwidth as students feel a sense of heightened vigilance related to one or more of their identities. Students are unable to just relax and bring their entire body and mind to the learning task. The "threat in the air" can become much more tangible in the case of microaggressions and bullying, the topic of chapter 4.

4

MICROAGGRESSIONS
AND BULLYING

For the purposes of this discussion, I have paired microaggressions with bullying, although I realize that there are differences. The "micro" in the term *microaggression* would seem to exclude the physical assault and hostile verbal harassment that is associated with serious bullying. However, we know that some of the most damaging kinds of bullying are psychological, especially since the advent of cyberbullying, so it seems appropriate to treat these two phenomena together. Related to bandwidth depletion, it is the subtle, just-under-the-radar acts and words that appear to be the most costly to the cognitive resources of young children and adolescents.

The term *microaggression* was first used by Chester Pierce in 1970 (DeAngelis, 2009) to describe the insults and dismissals that Black Americans experienced from non-Black Americans. He and his colleagues (Pierce et al., 1978) described these acts as "subtle, stunning, often automatic" (p. 66), hurtful in a way that can catch a person off guard. Children who hear such comments or sense such hostility feel helpless to do anything about it. Derald Wing Sue et al. (2007) have done extensive research on these microaggressions and their effects on Black people and members of other marginalized groups. They distinguished the following three categories of microaggressions:

1. A microassault is an explicit racial derogation characterized primarily by a verbal or nonverbal attack meant to hurt the intended victim through name-calling, avoidant behavior, or purposeful actions.
2. A microinsult is characterized by communications that convey rudeness and insensitivity and demean a person's racial heritage or identity.

3. Microinvalidations are characterized by communications that exclude, negate, or nullify the psychological thoughts, feelings, or experiential reality of a person of color. (p. 274)

As in the discussion of identity threat, we can substitute other identities for "person of color" or "racial heritage." The result of microaggressions and bullying for children is a scarcity of feeling safe and secure, belongingness, and certainty about the environment, each of which comes with a bandwidth tax.

Microaggressions are part of what is being referred to as "modern racism" (Carter et al., 2015, p. 242). Of course, the concept applies to classism, homophobia, xenophobia, and other "differentisms." Unlike racism before the civil rights movement, this racism is "a bit like air pollution; it is sometimes invisible but you always know it is there" (Verschelden, 2017, p. 33). Even though the old kind of racism was awful and painful, no cognitive resources were used up in recognizing a racist environment or that words or actions had racist intent. The Association for Psychological Science (2007) also linked this to what I am calling *bandwidth depletion*:

> The problem is that we have limited cognitive resources, so when we are solving one problem, we have difficulty focusing on another at the same time. Some psychologists reason from this that subtle racism might actually be more, not less, damaging than the plain antipathy of yesterday, sapping more mental energy. (para. 4)

In the broad definition of *microaggressions*, Sue et al. (2007) suggest that they are sometimes unintentional. Of the three kinds defined, assaults seem the most blatant and purposeful and are most likely intended. Insults and invalidations, however, can be unintended and rooted in ignorance, insensitivity, and thoughtlessness. Especially among children, who, I think, can be genuinely mean at times (many times out of their own pain and insecurity), microaggressions can originate from comments and attitudes they have learned from family members, peers, or misinformation in the media about groups of people who are unfamiliar to them. Although this does not make microaggressions any less hurtful to the target, it does suggest to me that it might be possible for teachers and schools to be very intentional and transparent about establishing environments in which microaggressions are treated as unacceptable, confronted calmly and consistently, and used as learning opportunities for everyone.

The research that I have seen about microaggressions has related to adults or to students in college, so I set out to find some examples from the pre-K–12 world. Liza Wyles (2017), a mother of two school-age children, wrote about microaggressions and described them as "how these tiny, yet powerful dings in my kids' confidence affect their feelings about school" (para. 2). I have included her observations in Table 4.1, along with others from my reading and conversations with kids, parents, and teachers.

Wyles writes about a conversation with her fourth-grade daughter about the project she was doing on Betsy Ross. Wyles asked if her daughter had chosen Betsy Ross, and she answered that they had picked a name out of a hat. That seemed fair to Wyles until she found out that there was a "male hat" and a "female hat"! In a short video by Eve Vawter (2016), young people talk about their experiences with microaggressions and why they are so harmful. She explained in the accompanying article:

> Microaggressions can be even more damaging than overt examples of bigotry, because they tend to make the recipient feel a sense of self-doubt about what they've experienced rather than outright anger. This can lead to feelings of isolation and contribute to poor self-image and depression. (para. 3)

In the video, young women reflect on the effects of microaggressions—for instance, that they can make you not like who you actually are and doubt yourself. Of LGBTQ respondents to the 2015 National School Climate Survey (Kosciw et al., 2015), almost all of them had heard homophobic and transphobic language at school, the word *gay* used negatively (98%), other words like *faggot* or *dyke* (96%), comments about gender expression (96%), and negative remarks about transgender students (86%).

The power of microaggression to make you "doubt yourself" is surely true for all targets of this underminer. And, because it is very difficult—and takes lots of bandwidth—to confront the person who does the microaggression, these words and behaviors mostly go unchallenged. This is more reason why teachers and school leaders need to be ever vigilant and willing to do the confronting and correcting on behalf of students, helping to create an environment that is safe for all.

TABLE 4.1

Examples of Microaggressions Toward Children in School

Microaggressions	Examples	Target
Microassaults	You look like a girl.	Native American boy with long hair
	Why are you so gay?	Boy who likes to hang out with girls, or likes nice clothes, or doesn't like sports
	Get out! Use the girls' (boys') room where you belong!	Transgender boy (girl)
	You don't belong here. Go back home.	Immigrant (or perceived immigrant)
	Can I touch your hair?[d]	Black child, usually.
	Retard! You're so stupid!	Child with intellectual disability
Microinsults	Where are you from? You are so interesting looking.[b]	Any child who is perceived as "not from here"
	You are good at math, for a girl.[b]	All girls (and boys, as the assumption is that they are all good at math)
	You look so handsome without your glasses.[b]	Kid who wears glasses
	Your skin is dirty.[c] You can't have two Moms.[c]	Black child.
	She has a Jew nose.	Child of lesbian couple Jewish (or assumed Jewish) child
	Why are you so weird?!	Child with autism spectrum disorder

(Continues)

TABLE 4.1 (*Continued*)

Microaggressions	Examples	Target
Microinvalidations	Wow! You sound American! [c]	Any child who, to someone else, doesn't look "American" (meaning English-speaking and white)
	Dress codes that objectify little girls[a]	Girls who want to stay cool in hot weather
	Gendered line-ups [a]	Transgender and gender-expansive children
	Gendered projects [a]	Boys and girls who want to choose a project on grounds unrelated to gender
	Gendered reading material [a]	All students, as the history and value of women is invalidated when most of the stories have male protagonists
	Equating sitting with success [a]	Any child who is hyperactive or whose body just needs to move.
	Passive exclusion	Child with a severe physical disability
	Active exclusion or separation	Child with intellectual or emotional disability

[a]Wyles (2017)
[b]Medini (2017)
[c]Jaime (2015)
[d]Vawter (2016)

5

SEXUAL ORIENTATION, GENDER IDENTITY, AND GENDER EXPRESSION

Ideas about sexual orientation and gender identity and expression among children and youth are still new to many people. Although there have been recent victories, like marriage equality, there have also been setbacks—for instance, court support of companies that refuse to do work with same-sex couples as an expression of "religious freedom" (*Masterpiece Cakeshop, LTD. v. Colorado Civil Rights Commission*, 2018). Most of the public discussion has been about these grown-up issues. Questions about use of gendered restrooms and freedom to present as the gender of choice (e.g., a girl wearing a tuxedo in a high school senior picture) have brought the discussion to elementary and high schools. Because the conversation is still new to many people, I have included a glossary in Table 5.1, from the Human Rights Campaign project "Welcoming Schools."

Life in school for LGBTQ students (the *Q* can stand for *questioning* as well as *queer*, which includes other gender-expanding terms like *gender-nonconforming, asexual,* and *intersex*) has been discussed related to belonging for transgender students and to some microaggressions. In this chapter, I give a bit more attention to this group of children and youth and what they need at school so they can have access to their full bandwidth for learning.

TABLE 5.1

Sexual Orientation and Gender Identity—Children and Youth

Term	Definition
Cisgender	When your gender identity (how you feel) is the same as what doctors/midwives assigned to you when you were born (girl/boy or sex assigned at birth).
Gender Binary	A way of seeing gender as two distinct and opposite groups—girl and boy. This idea doesn't include all the ways we can have a gender identity and express our gender.
Gender Expansive	Some people feel that the traditional ways of being a "boy" or "girl" do not fit for them. They live lives showing that there are many ways to be a girl, boy, both, or neither.
Gender Identity	How you feel. Girl, boy, both, or neither. Everyone has a gender identity.
Nonbinary	People who do not feel like the word *girl* or *boy* fits. They may feel like both or neither. They sometimes use pronouns such as *they, them, theirs.*
Sex Assigned at Birth	When a baby is born, a doctor or midwife looks at the baby's body/anatomy and says they are a boy, girl, or intersex.
Transgender or Trans	When your gender identity (how you feel) is different than what doctors/midwives assigned to you when you were born (girl/boy or sex assigned at birth).
Who You Love	
Bisexual	People who love people of two genders. [In Grades 3–5, you might say people who love or are attracted to people of two genders.]
Gay	People who love people of the same gender. [In grades 3–5, you might say people who love or are attracted to people of the same gender.]
Heterosexual	People who love people of the opposite gender. Also called straight. [In Grades 3–5, you might say people who love or are attracted to other people of the opposite gender.]
Lesbian	People who love people of the same gender. Two women. [In Grades 3–5, you might say people who love or are attracted to people of the same gender.]
Sexual Orientation	Who you love. [In Grades 3–5, you might say who you love or are attracted to.]

(Continues)

TABLE 5.1 (*Continued*)

Term	Definition
Gender and Who You Love	
LGBTQ	Acronym for lesbian, gay, bisexual, transgender, and queer.
Queer	People use this word as a way to identify with and celebrate people of all gender identities and all the ways people love each other. When used in a mean way, it is a word that hurts.

Note. From Human Rights Campaign (n.d.a).

I think there are at least five ways in which LGBTQ students are especially vulnerable:

1. Except in the case of economically secure, able, White children, all LGBTQ kids experience *intersectionality*, which means they have at least two identities about which there are negative stereotypes, like gay and Black, poor and trans, Hispanic and bisexual, or gay and physically disabled. Intersectionality often results in bandwidth-depleting life experiences that are more than just the sum of the two (or more) identities.

2. For most children and youth who have these identities, they are the only one in their family to have them. This means they do not necessarily have adults or older siblings from whom to learn the ropes of being who they are in the world. Unlike poor children who grow up in poor families and non-White children who mostly grow up in families with people who look like them, LGBTQ kids are often on their own to find a community of people who can identify with them and be role models for what it is like to be a happy and healthy adult. According to Emma Forbes-Jones, a psychologist who works with this population of children and youth, "the reality is that many are not only alone but also rejected by family members, and do not have family support, let alone family 'mirrors'" (personal communication, July 23, 2019).

3. Although a faith community is an important part of the lives of many children and youth, LGBTQ kids may be rejected by that community if they are open about their identity. Although the largest faith communities in the United States are not LGBTQ-affirming (Brammer, 2018), there are some "welcoming" faith groups (Masci, 2014); however, children—especially young

ones—may not have access to any church except where their parents attend. Being rejected by your faith community can be a devastating experience for a young LGBTQ person. "We need to recognize that the condemnation of LGBT people in churches leads to the abuse and rejection of LGBT children in far too many Christian homes" (Siciliano, 2013, para. 9).

4. Because of ignorance and misunderstanding about sexual orientation and gender identity, students may be not only be bullied and excluded due to their perceived identity but also blamed. Children are probably not often blamed for being poor (although their parents might be); they are not blamed for being Black or Hispanic or Muslim. Many people still think that sexual orientation is a choice, which is reflected in microaggressive statements like "How do you know if you're a lesbian if you've never dated a boy?" and "He's just going through an awkward time." Transgender kids are often treated like they are just going through a phase or that they are just trying to get attention. People think they should just decide to feel fine about their biological sex and get on with it.

5. In a patriarchal society like the United States, in which there is a clear hierarchy that puts heterosexual men at the top, people or groups of people who refuse to conform to a strict gender binary pose a threat to the system. People who are different make other people nervous, as if they might have to change their ideas about what is "normal," and that change might alter the power structure.

For all of these reasons, children and adolescents might decide that it is safest to just pretend they are cisgender and heterosexual to avoid the trouble they anticipate if they were to be honest about their true identity. I suggest that hiding any part of ourselves is one of the most bandwidth-depleting decisions we can make. When we are afraid to be our true selves, we are constantly on the alert, worrying that someone will notice we are different. I have had students describe to me how they are ever vigilant about how they dress, how they talk, how they move their hands, how they sit, how they interact (or not) with people of the same and the opposite sex. Fear of being found out—and then being mistreated, rejected, ridiculed, or worse—is always present, taking up precious bandwidth they need to learn and thrive in school.

From a 2012 study of more than 10,000 LGBT-identified youth (ages 13–17 years) in the United States (Human Rights Campaign, n.d.b), several findings are relevant to youth in school:

- 40% say that their home community is not accepting of LGBT people
- 26% report not feeling accepted by family; 21% report trouble at school, including bullying; and 18% report fear of being out as their biggest problems
- 90% say they are out to their close friends, and 64% say they are out to their classmates
- 75% say that most of their peers don't have a problem with their LGBT identity
- 92% report that they hear negative messages about being LGBT, mostly from school, the internet, and their peers

A 2017 survey (GLSEN, n.d.) of more than 23,000 U.S. students from 13 years to 21 years (mean age 15.6 years) in grades 6 to 12, affirmed that school is still a hostile environment for too many of them:

- 59.5% of LGBTQ students felt unsafe at school because of their sexual orientation, 44.6% because of their gender expression, and 35.0% because of their gender.
- Approximately 4 in 10 students avoided gender-segregated spaces in school due to safety concerns (bathrooms: 42.7%; locker rooms: 40.6%).
- Most reported avoiding school functions (75.4%) and extracurricular activities (70.5%) because they felt unsafe or uncomfortable.
- Almost all LGBTQ students (98.5%) heard *gay* used in a negative way (e.g., "that's so gay") at school; 70.0% heard these remarks often or frequently, and 91.8% reported that they felt distressed because of this language.
- 95.3% of LGBTQ students heard other types of homophobic remarks; 60.3% heard this type of language often or frequently.
- 94.0% of LGBTQ students heard negative remarks about gender expression; 62.2% heard these remarks often or frequently.
- 87.4% of LGBTQ students heard negative remarks specifically about transgender people; 45.6% heard them often or frequently.
- 56.6% of students reported hearing homophobic remarks from their teachers or other school staff.
- 71.0% of students reported hearing negative remarks about gender expression from teachers or other school staff.
- The vast majority of LGBTQ students (87.3%) experienced harassment or assault based on personal characteristics, including sexual orientation, gender expression, gender, religion, race and ethnicity, and disability.
- 70.1% of LGBTQ students experienced verbal harassment (e.g., called names or threatened) at school based on sexual orientation, 59.1% based on gender expression, and 53.2% based on gender.

- 28.9% of LGBTQ students were physically harassed (e.g., pushed or shoved) in the past year based on sexual orientation, 24.4% based on gender expression, and 22.8% because of gender.
- 12.4% of LGBTQ students were physically assaulted (e.g., punched, kicked, injured with a weapon) in the past year based on sexual orientation, 11.2% based on gender expression, and 10.0% based on gender.
- A sizable number of LGBTQ students were also bullied or harassed at school based on other characteristics—26.9% based on religion, 25.6% based on race or ethnicity, and 25.5% based on disability.
- 48.7% of LGBTQ students experienced electronic harassment in the past year, often known as cyberbullying.
- 57.3% of LGBTQ students were sexually harassed in the past year at school.
- 42.1% of transgender and gender-nonconforming students had been prevented from using their preferred name or pronoun.
- 46.5% of transgender and gender-nonconforming students had been required to use a bathroom of their legal sex.
- 43.6% of transgender and gender-nonconforming students had been required to use a locker room of their legal sex. (pp. 4–5)

In a study (Becerra-Culqui et al., 2018) of more than 1,300 transgender and gender-nonconforming (TGNC) children and youth (ages 3–17 years), the results were very clear that the children (ages 3–9 years) had higher rates of anxiety and attention deficit disorder than their cisgender counterparts. For adolescents, anxiety and depression were found to be common and often severe. "For all diagnostic categories, prevalence was severalfold higher among TGNC youth than in matched reference groups" (para. 3). In a meta-analysis of research on LGBT youth (Russell & Fish, 2016), the conclusion was very clear that global mental health problems are more prevalent in LGB youth than in their heterosexual peers. Further, there was preliminary evidence that bisexual and questioning youth were especially at risk for mental health problems. As LGBTQ children and youth struggle with mental health challenges, they may encounter yet another instance of the multiplier effect of intersectionality. According to TEAM (n.d.),

> LGBTQ people must confront stigma and prejudice based on their sexual orientation or gender identity while also dealing with the societal bias against mental health conditions. Some people report having to hide their sexual orientation from those in the mental health system for fear of being ridiculed or rejected. Some hide their mental health conditions from their LGBTQ friends. (para. 2)

Related to the increase in mental health problems, the incidence of suicide and thoughts of suicide are elevated in LGBTQ youth compared to their cisgender, heterosexual peers.

> The LGBTQ community is at a higher risk for suicide because we lack peer support and face harassment, mental health conditions and substance abuse. For LGBTQ people aged 10–24, suicide is one of the leading causes of death. LGBTQ youth are 4 times more likely and questioning youth are 3 times more likely to attempt suicide, experience suicidal thoughts or engage in self-harm than straight people. Between 38–65% of transgender individuals experience suicidal ideation. (para. 9)

In a study of nearly 6,000 LGBT students (ages 13 years–21 years), from all 50 states and Washington DC, researchers found that reported in-school victimization was related to negative educational outcomes, as measured by GPA and missed days of school (Kosciw et al., 2013). Related to the concept of identity threat, students do not often have out LGBT teachers because it is not safe for teachers to be out about their sexual orientation or gender identity. Only 20 states (and Washington DC) have laws prohibiting discrimination against people in the workplace based on sexual orientation or gender identity (another two states cover sexual orientation only) (Human Rights Watch, 2016). Sometimes teachers themselves are the perpetrators of microaggressions against LGBT students—for instance, from a transgender student in Utah, who described what it was like when teachers used the wrong pronouns as "like a little mental pinch. . . . It doesn't seem like a big deal, but eventually you bruise" (HRC, 2016, para. 18).

According to Russell et al. (2011), writing in the *Journal of School Health*, for many LGBTQ adolescents, "the simple, daily routine of going to school is fraught with harassment and victimization" (p. 228). This statement reminded me of what Chester Pierce called "mundane extreme environmental stress" (quoted in Carroll, 1998, p. 271) in writing about the experience of Black people in the United States. It is the kind of stress that is usually fairly low level but always there, stealing mental bandwidth from students who are just trying to learn, just like the rest of their classmates.

6

FOCUS ON RACISM

All social justice work is science fiction. We are imagining a world free of injustice, a world that doesn't yet exist.

—*adrienne maree brown (in Love, 2019, p. 100)*

After reading the first draft of this book, the publisher sent me an email message with the question "Are we doing enough about race?" My immediate thought was "Is it possible to do enough about race when we're talking about the lives of children in public school in the United States?" We live in a country that, during its formative years, created skin-color-based racism to justify slavery (Kendi, 2016). That legacy is still being played out today, blighting the hopes and potential of millions of children, like it has done for many of their parents and their parents for countless generations. I have cited statistics in other chapters about the inequities in educational opportunity for Black children as compared with White children. However, statistics seem inadequate to tell the story of what it means to grow up as a Black child, being aware that your skin color alone makes you vulnerable to low expectations, harsh treatment, prejudice, invisibility, zero tolerance, exclusion, and, personal violence.

In focusing on Black children and youth in this chapter, I do not mean to minimize the impact of racism, ethnocentrism, xenophobia, and other "differentisms" on other groups of children or the life-blunting effects of persistent economic insecurity for all people living in poverty. In chapter 2, I addressed the precarious and stress-filled lives of students living in immigrant families. The hostility against and rejection of Hispanic, Muslim, Asian, and other people who come to the United States seeking safety and opportunity mean that many students in these families live in a constant state of uncertainty, robbing them of precious bandwidth they need to thrive. When my children were young, we lived for 2 years in northern Alberta with the Lubicon Cree Nation, a people who had their livelihood of 2,000 years disrupted in the early 1980s by the oil and paper industries. I recently lived for 6 years in Oklahoma. I learned from Native people in both of these settings about the unique experience of indigenous people and their ancestors who live today. Bettina Love (2019) explained how the concept of settler colonialism helps us to understand that systemic oppression, noting

> the constant theft of Indigenous land, the extraction of resources, and the cultural genocide of Indigenous people. . . . In terms of schooling, the U.S. enacted cultural and linguistic genocide of Native American students. Indigenous children were taken from their families and put in boarding schools that viewed them as savages. In order to survive, they had to let go of their language, cultural traditions, and spiritual practices: cultural genocide. (p. 135)

Continued oppression has resulted in disproportionately negative health and social outcomes for Native children and their families.

Despite the amazing progress made during the civil rights movement of the 1950s and 1960s and the many pieces of legislation at the state and federal levels that make discrimination against the law, racism against Black people in this country today is pervasive, powerful, and deadly. In a recent conversation with the president of the community college where I work on the west side of Chicago, he suggested that if our Black students have to worry each day that they might be shot and killed on their way to the bus to come to school, they might not have much bandwidth left for learning when they arrive at our door. President and Director-Counsel Sherrilyn Ifill of the NAACP (National Association for the Advancement of Colored People) Legal Defense and Educational Fund talked about how Black people in the United States have to navigate the public space: "It's time we talk about what it means to not be welcomed as American citizens" (quoted in Nelson, 2018, 3:44).

I feel strongly that we must address the national shame of what we have done and continue to do to Black children in this country. Maybe it is because I raised two Black sons since their infancies and so got a glimpse, as a White person, into what it is like to "navigate the public space" as a person who must always question whether or not they are welcome—or even safe— in their own community and school. Maybe it is because, as a 13-year-old, I saw on television the raised fists of Tommie Smith and John Carlos at the 1968 Mexico City Summer Olympics, an image that has stayed with me all of my life. And almost 50 years later, Colin Kaepernick began what became a similar symbolic movement of athletes in protest against police violence toward Black people. Why can't we get past this? The truth is that we (humans) have made a mess of things, holding on to racism for centuries, so that we find ourselves, in 2020, living in a country where millions of children are denied the chance to truly thrive at school.

For Black children, the lack of being welcomed starts before birth. Negative childbirth outcomes for Black women and their children are significantly higher than for women and children in other groups in the United States. Infant mortality, which is the number of babies who die before they reach their first birthday, is 11.1 per 1,000 births for Black children as opposed to 4.8 for non-Hispanic White babies (Kids Count Data Center, n.d.). Low birth weight is the second leading cause of infant death (after birth defects) in the United States and, in 2016, Black babies were twice as likely (14%) as non-Hispanic White ones (7%) to be born at low weight (Child Trends, n.d.). These disparities hold true for women across income levels, prenatal care, and mother's education (Gross et al., 2019).

To explain the science behind this cyclical generational disadvantage that Black girl babies grow into and then experience as mothers, I share this excerpt from my first bandwidth book (Verschelden, 2017):

> The path toward adverse birth outcomes for Black women starts when they are infants and young girls. A life of racism causes wear and tear on people's bodies, in what some people refer to as *weathering*, and contributes to racial health disparities. Weathering is a result of persistently elevated allostatic load, which is highest among Black women (compared to both White women and Black men), possibly due to the double discrimination of racism and sexism (Geronimus, Hicken, Keene, & Bound, 2006). Of course, any condition of ill health can contribute to negative birth outcomes for pregnant women. The inflammation caused by stress can negatively affect birth outcomes (Christian, Glaser, Porter, & Iams, 2013) . . . during pregnancy, cortisol can cross the placental barrier and affect fetal development and have lifelong health consequences for the child (Challis, 2004; de Weerth & Buitelaar, 2005; Kuzawa & Sweet, 2009). Tollenaar, Beijers, Jansen, Riksen-Walraven, and de Weerth (2011) identified three potential pathways for stress to cause changes in fetal programming: Cortisol could cross the blood-brain barrier to affect brain development in the fetus; stress may constrict blood flow to the fetus, decreasing available nutrients and oxygen; and stress might cause changes in the mother's behavior, such as eating patterns or increased tobacco and alcohol consumption. And the pattern starts over with the new child. (p. 17)

Being not welcomed into this world, even before birth, takes a toll on Black babies and children, resulting in bandwidth issues that impair their ability to learn and thrive in school.

Early in a child's life, racism affects so many things. In chapter 2, I gave the statistics on the disproportionate suspensions and expulsions of Black children, starting in preschool. The physical removal of Black children from the learning environment brings with it a very clear message that "you don't belong here" and/or "you pose a danger to other children" or "we don't really expect you to succeed." These messages can thwart the hopes and aspirations of children from their earliest years in school and, I suggest, cause acting-out behavior that results in more exclusion, keeping the cycle going to the continual detriment of Black children.

Much attention has been given to the plight of Black boys in high schools and colleges, for very good reasons related to completion rates, vulnerability to profiling and potential violence, and many other negative societal realities. Black girls have their own struggles, which are, I think, often overlooked because the attention is on the boys. In *Pushout*, Monique W. Morris (2016) wrote movingly about the precarious situation of Black girls in school because they are seen as "loud" (an attempt to be heard?) and that they have "attitude" (p. 19), the hypersexualization of their bodies, the disproportionate victimization in sex-trafficking, and likelihood of being involved as adolescents in juvenile lock-up. When the trauma of all of these manifestations of racism works its way into the lives of girls at school, it has the effect of "disrupting one of the most important protective factors in a girl's life: her education" (p. 3).

Restorative practices, which I write about in chapter 12, are especially critical for Black and Brown children who come to school within a society that does not value them and from which they get many messages that they are not worthy and that little is expected of them. Like all children who have experienced trauma (and I suggest that racism is a daily trauma for many Black and Brown children), school needs to be a place where there is safety, predictability, and support and where exclusion is used as a last resort.

It is not in the purview of this book to cite all the statistics that could be used to make the case that racism against Black and Brown people is as strong as ever in the United States. I will add this short list of facts to the already-cited data related to school exclusion and school-related statistics to further illustrate the gross inequities in our social systems.

- In the United States, "Black youth were more than five times as likely to be detained or committed compared to white youth, according to data from the Department of Justice collected in October 2015"

Sentencing Project, 2017, para. 1). Of detained youth, 44% were Black, even though Black youth are only 16% of all youth in the United States (Sentencing Project, 2017).

- In July 2019, the unemployment rate for young Black people (16 years–24 years) in the United States was 14.6%, compared to 8% for White youth and 11.3% for Hispanic youth (Bureau of Labor Statistics, 2019).
- Hiring discrimination is still a significant factor for Blacks. In a meta-analysis of 24 field experiments, among job applicants with identical résumés, White applicants received 36% more callbacks than Black applicants (and 24% more than Latino applicants; Quillian et al., 2017).
- "Black adolescents and young adults are at higher risk for the most physically harmful forms of violence (e.g., homicides, fights with injuries, aggravated assaults) compared with Whites" (Sheats et al., 2018, p. 462). "Minority populations are disproportionately exposed to conditions such as concentrated poverty, racism, limited educational and occupational opportunities, and other aspects of social and economic disadvantage contributing to violence" (Sheats et al., 2018, p. 463).
- At 20.8%, in 2018, Black people in the United States had the second highest poverty rate, behind Native Americans at 25.4%, compared to Hispanics at 17.6% and Whites at 10.1% (Poverty Facts, n.d.)
- Black people in the United States make up just 13% of the population but are 40% of people who are homeless (National Alliance to End Homelessness, 2018).
- A comprehensive study of the economic trajectory of Black boys in the United States concluded, "The worst places for poor white children are almost all better than the best places for poor black children" (Badger et al., 2018, para. 36).

Although we would like it not to be true, public schools, like other societal institutions, mostly replicate the qualities of the larger society. By nature of being part of U.S. society, public schools—without very intentional efforts not to be—are characterized by racism, sexism, classism, xenophobia, homophobia, and so on, and it seems to me that we need to acknowledge this and decide together to create a new normal for students and for the teachers, parents, and school leaders who are partners in their learning and development. This will require a willingness to have honest conversations with each other and hold each other accountable for changing how we treat each other and protecting our children and youth from the negative effects of the trauma of racism and the debilitating effects of persistent economic insecurity that blight the hopes and dreams of so many of our students.

PART TWO

BANDWIDTH STEALERS— PARENTS AND TEACHERS

7

PARENTS

I n most families, it is probably fair to say that the bandwidth of the children can be significantly affected by the bandwidth of their parent or parents. (I use the term *parent* to represent those adults who have primary responsibility for children, including legal guardians, grandparents or other relatives, or other persons.) The ability and possibility of parental support for children in school is certainly enhanced or limited by the amount of bandwidth available to the parent. Parents who are living in poverty or persistent economic insecurity, who have their own challenges with physical or mental health, who have unmet relational needs, who are unemployed or underemployed, who are LGBTQ, who have themselves been victims of violence, who live in unsafe and polluted neighborhoods, who encounter the same social-psychological *underminers* as do their children, and who face many other life struggles might not have the mental bandwidth to do the things they know would be supportive of their children's education. In addition, these parents have children who are members of negatively stereotyped groups, are differently abled physically, have mental health challenges, who are LGBTQ, who have emotional or learning needs that are not met in most classrooms, who are victims of bullying, or whose behavior in school is considered disruptive or unacceptable. In families who live in poor neighborhoods, parents have to worry about the physical safety of their children in school. In a United Negro College Fund study (Bridges et al., 2012), 87% of low-income parents reported that a "safe, secure, and violence-free environment" (p. 10) was the major factor in choosing a school for their child.

In a recent faculty meeting at a community college, the conversation was about how to get high school students in certain underserved groups to come to a meeting about the various opportunities that were offered. It was mentioned that it was even more important that the parents be at the meetings as they are the ones who will encourage (or not) their children to go on with schooling after high school. Someone was quick to point out that that was the problem, saying that parents of "those kids" (Black, Brown, poor) didn't care enough to come to a meeting about education. In my experience, most parents care about their children and want them to get a good education. However, parents who are working more than one job, and/or who are operating with severely limited bandwidth, may not be able to come to school meetings. The fact that some people interpret this as a lack of caring seems to me like a microaggression in itself. If we assume that what is really happening is a lack of bandwidth rather than a lack of caring, we must be interested in and concerned about the things that steal bandwidth from parents.

As is the case for their children, parents who live in poverty or with persistent economic insecurity experience bandwidth depletion due to the constant worry about money. As has been shown by Baddeley and Hitch (1974), our brains cannot do more than one thing at a time. So when parents are worried about the things that they and their children need, and which they cannot afford, they have fewer cognitive resources for everything else, including things that would support the educational success of their children. I suggest that the situation is even more taxing on bandwidth for parents than for their children for several reasons.

- Parents are expected to provide for their children, both by society and by the children. Failure to do that adequately comes with negative judgment from others, from themselves, and sometimes from their children. This kind of persistent negative judgment eats away at self-confidence and mental bandwidth.
- One of the ways parents try to protect their children is by hiding their worries about money, or trying to. Parents want their children to be free of adult concerns, concentrate on school, have fun and play, and grow and develop without stress. So parents add to their own level of stress by carrying the full burden of poverty so their kids do not have to. This can be especially true for single parents as there may not be many outlets for them to express the frustration, stress, and fear that come with persistent economic insecurity. From a colleague who teaches 3- and 4-year-olds: "But the kids tend to carry it anyway, so then parents are dealing with their increased stress as well as the ways the children react to stress" (Mercier, personal communication, July, 2019).
- Many people, even those who are economically and politically conservative, have sympathy for children who are living in poverty. There are programs to help them access food (e.g., in public

schools), warm clothes, and publicly run recreational activities. For parents, however, there is often less sympathy and, as mentioned previously, plenty of criticism related to their capabilities to properly care for their children.

- Ever since the Reagan years, there has been a societal story line about the "welfare mother" and the people who are just "living off the system." Remember, that was the time of what was called *trickle-down economics*, which was the idea that tax breaks for the rich would create jobs, and the economic advantages would trickle down to help workers and people living in poverty. The trouble is, it did not work. The economic advantage stayed at the level of rich people, but the sense that poor people should have been able to "pull themselves up by their own bootstraps" remained. In the mid-1990s, so-called welfare reform was passed in the United States, ending entitlement programs and making our system of public support for low-income and poor people much meaner, and that situation continues today.

All of these factors exacerbate the bandwidth tax experienced by parents who are living with their children in poverty or near-poverty.

Economic Inequality

The United States is a very rich country in many ways, including money, natural resources, educational institutions at all levels, and physical infrastructure. However, it is also one of the most unequal countries in income and wealth distribution. Since 1980, the gap between the richest and the poorest in the United States has been increasing and is currently the largest in the history of the country (Ryscavage, 1995; Stone et al., 2018). International data indicate that it is not the actual amount of money that people have within a country but the inequality in distribution of the money that seems to be highly correlated with many measures of health and well-being for individuals and societies. Wilkinson and Pickett (2010), in *The Spirit Level*, offered ample evidence of this phenomenon. The United States was compared to a group of 20 to 23 countries the authors referred to as *successful democracies* wherein they demonstrated that more equal societies are better, based on metrics related to levels of trust, mental illness, life expectancy, infant mortality, obesity, children's educational performance, births to teenage mothers, homicides, imprisonment rates, and social mobility. Figure 7.1 presents a summary of these indicators.

Figure 7.1. Comparative health and social problems.

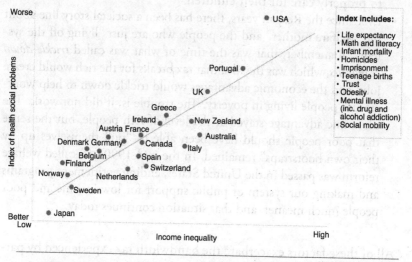

Note. From Wilkinson and Pickett (2009). Reprinted with permission.

Figure 7.2. Life expectancy and income.

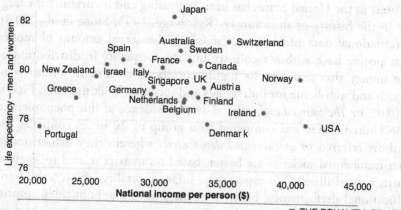

Note. From Wilkinson & Pickett (2009). Reprinted with permission.

These issues of physical and social well-being are not matters of money per se. For instance, as you can see in Figure 7.2, life expectancy is not related to comparative income. The United States has the highest national income per person and is among the lowest in life expectancy.

Another example is child well-being. As indicated in Figure 7.3, child well-being is not related to per-person income in these rich countries. Although the United States has the highest per person income, it has one of the lowest levels of child well-being. There are similar graphs that show the same relationships between inequality and negative outcomes for factors like homicides, depression, levels of trust, obesity, mental illness, and so on. Why is this, and how does all of this affect the mental bandwidth of the parents of children in our public schools?

This is my understanding of the dynamic: As fewer and fewer people own more and more of the income and wealth in the United States, there are more millions of people—adults and the children they are raising—who are left out of the promise of the opportunity for a decent life that has been a foundational part of the "American Dream." Living in poverty or near-poverty in any country is debilitating, both physically and mentally. Poverty comes with hunger, ill health, exposure to weather and other environmental hazards, violence, and constant worry and stress related to meeting the basic needs of existence, which often lead to hopelessness, depression, and despair.

Figure 7.3.   Child well-being and income.

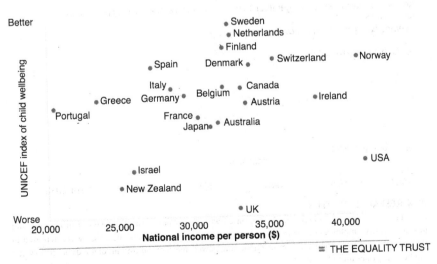

Child well-being is unrelated to average incomes in rich countries

Note. From Wilkinson and Pickett (2009). Reprinted with permission.

Living in these conditions in a country where there are clearly enough resources for everyone to live decently, but where social and economic policies actually exacerbate inequality, adds to bandwidth depletion.

According to Robert Reich in his documentary *Inequality for All*, in the years after the Great Depression and especially after World War II, the United States experienced unparalleled economic growth and increase in levels of education (Kornbluth, 2013). Veterans (mostly White) took advantage of the GI Bill and went to college in record numbers. There were low-interest loan programs that enabled middle-class families to buy a home (again, mostly White families). The gross domestic product (GDP), a measure of economic productivity, was on a constant upward trajectory from the 1950s well into the early 2000s. However, in the early 1970s, while GDP continued upward, wages stagnated, with the result that the wealth generated from this collective productivity began to be concentrated not in the workers but in the owners of corporations. That distributive pattern has continued, unabated, to the present, resulting in the wealthiest 10% of families in the United States owning 76% of all the wealth of the country in 2017 (Sahadi, 2016). The lack of the political will to change this by, for instance, establishing and enforcing a universal minimum wage and taxing wealthy people at the same rate as middle-class people, has allowed the levels of inequality to increase every year.

Even though average wages are higher today than in the 1960s, those wages have little more buying power, as seen in Figure 7.4.

Figure 7.4.   Stagnant purchasing power of wages.

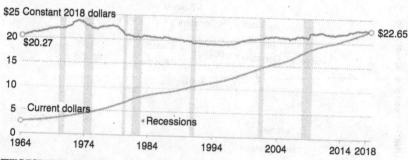

Americans' paychecks are bigger than 40 years ago, but their purchasing power has hardly budged.
Average hourly wages in the U.S., seasonally adjusted

PEW RESEARCH CENTER

Note. From Wilson and Pickett (2009). Reprinted with permission. Data for wages of production and non-supervisory employees on private non-farm payrolls. "Current dollars" describes wages reported in the value of the currency when received. "Purchasing power" refers to the amount of goods or services that can be bought per unit of currency.
Source: U.S. Bureau of Labor Statistics.

Figure 7.5.   Wage increases for top workers.

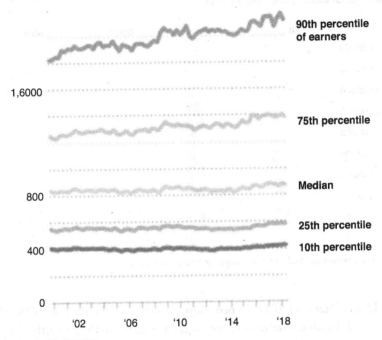

Wage increases in the U.S. rise to the top earners.
Usual weekly earnings of employed, full-time wage and salary workers, no seasonally adjusted, in constant 2018 dollars

90th percentile
of earners

1,6000

75th percentile

Median

800

25th percentile

400   10th percentile

0

'02   '06   '10   '14   '18

PEW RESEARCH CENTER
Note. From Wilson and Pickett (2009). Reprinted with permission.
Source: U.S. Bureau of Labor Statistics.

After adjusting for inflation, however, today's average hourly wage has just about the same purchasing power it did in 1978, following a long slide in the 1980s and early 1990s and bumpy, inconsistent growth since then. In fact, in real terms average hourly earnings peaked more than 45 years ago: The $4.03-an-hour rate recorded in January 1973 had the same purchasing power that $23.68 would today. (Desilver, 2018, para. 5)

Meanwhile, increases in real wages have gone up for the top 10% of wage earners, shown in Figure 7.5 (Desilver, 2018).

When wages are held down, that means more profit for the people who own the companies that employ workers, adding to the wealth gap between the richest citizens and the rest of us. According to the Institute for Policy Studies and Forbes (Inequality.org, n.d.), in 2016 the richest three people in

Figure 7.6.   Median wealth by race and ethnicity.

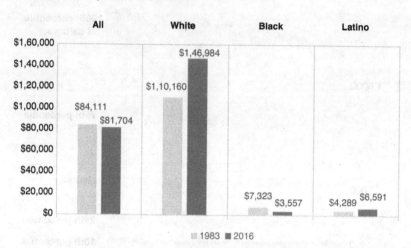

The racial wealth divide has grown over 3 decades

U.S. median wealth by race, 1983 and 2016

Note. From Wilson and Pickett (2009). Reprinted with permission.

the United States in 2018 owned more wealth than the bottom 50%. Over the past 3 decades, whereas the very rich have added to their wealth, the people at the bottom have dropped into "negative wealth," meaning that they owe more they own. The richest 1% own over half of all wealth in stocks and mutual funds, whereas the bottom 90% have the majority of their wealth in their homes. When we look at economic inequality by race and ethnicity, the gaps are even more staggering (see Figure 7.6).

It is bad enough that the majority of citizens in the United States own virtually no wealth and have no hope of accumulating it and have wages from full-time employment that are not enough to provide a decent standard of living for themselves and their children; however, what is more offensive than just the daily grind of that life is the fact that as a country we seem to be okay with that. People who are not valued and who are, for all practical purposes, left out of economic opportunity get persistent messages that their lives do not matter and that they do not belong in this society. And we know that not belonging consumes significant bandwidth. The psychological cost for parents of being, in essence, cast off by their own country leaves a huge dent in available bandwidth, including what is needed to support children in school.

Microaggressions

Schoolchildren and adolescents experience microaggressions while at school and in their neighborhoods and other public spaces. Their parents do as well. Remember that microaggressions are those small, everyday slights, insults, and invalidations that happen to people who are members of minoritized or undervalued groups. Closely related to the discussion about economic inequality, parents who are on the lower end of the scale of income and wealth may often feel the invalidation and indignity of not being thriving participants in the legitimate economy. Parents who are recipients of public assistance in the form of food or housing subsidies and whose children get free or reduced-priced breakfast and lunch at school may experience the stigma of negative judgment from people who think that each family should be able to take care of its own needs. Schoolteachers and staff often make assumptions about low-income and poor families, thinking that because they lack financial resources they also "lack intelligence, knowledge, propriety, and responsibility" (Potter, 2008, p. 67). As we know, microaggressions eat away at self-confidence and can make parents even less able to advocate for their children at school and to meet the other physical and emotional needs of their families. Microaggressions act to deplete the bandwidth of parents, leaving them with fewer cognitive resources to apply to all of the other responsibilities of life.

Parents, like many adults who have the responsibility for people other than themselves, try to maintain their equanimity when they are the target of microaggressions. They use up bandwidth wondering if the insult or slight was intended or not and whether or not they are safe in the environment where it happened, such as at work or in the social service agencies where they go for help. The psychological cost of experiencing these negative words or behaviors is high for anyone, and parents, especially single parents, may also have the added disadvantage of not having anyone with whom to talk about their feelings and not wanting their children to see they are stressed. On top of that, parents may witness or hear about from their children microaggressions aimed at their children in their school, neighborhood, faith community, or within their own extended families. Children who are the targets of microaggressions rooted in racism, sexism, classism, ableism, ethnocentrism, homophobia, transphobia, and so on, count on their parents to defend and comfort them. Parents experience vicariously the pain, anxiety, and fear their children might be reporting, adding to their own bandwidth depletion.

As is true when anyone attempts to confront a microaggression, parents walk a thin line in deciding what action to take, if any, in response to reports from their children of insults or slights or invalidations they may be experiencing at school. Intervention by parents with the intention of standing up for their children's rights, comfort, and safety can be a delicate and difficult undertaking, especially for parents who lack the social capital to feel capable and equipped to communicate within the formal school environment. When and if a parent does manage to have a conversation with a teacher, principal, or counselor, there is no guarantee that the outcome will be positive for the child. The culture in some schools and classrooms is not open, and may even be hostile, to reports that assert that a child has been treated unfairly or in a manner that impedes learning. Responses can be defensive, denying that anything unpleasant is allowed to happen and that the child is exaggerating, overly sensitive, or imagining things. There is a danger that the situation may worsen for the child if the parent is not believed and the child is labeled as a troublemaker for reporting her experience. Just like for adults who try to confront and correct microaggressions, although it sounds like the reasonable thing to do, it often does not turn out well. Clearly, microaggressions are major bandwidth stealers for parents, both in the experience of being the target and in the process of deciding what to do or not to do about them for themselves or on behalf of a child.

Worry

Most parents (and grandparents and aunts and uncles) worry about their children. I know I've been worrying for 39 years—and counting. A friend once told me, "A parent is only as happy as her saddest child." Parents who are economically secure and whose children are physically and mentally healthy and are not members of one or more negatively stereotyped groups worry about their children and that worry takes a bit of their bandwidth on most days. Parents who are poor or near poor, whose children have physical or mental health challenges, and/or who are members of one or more negatively stereotyped groups worry more. In addition, parents in the former category, when their children experience ill health or injury or run into obstacles, are much more likely to have the economic and social capital to get the help they need to deal with the situation and lessen the impact or eliminate the obstacle. Parents in the latter category are much more likely to lack both economic and social capital, including things like good health insurance, time flexibility, connections to services, and other help, so they may not only be worried but also feel helpless and useless, adding to the bandwidth tax.

Like the emotional stress that comes from the negative experiences of microaggressions, when parents are worried about money and many other things related to their children's well-being and success in school, they try to hide the extent of that worry from their children so that they do not also have to pay any more of a bandwidth cost than necessary. Parents try to reassure their children and support them as well as they can when they are struggling at school and when they know they do not have the same resource base as their classmates. Parents sacrifice in many ways to protect their children from physical and emotional stress, like giving up meals themselves or not buying better clothing to save the money to feed and clothe their children. They also suppress their needs for the emotional support they could get from talking about their worries and problems and speak in encouraging ways to their children and listen to *their* worries and anxieties, offering comfort and support. In this way, they are, ironically, sacrificing their own bandwidth to protect their children's. They know the damaging effects of vicarious racism (classism, xenophobia, homophobia, etc.) on their children, the need for them to "cognitively make sense of a world that systematically devalues and marginalizes them" (Heard-Garris et al., 2018, p. 236). Protecting their children from these effects takes a great deal of bandwidth from parents, thus robbing them of internal resources to meet the demands of daily life and advocate for their children at school.

8

TEACHERS

T eachers, who may be the most critical players in helping students recover bandwidth, can themselves live and work in conditions that seriously deplete their own. I recognize that many teachers are also parents and may be low income and/or members of negatively stereotyped groups; however, this chapter will focus on conditions specific to work that might steal bandwidth from teachers. In regard to teacher bandwidth, I want to focus on three main areas: inadequately funded schools, high-stakes testing, and comparative salaries that communicate a lack of respect and value for teachers. Although teachers are faced with many challenges, these three factors are significant in that they often present complex moral dilemmas for teachers who are discouraged about their ability to solve them. Working within systems that are fundamentally unfair takes a toll on bandwidth when this condition persists over many years.

School Funding

From the professional literature and research, and from interactions with public school educators, it is clear to me that teachers in many areas of the United States work in environments that overwhelm them with bandwidth demands that result in less-than-optimal work performance as well as costs in health and well-being. There are public schools in the United States that are well-resourced, where teachers get paid a fair wage, where educational supplies and technologies meet the needs of a modern learning environment, and where best practices are applied for all students. However, millions of children and youth attend schools that fall short on most or all of these measures and in which the teachers cannot meet their own expectations as professionals because of these structural barriers. The reality that you cannot be the professional you intended to be can be extremely taxing on bandwidth, making the effort of doing a good job even more challenging.

To reach equity in student outcomes, school districts with the highest proportion of poor and near-poor students need the highest levels of state and local funding to meet the needs of students who are likely to have fewer of their educational needs met in financially strapped households. The realities of school funding, however, do not bear out this equitable funding pattern. The data indicate, conversely, that states in which the highest number of public schoolchildren come from families living in poverty, the per-student spending is lagging behind the states where children live in more economically secure homes. Exacerbating these inequities are the facts about early childhood education; in the vast majority of states (46), children in low-income families are "considerably less likely to be enrolled than their [higher-income family] peers" (Baker et al., 2018, p. 23), when these are the children who need the early learning the most.

In the case of elementary and high school funding, most states do not have *fair school funding*, defined as

> a state finance system that ensures equal educational opportunity by providing a sufficient level of funding that is distributed to districts within the state for additional needs generated by student poverty. (Baker et al., 2018, p. 2)

In fact, in the majority of the states (37), schools in which 30% or more of the students come from low-income or poor families were funded at just equal to (20) or lower levels (17) than schools with fewer of these students (Baker et al., 2018). This is a critical flaw that significantly impacts both students and teachers in these underresourced schools. Baker et al. (2018) asserted that states should provide higher levels of funding to schools where there are the highest concentrations of children from low-income and poor families.

> Student and school poverty correlates with, and is a proxy for, a multitude of factors that increase the costs of providing equal educational opportunity—most notably, gaps in educational achievement, school district racial composition, English-language proficiency, homelessness, and student mobility. (p. 3)

In other words, the reality is that it costs more, not less, in teacher time and energy, educational resources, support services for children and families, remediation efforts, and so on, if schools are to provide truly equal access to educational opportunities for children whose families are less able to provide educational enrichment, let alone the basic needs of food, clothing, and shelter.

Teachers who work in comparatively well-resourced schools can gain great satisfaction in providing learning environments in which students can achieve their full potential in spite of living in homes and in families who are challenged by the bandwidth tax of persistent economic insecurity. However, teachers who work in high-poverty schools that are under resourced experience the daily grind of knowing that they are hardly making a dent in closing achievement gaps and some suspect that their school might even be making things worse for some children. And that is thinking just about economics. Add on to that teachers who work in schools where racism, classism, homophobia and transphobia, and other "differentisms" are daily hindering the growth and development of their students in environments in which teachers feel helpless to make things better.

In her book *Demoralized*, Santoro (2018) stated that

> the process of demoralization occurs when pedagogical policies and school practices (such as high-stakes testing, mandated curriculum, and merit pay for teachers) threaten the ideals and values, the moral center, teachers bring to their work. . . . Demoralization [is] the inability to access the moral rewards offered and expected in teaching. (pp. 5, 8)

I suggest that teachers who work in poorly resourced schools that serve high proportions of poor and near-poor students are likely to be demoralized by their inability to be the effective teachers they know they can be. In addition to pedagogical policies and school practices, these teachers have to contend with students who are dealing with the everyday bandwidth taxes of living in poverty and all that brings with it. Schools, like individual teachers and staff, have bandwidth limits. When schools are focused on the lived realities of their students related to food and housing insecurity, trauma from exposure to neighborhood violence, lack of resources at home that support learning and development, among other problems, it is not surprising that there is little bandwidth left to address issues such as racism, classism, religious intolerance, homophobia, and the other social-psychological underminers that plague their students and their families.

Over half of children attending public schools are living in poverty (Southern Education Foundation, 2019). The many needs of these students are very obvious to teachers and they know that they need more, not less, than other students to achieve in school. However, due to inadequate funding, too-large class sizes, deteriorating physical structures, and other persistent challenges, teachers find themselves unable to meet student needs. According to Santoro (2018), the difference between what teachers believe students need and deserve and what they are able to provide is what contributes significantly to teacher demoralization.

> For teachers experiencing demoralization, the moral dilemma is not *what* they should do to be good teachers, but that they *cannot* do what they believe a good teacher should do in the face of policies, mandates, or institutional norms. The source of the problem is the dissonance between educators' moral centers and the conditions in which they teach. (Santoro, 2018, p. 43)

High-Stakes Testing

Standardized testing of schoolchildren and youth increased significantly with No Child Left Behind (Walker, 2014b).

> The law, with its sweeping mandates for standardized English and math tests in grades 4–8 and its crushing consequences for schools that fail to make "adequate yearly progress," merely created a toxic culture of "teaching to the test" in order to raise test scores. It wasn't long after its passage that a narrow, scripted curriculum blanketed schools coast to coast. (Walker, 2014b, para. 14)

In a 2013 survey of teachers by the National Education Association (NEA, 2015), teachers reported that they spent a disproportional amount of time preparing students to take the tests and very little time using the results to improve learning. Teachers who taught classes in states in which students took a state standardized test reported spending the equivalent of 54 school days (out of about 185) on preparation and testing and only 2 days reviewing the results with students or parents. Half of the teachers thought that they spent too much time on standardized testing and 42% reported that their schools put moderate or extreme emphasis on test scores as part of teacher performance evaluation; 72% of respondents reported that they felt "'moderate' or 'extreme' pressure from both school and district administration" (Walker, 2014a, para. 3) to improve test scores. Even though 70% of teachers reported that they were satisfied with their job, 45% had considered leaving the profession "because of standardized testing" (para. 10).

In addition to the number of days devoted to preparing for and administering exams, teachers felt like high-stakes testing negatively affects students in the classroom. According to Walker (2014b), No Child Left Behind is uniformly blamed for stripping curriculum opportunities, including art, music, physical education and more, and imposing a brutal testing regime that has forced educators to focus their time and energy on preparing for tests in a narrow range of subjects: namely, English/language arts and math. For students in low-income communities, the impact has been devastating. (para. 3)

Walker reminded us that, although these same testing requirements might be affecting better resourced schools, children in those schools may get to go on field trips to museums and probably live in families that have the financial means for this kind of enrichment outside of school. Children from poor and near-poor families count on school to provide exposure to art, history, music, and other enriching experiences. When those activities are sacrificed to test preparation in an ever-more-restricted curriculum, these children are the ones who lose the most. Teachers, knowing this, can get very discouraged at the low quality and quantity of rich educational opportunities they are offering to the students who will benefit so much from them. One frustrated teacher commented about "the way critical subjects have been crowded out of schools or even eliminated entirely by the lethal one-two punch of deep budget cuts and the singular focus on improving reading and math" (para. 5).

Teacher Salaries

Most teachers did not go into the profession to make loads of money but because they want to help children and young people learn and develop. They want to contribute to their communities and society by helping to educate the next generations of workers and citizens. However, I suggest that it is a bandwidth-depleting experience to realize that, year after year, your work is less and less valued when measured by the willingness of the public to pay you a fair wage compared to others with similar educational requirements and work responsibilities. Especially for teachers who are working in schools where there are high numbers of students who come from low-income and poor families who accordingly need more care and attention, being undervalued in terms of salary can be demoralizing.

Because the bulk of school budgets are teacher salaries, the data on school funding related to schools with high proportions of students from low-income and poor families tell us that teachers in these schools are probably not being paid fairly for the work they do. When the salaries of teachers are compared to other professionals who are in the same labor market, are of similar age and degree level, and have similar work hours, the results are disappointing, to say the least. In only three states do teachers get paid virtually the same as their professional peers. In all the other states, they are paid far less, from a low of 69% to a high of 91%. In 41 states, teacher salaries are 85% or less than the salaries of their professional peers (Baker et al., 2018). According to the National Center for Education Statistics (2017), "In constant (i.e., inflation-adjusted) dollars, the average salary for [public school] teachers was one percent lower in 2015–16 than in 1990–91" (Table 211.50). (Add to this that most teachers find themselves spending part of their salaries on school supplies for their classrooms and for their students whose families cannot themselves afford to buy them.)

Further exacerbating salary inequities, teachers in high-poverty schools in most states have the same number or more students in their classrooms, even though children in these schools need more, not less, attention. Although 19 states have a progressive distribution of teachers (at least 5% more teachers per student in high-poverty districts), the rest of the states have little difference across districts according to student poverty rates (19) or have higher student:teacher ratios in high-poverty schools than in other schools (10; Baker et al., 2018). So, in addition to uncompetitive salaries, teachers in the highest poverty schools can also have more students needing even more from them. This is clearly a situation that can cause demoralization among the teachers who care the most about students.

BANDWIDTH
RECOVERY—STUDENTS

PART THREE

BANDWIDTH
RECOVERY—STUDENTS

FUNDS OF KNOWLEDGE

I will return to the consideration of parents and teachers in Part Four, but in Part Three I want to focus on ways in which classroom and school environments can be created to help students recover bandwidth that might be lost to poverty and persistent economic insecurity and to other kinds of scarcity based on individual or group identity and other challenges. In Part One, I made the case that the bandwidth of children and youth was depleted by insecurity about belonging, by stereotype and identity threat, and by microaggressions and bullying. In the next few chapters, I discuss some ideas for helping students recover bandwidth that relate to how we view students' strengths and resources; how we help all students feel like they belong by creating community within the classroom and school; and the importance of certainty, growth mind-set, and communication. The chapters in Part Three are meant to encourage teachers and others in schools to think about practical ways that we can be accountable to students, their families, and the community by creating learning environments where every student can not only survive and learn but also thrive. This can only happen when students have access to all of their bandwidth.

The specific order of the chapters is not significant. I could have started with basic needs using classic Maslowian architecture, but I decided to begin with the acknowledgment of what students and families bring to the learning environment. It is true that it is difficult for a child to learn when they are hungry, but in some ways those basic needs are more manageable than are the psychological needs for respect and affirmation. Fundamentally, children and youth need to be both physically and psychologically safe and secure for the best learning to occur, and that starts by acknowledging what they bring to the learning environment.

Growing up in poverty or persistent economic insecurity and/or as a member of a group that is in some way marginalized can result in feelings of exclusion, even invisibility, in the larger culture, beginning in early learning environments. Sometimes, it is assumed that children who come from working-class and poor families come to school without resources related to intelligence, knowledge, organization, and enriching experiences. As a result, teachers can hold low expectations for them and assume they are not as able to learn and grow in the ways that children from more economically secure families can. Because of racism, classism, and many other kinds of "different-isms," Black and Brown children, immigrant children, children with disabilities, and children who do not conform to someone's idea of "normal" may be treated as less able and less deserving than others. These children experience a scarcity of respect and belonging and, consequently, might have depleted mental bandwidth for learning.

One concept that I think perfectly addresses this scarcity issue is *funds of knowledge*. The idea, developed by Moll et al. (1992), is that even very young children have significant knowledge and skills they have learned from their family's culture, work, household management, neighborhood and family connections, and faith community that have helped the family to survive and thrive. So, instead of seeing children through a deficit lens, we can look for and see all the wisdom and skills they bring from home. In interdependent communities and families, children learn from the adults in their lives through everyday exchanges. This learning is achieved by asking questions rather than learning being imposed by adults for its own sake. As part of the family and community, children learn skills like a second or third language, music and other artistic expression, sewing and other crafts, sports skills, strategies to navigate between cultures, home repair, gardening, carpentry, and cooking, as well as knowledge about nutrition, spirituality, childcare, mechanics, history, and herbal medicine. All of these skills and knowledge add to the confidence and competence of children outside of school. In regard to school,

> Our analysis of funds of knowledge represents a positive (and, we argue, realistic) view of households as containing ample cultural and cognitive resources with great, *potential* utility for classroom instruction (see Moll & Greenburg, 1990; Moll et al., 1990). (Moll et al., 1992, p. 134)

This concept is especially important when teachers are working cross-culturally with their students. Most teachers in public pre-K and elementary schools are female and White, and, in many public schools, more than half the students are not White; accordingly, classrooms are cross-cultural environments. I would argue that social class differences are often, in essence, cross-cultural as well, as there may be disconnects among teachers, students, and families based on socioeconomic factors.

Teachers who embrace the funds of knowledge of their students can then leverage those to help students learn the concepts and skills in the school curriculum. González et al. (2005) developed a worksheet they have used with parents and families to learn about students' funds of knowledge. In some pre-K and early learning settings, teachers actually do home visits, which, in my view, would be ideal for all teachers of children in elementary grades as well (although probably impractical logistically).

In their discussions around culturally relevant classrooms, Baines et al. (2018) asserted,

> Building mutually supportive relationships with families is an essential anchor in the commitment to "good love" that grounds culturally relevant teaching. In our experiences, we've found that those relationships center on (1) building trust, (2) engaging in home visits that connect rather than condescend, (3) getting to know the community, and (4) supporting families' right to be heard and respected. (p. 28)

If home visits are not possible, teachers can work with parents in individual conferences or group parent meetings to learn from them about their home and work lives and the things their children know and can do. As some parents have little flexibility in their work schedules, consideration could be given to evening or weekend meetings, phone conferences, or available times before the school day begins. González et al.'s (2005) list of categories of household factors include home language, family values and traditions, caregiving, friends and family, family outings, household chores, educational activities, favorite TV shows, family (adult) occupations, or scientific knowledge (e.g., health, recycling, exercising). By learning about these aspects of family life, teachers can appreciate the resources of knowledge and skill that each child brings to the classroom. Teachers at a bilingual school in California wholeheartedly embraced this idea when they said of their students that "all were brimming with knowledge, ideas, and resources for life and learning" (Stillman & Anderson, 2017, p. 79).

How could teachers use the concept of funds of knowledge to help students recover bandwidth so they can learn better? This discussion overlaps with the one about belonging, which is in the next chapter, but here I will assert again that there are costs to not feeling valued and respected, kinds of scarcity that steal bandwidth. So, to the extent that children and their families are valued and their experiences acknowledged and respected, bandwidth can be reclaimed. Practically, what does this look like once a teacher has found out about a child's funds of knowledge? I suspect that just being asked about their traditions, work, household practices, activities, and so on is affirming enough that some bandwidth recovery may come from the sharing exercise itself. Beyond that, teachers can leverage student and family funds by inviting children to share with the rest of the class something they know or can do that is unique to their family or culture. Teachers can ask family members to come to school and share a skill or interest (e.g., cooking, painting, music, dance, or storytelling) with the class and then talk about that activity in the days and weeks following the visit to affirm that connection (No Time for Flash Cards, 2018). Based on the cultural practices and traditions of students' families, teachers can have small celebrations in the classroom and incorporate appropriate history lessons that affirm the heritage of each student.

From a learning perspective, recognizing students' funds of knowledge allows the teacher to build on them for optimal learning. We know that students learn best when they can connect new knowledge to prior knowledge—connecting the unknown to the known. As Glisczinski (2011) told us, when we connect knew information to concrete experiences from students' lives, their brains light up and learning happens. In a study involving 262 high school students and 7 science teachers, students in the experimental group wrote about the usefulness and value of the course material for their lives. This intervention resulted in improved grades for students who had low expectations for success in the class (Hulleman & Harackiewicz, 2009). Interestingly, there was a negative effect on the grades of the students whose teachers *told* them why the content of the class was relevant, suggesting the importance of student self-reflection and connection-making.

This idea of connecting the known to the unknown will, of course, look different based on the age, developmental stage, and needs of each group of students. In early learning environments, toddlers and pre-K children would not be asked to write about how science or history or math relates to them, but there are many other ways they can relate what they know to these topics. Is this a reason that the concept of "show and tell" has lasted for generations? Children are asked to bring something from home to share with the class as a way to connect home to school and to honor children's funds of knowledge. As children progress into early elementary and then into middle school, the invitations and prompts related to this kind of activity can get more specific. For instance,

"Bring something to share that relates to the following. . .

- Your grandparents or great-grandparents and how they lived that's different than today
- The language you speak at home
- A story that often gets told at family gatherings about something that happened in the past
- A special day you had with family or friends
- Someone really important in your life who is part of your "family," but not an official relative
- The story of how your parents or grandparents learned English and how to live and work in the United States
- What your parents or aunts or uncles do for work
- Something pretty or interesting in your house that is part of your culture or your family history
- Food you eat in your family and how it is prepared
- A favorite book that was read to you by a parent, older sibling, or other family member
- Something you dream about doing in your life and where you got the idea"

When we start out with the appreciation of what students already know and can do, we take advantage of what Vygotsky (1930) called the "zone of proximal development" (p. 79). This zone encompasses the space in which a child almost knows something or how to do something but needs just a bit of help to know or do it independently. "The zone of proximal development today will be the actual developmental level tomorrow—that is, what a child can do with assistance today she will be able to do by herself tomorrow" (Vygotsky, 1978, pp. 87–89). In order to leverage students' funds of knowledge for the learning of new knowledge and skills, the following conditions need to be met:

- The presence of someone with the knowledge and skills to guide the learner
- Social interactions that allow the learner to observe and practice their skills
- Scaffolding, or supportive activities provided by the mentor or teacher that help guide the learner through the [zone of proximal development] (Cherry, 2019, para. 5)

The "someone" can be an adult or a fellow student. Peer instruction, according to Mazur (Lambert, 2012), has been shown to be extremely effective, especially when the time that the teacher first learned the concept or information is in the distant past. A student who has recently learned something might remember when they did not know it and be able to explain it to another student in the way that helped them understand. Asking one student to do the scaffolding for another has significant benefits for both students. The "student" learns a new thing and the "teacher" feels affirmed and empowered. The "teacher" also usually develops a deeper understanding of the topic or lesson as they try to communicate it to someone else.

Social interaction is critical in many ways for children and youth at various developmental stages. During times when children and adolescents are establishing their own identities, they may look to peers more readily and willingly than to adults. Providing consistent scaffolding is critical to learning within the zone of proximal development; the idea is to give just the right amount of support so the student can take over the problem-solving process on their own as soon as possible.

To get to the next level of development or to solve a problem at the next level of complexity, students need to take some risks and try things that might not work the first time. If we know that students are bringing funds of knowledge to the learning task, we will have confidence that they can take some risks and, with support, reach their learning goals. However, if we assume they are coming from deficit home environments because their families are poor or speak a different language, we will be less likely to trust them to reach for that new achievement. Because bandwidth can be taxed by a scarcity of confidence and trust, it is critical for bandwidth recovery for students to experience frequent small forward steps so their confidence is bolstered and they are adding to the funds of knowledge they have to apply to the next task.

Both confidence and trust are undermined by frequent (or constant) correcting of "bad" behavior. I suggest that some of what we see as dysfunctional or disruptive behaviors are themselves actually funds of knowledge—adaptive, complex skills developed to respond to unhealthy environments. For instance, a child who has learned that he gets his needs met only by loud demands will continue that behavior in school. How could those learned survival skills, and certainly that adaptability, be celebrated and guided toward integration into a peer group and, eventually, to positive achievement?

The application of the concept of funds of knowledge looks different for students at various stages of growth and development. In early learning centers, pre-K, and elementary school, children's primary identification group is most likely to be their family and so getting to know what they learn from and with people in their household is critical. Students' home cultures, traditions, and practices are probably the primary resources for them as they learn and grow. Beginning in middle school and through high school, many students will be acquiring funds of knowledge from outside the households of their families. Students may have jobs where they are learning important technical and interpersonal skills. They may play on sports teams, be part of a band, or be active in clubs like scouting or 4-H, or participate in youth groups in their faith community. The idea is the same, though. Teachers can reach out to students and their families and communities to find out what students know and can do and build on that in school.

In 2014, Luis Moll, one of the original researchers who developed the concept of funds of knowledge, joined a new colleague, Moisès Esteban-Guitart, to discuss "funds of identity," building further on Vygotsky's work on learning in interaction with other people and through life experience. They wrote about the analysis of funds of identity as they are expressed through writing, voice, music, and visual art, and in which students incorporate their culture, language, and life experiences, connecting learning from within the school to that outside the school. To learn about students' funds of identity, the focus is no longer necessarily on conversations with the family about household activities and practices. Instead the focus is more on the expression by the students about what they know and can do. The expression of funds of identity can take a variety of forms that could include the many kinds of media and technology that are available to students today (Esteban-Guitart & Moll, 2014).

For many years, I have had my college students do what I call a "Life Report" as a way to affirm that they come to the class with experience and wisdom worthy of being shared and valued. The report is done using the PechaKucha presentation method (Klein Dytham Architecture, 2003), which is 20 PowerPoint slides, 20 seconds per slide, using mostly pictures. I use this method for several reasons: The use of pictures to tell a story lets students be effective presenters even if they are not proficient in English (writing, spelling), it is time limited so everyone has a chance to present, it honors life experience, and it builds community within the class. When teachers acknowledge students' funds of knowledge and identity at all ages and stages, they are helping them to recover bandwidth so they will be more likely to thrive at school. High school students might do a Life Report that tells about their family, their school experiences, their work and hobbies, their plans for college or technical training, and/or their career aspirations.

As the teacher, I have always done my own Life Report during the first class meeting as a way to introduce myself, demonstrate the presentation method, and model sharing about my life. For the past several years, after everyone has done their Life Report, I have had students do a guided written reflection about what they learned about their classmates, about themselves, and about how what they learned will affect their life and work in the future. The following themes have been consistent over the years:

- *Resilience.* Many of us have been through struggles and survived.
- *Solidarity.* Even though we have different backgrounds and different experiences, we are all here in this class together to get an education.
- *Nonjudgment.* "Don't judge a book by its cover"; you don't know what people have gone through in their lives that is affecting how they think and behave today.
- *Self-confidence.* In spite of some challenging things in my life, I'm still persisting and trying to reach my goals.

The concept of a Life Report could be adapted for students at any age. The specific prompts need to be age and situation appropriate, but the idea of telling about your life, experiences, and aspirations is doable for people at any age. For young children, teachers can determine what is appropriate and possible for their students, but prompts could include family makeup, extended family, pets, favorite toys or movies, fun trips or activities, involvement in sports, music, community or interest groups, and favorite foods. In upper elementary grades and high school, students can begin to reflect on things that make their family unique, including strengths and challenges; cultural practices that have had meaning for them; involvement with a faith community; or activities like sports, music, dance, volunteer work, and other interests. Guided articulation of these aspects of life experience can help students gain insight into their own funds of identity and into the lives of their classmates and teachers, contributing to a sense of belonging for everyone.

With the accessibility of images on the internet, students can create presentations about their lives even if they do not have family pictures available. Some of my students have had almost no pictures from their childhoods because their houses had been lost to fires or floods or there had been periods of homelessness or because they were no longer connected with their parents. They have still been able to find pictures online of their elementary school and high school, the towns where they grew up, and images that reflect other important things in their lives. If technology is not accessible, Life Reports could be done in some other media, like visual art, spoken word, or movement. In summary, Life Reports allow students to bring themselves authentically into the classroom, inviting them to meld their personal and cultural identities to their growing concept of themselves as successful students and scholars who truly belong in school.

If time does not allow for individual presentations in the form of Life Reports, an anonymous survey could be done early in the year to gather data about the students as a group related to their families, life experiences, interests, and preferences, gauged to appropriate age levels. (Maybe technology could be used so the exercise also includes learning about data collection and reporting.) A survey might include items about favorite foods, books, songs, television shows, movies, colors, video games and toys, leisure time or sports activities, places that students have visited, local places where students have found solitude or beauty, demographics like number of siblings or grandparents or family country of origin, occupations or hobbies of family members, and so on. Shared with the class in aggregate, the results could illustrate both diversity and commonalities among class members.

In Box 9.1, author and 25-year public school teacher Julie Landsman writes about using themes as a way to let students express their funds of knowledge.

BOX 9.1.
Ideas in Practice: Teaching Using Themes

Courage
You can use examples from history and language arts and even science that involve people of color or immigrants and both women and men as examples of courage. Students can write about people in their lives who have been courageous.

Leaving and Arriving
Students can study immigration in history and in stories, and even connect that with their own family's journey from where their parents grew up to where they are. Often, students' parents immigrated to other parts of the country or an entirely new country for work or a new life. This theme takes in so much that students can relate to; they can write about their own journey, where they hope to go next.

Timeline
Students do their own timelines, indicating years when something happened that was important for them; timelines can also involve artwork.

Innovation and Discovery
There are many examples of people and peoples who have invented new things, discovered old things and places, and made important contributions to the world. A class project could involve finding innovators in the local community, especially students' family members, and have them come to class to talk about their work.

10

BELONGING

It is human nature to want to belong and, according to Maslow's (1943) hierarchy, a human need as well. People may have very different ideas about what that looks like in their lives or in the lives of children at various stages of development, but most people would agree that it is a basic need. Maslow ranks belonging just above the basic needs of food and water, shelter, and safety and security. Belonging is about feeling like you fit in, that someone likes and accepts you, that someone will play with you and value you as part of the group. Belonging means being loved and included. If you belong, you have the feeling that you matter, that someone thinks you are worthy of attention, and that you can contribute. Feeling like you do not belong takes up lots of bandwidth. If you sense that your status of belonging is not reliable, that it could easily disappear, that takes up even more bandwidth. If belonging in a classroom, for instance, is dependent on being a certain kind of student or behaving in specific ways, then belonging can feel very tentative. Belonging at school is the most critical for students in the following situational or identity groups: those who live with persistent economic insecurity; those who are part of marginalized racial, ethnic or other minority groups; those who have a physical, mental, or intellectual disability; or those who do not fit into a clear girl/boy gender binary. School can be very precarious for these students, and the degree to which they feel a sense of belonging might strongly influence their ability to learn and develop.

How do we create school environments in which all students feel like they belong? There are many ways to talk about belonging in schools, and some of them will be included in the next two chapters on community and certainty. In this chapter, I focus on three aspects of belonging: unconditional love, affirmation, and respect; freedom to be your whole self; and identity safety.

Unconditional Love, Affirmation, and Respect

I have often heard my faculty and student services colleagues say, "I try to treat students like I would want someone to treat my children or my grandchildren." Someone approached me after one of my bandwidth recovery talks and asked, "Aren't you just telling us to treat people the way our grandparents taught us?" Yes and yes. When we love unconditionally, we affirm that each person is valued as a precious person deserving of our respect and care. That is all well and good, but how do we actually make this happen in classrooms in which the realities of the economy and society bring increasing challenges (poverty, racism, classism, and all the other "differentisms") into the crucial work of education?

Beginning in early childhood learning settings, teachers and school staff set the tone for the way children and families are treated at school. Because young children need more guidance in basic social interactions and have not developed full impulse control, teachers often need to implement logical consequences that might include moving away from a desired area, which can feel to children like "conditional love." However, when teachers use behavior-centered language ("That behavior is not acceptable" or "That seems like a bad choice" versus "You are a bad person"), they empower children's understanding of their ability to make positive choices and modify behavior within the secure relationship, because they are saying it is the behavior that is inappropriate, whereas the child is loved no matter what.

In what is sometimes called the *hidden curriculum* (Alsubaie, 2015), teachers and administrators communicate the standards and values of schools by how they treat students and parents. The hidden curriculum might determine what kinds of behaviors are acceptable, what groups seem to be more valued than others, what kinds of knowledge are privileged, or what language patterns are legitimate. When students see that everyone is loved and respected at school, they are more likely to feel they belong themselves and are more likely to follow that lead and show respect to others. In the hidden curriculum, teachers are key role models for students and have a great deal of influence in establishing an affirming culture in the classroom. Critically, a sense of belonging significantly affects school attendance:

> Attendance rates are evidence of the attachment students have to their school and the people who work and learn there. . . . The relationships educators build and maintain with students and their families make school feel like a valuable place. They are what make children feel that

they are cared for at school and missed when they are absent. (Smith et al., 2017, p. 49)

Respect is shown to students and families in many ways that are related to the concept of funds of knowledge (discussed in chapter 9). When teachers and school staff are interested in the lives, cultures, and life experiences of students, they are showing respect and valuing the diversity their students represent. Respect is modeled by teachers and staff in the ways they treat each other, students, parents, and community members. Respect communicates that each person has a vital contribution to make to the learning of everyone and that each person's voice should be heard. When students are in a respectful environment, their bandwidth is freed up because they know they can apply their whole selves to the tasks of learning and growth. Margaret Martelle, who has taught children in first grade for more than 20 years, encourages students to affirm each other each school day through a

> Thankful Circle at the end of the day. Kids get the opportunity to thank a classmate. We practice social skills like making eye contact, but the most powerful part is watching the kids burst with pride when someone acknowledges them. (personal communication, July 30, 2019)

Respect is shown when we acknowledge that students and their families have values that inform their lives and choices and affirming those values can free up bandwidth. Research by Cohen et al. (2006) and many similar intervention experiments by a variety of people have shown that having students identify important personal values and write about them resulted in an end to a downward spiral of grades (Sherman et al., 2013), more resiliency in the face of setbacks, and decreased physiological responses to stress (Sherman et al., 2009; Creswell et al., 2005). The simple intervention consisted of presenting students with a list of values and asking them to choose which were the most important in their lives and then complete a short writing exercise in which they explained why those values mattered to them. Sometimes this was done only once in a semester or only before major exams or several times over a school year. In all cases, students who were part of the intervention did better than control groups in measures including semester grades (Cohen et al., 2009), reduced achievement gaps between White and Latino students over 3 years, and positive self-reported feelings of health and well-being 3 years later (Sherman et al., 2009)

Figure 10.1 shows the personal values exercise that I have used with college students and adults. I have included the writing prompt I often use, but the prompt could vary depending on the setting. The prompt could relate to career aspirations or the vision students have for their lives. Alternative prompts could

Figure 10.1. Personal values affirmation exercise.

Wisdom	Reliability	Integrity	Enthusiasm
Winning	Productivity	Inspiration	Efficiency
Well-being	Power	Initiative	Dignity
Wealth	Personal growth	Independence	Dependence
Volunteering	Perseverance	Humor	Curiosity
Understanding	Peace	Humility	Creativity
Truth	Patriotism	Hope	Courtesy
Trust	Patience	Honesty	Courage
Tradition	Orderliness		Cooperation
Teamwork	Optimism	Health	Conflict resolution
Success	Openness	Harmony	Confidence
Spirituality	Open communication	Generosity	Competitiveness
Simplicity	Nature	Fun	Competence
Service	Mercy	Friendship	Compassion
Self-reliance	Making a difference	Freedom	Community
Self-esteem	Loyalty	Forgiveness	Commitment
Self-discipline	Love	Flexibility	Collaboration
Safety	Listening	Fitness	Civility
Sacrifice	Learning	Financial stability	Caring
Romance	Leadership	Family	Boldness
Risk-taking	Knowledge	Fame	Beauty
Responsibility	Kindness	Faith	Ambition
Respect	Justice	Fairness	Adaptability
Resilience	Joy	Excellence	Achievement
Reputation	Job security	Ethical behavior	Accountability
Religion	Intuition		

1. From the list, circle the 10 values that you consider to be the most important in your life.
2. Think for a bit about each of those 10 values. Put a second circle around the three that are the most important of all of them.
3. Write a letter to a friend or family member explaining why these values are important to you and the difference they have made in your life. Give some examples of things you have done or choices you have made in your life based on these three values.

include: "Write about how these values have influenced your thoughts about what job you would like to do as an adult" or "Write a letter to someone close to you telling them how these values have made you think about what kind of family you would like to have as an adult." I often have students write and then talk with each other about the values they chose and why.

For youth and younger children, teachers can use a shorter list with words that are at the reading level of the students in the class (or parents in a family or school community meeting). My understanding of why this simple exercise is so powerful is that children and families who are poor or near-poor, are members of groups about whom there are negative stereotypes, and who already feel left out in many ways, are seldom asked about what they value. In fact, I think there are many messages in society, the media, and even from our schools that what these students value from their culture and life are not the things that will help them be successful at school. Just having their values acknowledged, and having them reflect on how they are important to them, increases students' sense of belonging and helps recover bandwidth.

The list of values would not need to be in writing, of course, especially for young children or students for whom English is not their first language. Values could be portrayed in picture books or through storytelling. Students could draw their values or speak them in a group or ask a parent or grandparent to come to school and talk about cultural values that undergird their family. In Figure 10.2, I have suggested a list of value words that might be appropriate for early elementary students.

It seems to me that it does not much matter what words are in the list. The important thing is that students are asked about what matters to them and someone listens to their answers. Even very small children can think and talk about what is important to them and how they want to be treated (see Box 12.2). Landsman, in Box 10.1, suggests supportive ideas for a sense of belonging in the classroom.

Figure 10.2. Personal values affirmation exercise for elementary school students.

Being nice to other people	Being good at sports	Not fighting
Telling the truth	Running fast	Speaking quietly
Loving your family	Sharing your toys	Helping
Listening to the teacher	Reading well	Taking care of other people
Doing math well	Telling stories	Being nice to animals
Playing outside	Doing your schoolwork	Staying safe

BOX 10.1.
Ideas in Practice: Supporting a Sense of Belonging

1. "I Am From . . ." Many schools begin their year having students write a list of things they are from—the food they eat, the songs they sing, the celebrations, the holidays, things they value, and so on. Students of any age can do these lists. Once students have them, they can be read aloud or posted on a board. Eventually a class "I Am From" poem can be created using lines from each student's poem. (See iamfromproject.com for more information.)

2. A curriculum that empowers students around issues that are important is a way of creating a sense of belonging. For instance, they can work together to write letters to the editor about a park they want for a place to play but has been vandalized or filled with trash.

3. Students can interview elders in their family or neighborhood and present those interviews to the class.

4. Community members can be invited to come and talk with students about issues that concern them; students are asked to prepare questions ahead of time.

5. Artists, poets, engineers, and activists who look like the students themselves can be invited as guest speakers and performers.

Unconditional love and respect may be especially important (and elusive?) for students with disabilities. I suspect that many of them would tell you, "It's not easy being me." It is sometimes challenging to interact with students who communicate in different ways and whose learning needs present unusual demands on teachers and classmates. Maintaining an attitude of affirmation and respect can surely be challenging at times. In Box 10.2, Jennifer Bronski, an instructional resource teacher in metropolitan Chicago for 16 years, shares how she attempts to provide a consistently positive learning environment.

BOX 10.2.
Ideas in Practice: Clean Slate

I think one of the most important things I can do for my students is to start with a clean slate at the beginning of every class. The majority of them struggle with impulse control, confidence, and motivation. This is also why I have fun class activities that do not need to be earned. All students need to know they are part of our classroom family unconditionally. This has helped significantly in building trustful relationships.

Freedom to Be Your Whole Self

I went to a Catholic elementary school in a small town in Kansas. About 90% of the kids in town went to this school. All of us were White and, although there were a few families that could probably be described as "upper class," most of us were from families who, in general, were just getting by economically. My family owned the local funeral home, which had been in my father's family for generations, and my parents were very highly regarded in the town. In other words, my sense of belonging was never in question. None of my bandwidth was used worrying about fitting in or being accepted.

The situation can be very different for students who are, in the context of U.S. society and within their school environment, considered to be somehow different and not quite good enough. This could be because their families are poor or near-poor, they are Black or Brown, their first language is not English, they are differently abled physically or mentally, they identify as LGBTQ, or their gender identity does not conform to a strict girl/boy binary. For students in these groups, a true sense of belonging must include an acceptance of all of their identities, fully and lovingly. The school environment must provide a space in which they are protected from the negative effects of the social-psychological underminers they experience in society, like stereotype threat, microaggressions, and even threats to their physical safety.

Being their whole self means that each student brings unique strengths and challenges into the learning environment. Teachers need to embrace both and help students see that this kind of diversity is not only tolerated but also celebrated. They need to help all students understand that each student has different gifts and abilities and areas in which they need a bit of extra support. For instance, students who grow up in families that experience persistent economic insecurity may exhibit behaviors that are off-putting or misunderstood by other students, and teachers need to help all students realize this and make the classroom work for everybody.

Children who grow up in poverty may have a narrower set of emotional responses available to them. All children have the emotions that are automatic, like fear, joy, and sadness, but some may lack those that need to be taught, like compassion, cooperation, patience, humility, and optimism. Emotional dysregulation may get in the way of students succeeding in school. Peers working in groups with these students might feel like they are not doing their share or that they are not invested in the project, so they do not want to have them as part of the group. This exclusion adds to their sense of not belonging and contributes to further discouragement. (Jensen, 2009, p. 19)

Teachers can help all students understand that growing up in different environments can make students behave in different ways that have little to do with their capabilities or their willingness to work hard and contribute. When students learn to understand each other, they can be encouraged to include everyone and to respect and value what each person brings to the table and, in the process, discover talents and skills that might not otherwise be revealed. When students understand and empathize with each other, they can celebrate when a classmate who is facing some exceptional challenge experiences success.

Expressing themselves in daily or weekly journals can help students articulate some of the challenges they encounter related to their identities and the realities of their lives. Journals can be class- or subject-specific or be part of the routine of any class. Students can share journal responses as a way to connect with their teachers or other students. Teachers might have students respond to a prompt in writing and then let them choose a part of their writing to share out loud. This exercise, done routinely and respectfully, could increase empathy and help put student behavior in context. Consider prompts such as the following:

- I wonder about . . .
- Once I dreamed that . . .
- I used to think that . . .
- Someone once told me that . . .
- I don't really believe in . . .
- One of my favorite memories is . . .
- I wish . . .
- The most beautiful place is . . .
- I once visited . . .
- I would really like to meet . . .
- Sometimes I just want to . . .

If this writing and sharing works for students, they could generate their own set of prompts.

Students who are part of the minority related to sexual orientation, gender identity, or gender expression are often expected (or feel like they are expected) to leave important parts of their identities outside the school or classroom doors. Though acceptance of LGBTQ people in the United States has increased over the past few decades, it is still a tenuous situation for many schoolchildren and youth in public schools. According to Carter et al. (2018), schools can be considered "performance venues" within which "identity formation takes place in a social context" (p. 108). Their concept of "impression management" involved a "process by which people attempt to present a public image of themselves in the service of 'fitting in'" (Goffman, 1959, p. 108). They explained that, in a social context in which it is important to establish that one is not gay, students can bully or ostracize other students who they think might be LGBTQ as a way to separate themselves from those identities. Obviously, this can create a very hostile environment for students who do identify within these categories. The authors wondered how we can "prepare teachers to assist students in forging their own personal stories without building their identity at the expense of others" (p. 109). This seems like the central task of creating learning environments in which all students (and teachers) can bring their whole selves, including all of their identities, freely into the school space.

Identity Safety

In *Whistling Vivaldi*, Claude Steele (2010) wrote about the nearly 20 years of research by him and his colleagues and others related to the concept of stereotype threat, what he termed the *threat in the air*. Identity threat is even more diffuse. Steele explains that we all have identity contingencies, qualities that people associate with us based on real or perceived group membership. If those associations usually or often result in the expectation of unpleasant, or even dangerous responses from others, the person is in an identity threat situation. Steele described this phenomenon as

> the threat of something bad happening to you because you have the identity. You don't have to be sure it will happen. It's enough that it could happen. It's the possibility that requires vigilance and that makes the identity preoccupying. (p. 75)

In fact, the not knowing actually takes up more bandwidth than if you were sure something bad was going to happen, because at least then you could expect it. Identity threat in school environments steals lots of bandwidth from students. And Steele indicated that it is not just a passing threat, something that happens in the classroom or during tests. He called it a "cloaking threat that can feed on all kinds of daily frustrations and contextual cues and get more disruptive over time" (p. 177). So schools need to do what they can to create identity-safe spaces for every student.

Identity safety relies on several factors in a learning environment. In an identity-safe school, students see images of themselves in art and photographs that are publicly displayed. Identity safety is increased if students at least sometimes see teachers and school leaders who share some aspect of identity with them. There are consistent messages in identity-safe schools that all children and their families are welcomed and valued. We should not forget that the identities of family members, even though they may seldom be present in the classroom, must also be safe. Children whose parents or siblings identify as LGBTQ, for instance, need to feel they can talk openly about members of their families. When teachers clearly communicate acceptance of LGBTQ family members, students "can stop censoring themselves and instead be honest about the people they live with and love, focusing on being kids and learning rather than on hiding or making other people feel comfortable with their families" (Ryan & Hermann-Wilmarth, 2018, p. 6).

The Stanford Integrated Schools Project, in research involving observations in 84 elementary classrooms, found that there was a positive relationship between identity-safe teaching and student performance. "Students in identity-safe classrooms performed at higher levels on standardized tests and felt a greater sense of belonging and inclusion" (Cohn-Vargas, 2015, para. 5). In Figure 10.3, Cohn-Vargas describes key aspects of identity-safe classrooms in four areas.

As you can see, this list includes concepts from funds of knowledge, affirmation, respect, and other aspects of student engagement and positive relationships, and the intentionality of forming and maintaining community, which I will address in chapter 12.

Identity safety can also be inculcated in a school when teachers teach in culturally relevant ways. Carmen Tisdale described what she called an All-Male Reading Blitz through which she invited Black men from the community to come into her kindergarten classroom to read to and interact with the children (Baines et al., 2018). These men provided role models of strong and competent Black men, and she observed an increase in self-confidence in her young Black boys. "At a time when schooling and society often positioned Black males with a kind of nobodyness (Hill, 2016), Carmen wanted her students to know that they were somebodies, already filled with greatness" (Baines et al., 2018, p. 30).

For students with disabilities, I suspect the feeling of "nobodyness" is common. These students struggle to belong and to find a place where they fit in and have people they can call friends. I read about how lonely many

Figure 10.3.   Key aspects of identity-safe classrooms.

---

1. Child-Centered Teaching

Such instruction promotes autonomy, cooperation, and student voice.

- *Listening for student voices* ensures that each student can contribute to and shape classroom life.
- *Teaching for understanding* assures that students learn new knowledge and incorporate it into what they know.
- *Focusing on cooperation rather than competition* encourages students to learn from and help others.
- *Classroom autonomy promotes responsibility* and belonging in each student.

2. Cultivating Diversity as a Resource

Approaching diversity in this way provides challenging curriculum and high expectations for all students in the context of the regular and authentic use of diverse materials, ideas, and teaching activities.

- *Using diversity as a resource for teaching* draws from all students' lives as part of the curriculum and daily life in the classroom.
- *High expectations and academic rigor* support all students in learning to analyze, synthesize, evaluate, and strive to grow intellectually at every academic level.
- *Challenging curriculum* motivates students with meaningful, purposeful learning as opposed to rote teaching and remediation.

3. Classroom Relationships

Classroom relationships are based on trusting, positive interactions with the teacher and among the students.

- *Teacher warmth and availability to support learning* builds a trusting, encouraging relationship with each student based on belief that can succeed and achieve at high levels.
- *Positive student relationships* promote interpersonal understanding and caring among students in a climate free of bullying and social cruelty.

(Continues)

Figure 10.3. (*Continued*)

4. Caring Classroom Environments
In caring classroom environments, social skills are taught and practiced, and they help students care for one another in an emotionally and physically safe space. • *Teacher skill* is the capacity to establish an orderly, purposeful classroom that facilitates student learning. • *Emotional and physical comfort* are crucial so that each student feels safe and attached to school and to other students. • *Attention to prosocial development* incorporates social and emotional learning (SEL) into all aspects of daily life, teaching students how to live with one another, feel empathy for one another, and solve problems with respect and care for others.

Note: Reprinted from Cohn-Vargas, 2015, paras. 7–11

of these students feel because they do not have friends, or maybe they have a few people they can relate to at school, but they are only at-school friends (Robinson & Truscott, 2014). Inclusion in regular general education classrooms is the best for most students (Kimbrough & Mellen, 2012; Robinson & Truscott, 2014); however, when a student is the only "special" student in a classroom, it can be more difficult for them to feel comfortable and connected. Reading this, I thought of Black college students who have told me how they feel when they walk into class on the first day and see they are the only person of color in the room and experience that sinking feeling of isolation. This sense of "onliness" is a potential identity threat for students in a variety of situations.

It seems like there could be strategies to eliminate the sense of onliness for students with disabilities. Teachers could encourage students to see ability, communication style, approach to learning, and other individual differences as neutral variables—not good or bad—and help all students assess where they each fall on a series of continuums. For instance, if students thought about their physical abilities, some would be left- or right-handed, and some would be able or would not be able to run fast, do a cartwheel, sit cross-legged, and so on. By making a class continuum of various physical abilities, students would see that their classmate in a wheelchair is just at a different place on the line, not an "other" completely different than everyone else. Students could demonstrate different ways of explaining a situation or describing an object or meeting a person for the first time, learning that a classmate on the autism spectrum just has a unique way of relating that is not right or wrong, just different. Removing the onliness could make a significant difference to a student who has the label of "disabled" or "special" and facilitate their sense of belonging and of being somebody.

11

CERTAINTY

ne of the most insidious bandwidth stealers is uncertainty. As I
mentioned previously, significant bandwidth can be taken up
with trying to figure out if an insult or slight was intended or not
and whether or not it seriously threatens safety. That process is exhausting
and can chip away at not only cognitive resources but also self-confidence.
Uncertainty leaves us wondering, which takes up cognitive capacity. Children
who live with persistent economic insecurity or who experience the frequent
underminers of racism, classism, heterosexism, xenophobia, and so on need
to be able to count on their school to be a place that is predictable, where
they can use their bandwidth for learning instead of for the vigilance that
marks a state of uncertainty. The more insecure home life is, the greater the
need for security at school if students are to have access to their full bandwidth for learning. In this chapter, I discuss student needs related to food,
water, and exercise; physical and emotional safety; and reliable routines.

Food, Water, and Exercise

Physical security begins with having basic needs reasonably satisfied. Good
breakfast and lunch programs at schools are critical to address the needs of students for nutrition. In the second edition of *The New Science of Learning*, Doyle
and Zakrajsek (2019) discussed the brain's need for food and water to achieve
optimal learning because the brain uses a significant amount of the body's energy:

> This means if you do not have a healthy diet and eat regular meals, you are
> starving your brain of the energy it needs to function properly, causing your
> brain to work much less efficiently. . . . It is crucial that you eat properly
> before you try to learn. . . . Water is essential for optimal brain health and
> function. (pp. 11–12)

Students who live in food-insecure families need to have healthy meals and snacks at school. Mullainathan and Shafir (2013), in *Scarcity*, talked about the concept of "tunneling" (p. 29), which happens when a person focuses on a specific thing to the exclusion of everything else. Focus is often a good thing; it makes us most attuned to the things that are most important. When students are focused on how hungry they are at school, that is not such a good thing. "*Focus* is a positive: scarcity focuses us on what seems, at that moment, to matter most. *Tunneling* is not: scarcity leads us to tunnel and neglect other, possibly more important things" (p. 29). When students are hungry or thirsty, they will be thinking about food and drink instead of focusing on learning or effective interactions with peers and teachers. This may look like the student is intentionally "not paying attention," or it may result in less than optimal levels of learning and development even when students seem to be engaged and trying to learn.

Access to clean water to drink seems almost too basic to mention, but it is critical to brain health and, therefore, to learning. In some crumbling school buildings, water fountains might be dysfunctional, but in most schools, students are able to drink clean water from accessible fountains. It is important that drinking water is encouraged.

Healthy hydration improves cognition and attention and can even improve students' test scores. It allows organs and body systems to perform at their best. . . . Yet, studies show that schoolchildren are often under-hydrated (Drewnowski, Rehm, & Constant, 2013; Kenney, Long, Cradock, & Gortmaker, 2015). (Hecht, 2018, para. 3)

Student health and learning can be enhanced by drinking more clean water, so efforts to increase water intake could add positively to the productivity of school days. For youth ages 14 years to 18 years old, 36% of the calories from added sugars come from sweetened drinks (Hecht, 2018). The easy access to and affordability of sweetened and carbonated drinks offer students many less healthy choices; school leaders should ensure that they follow USDA regulations related to vending machine products sold in schools (USDA Food and Nutrition Service, 2019).

We can help students recognize their need for water. Children, especially young children, do not necessarily know how to recognize and label their bodies' needs. We may, as adults, assume that children will maintain adequate hydration by drinking when they feel thirsty, but they may not understand what that feeling is, or that it means they need water. We can support them by encouraging them to drink frequently and by teaching them what it feels like to be thirsty or dehydrated.

A side note: How can we be firm about expectations at school regarding good health and behavior choices without undermining parents or causing children to worry about what happens at home? For example, "If we're learning about the importance of drinking water, but all Mom ever drinks at home is soda, is my teacher saying that Mom is bad?" (This should be less and less of a problem as children mature, but young children worry about these things.) Teachers can handle this by prefacing statements with "In our classroom" (e.g., "In our classroom, everyone gets their turn"). When children need more explanation, one helpful strategy is to say, "Mom and Dad get to choose at home, and we choose here." This allows the children to have certainty about expectations in this place, rather than questioning, worrying about, or judging how things are at home.

Movement is also important to students' health and well-being. Children and youth need to move their bodies to be healthy and to encounter the world in ways that help them orient themselves and develop properly. In *Balanced and Barefoot*, Angela Hanscom (2016) lamented the fact that even very young children are told to sit still in school when it is more natural for them to be in constant motion.

> If they keep their body and head still, it reduces activation of the brain, making it harder to do what the teacher wants them to do—pay attention and learn. But in order for children to learn, they must be able to pay attention. And in order to pay attention, children need to move. (p. 66)

Hanscom recommended large doses of free play for young children as having many advantages for learning and healthy development. She asserted that in free play, where children are left on their own with no coaches and no rulebooks, "lasting changes are made in the frontal brain, which plays a critical role in regulating emotions, making plans, and solving problems" (p. 93). When children play together—ideally outside—they work things out, problem-solve, take turns, and interact actively with the physical world. The U.S. Department of Health and Human Services (2018) advocates physical activity for schoolchildren:

> Regular physical activity in children and adolescents promotes health and fitness. Compared to those who are inactive, physically active youth have higher levels of cardiorespiratory fitness and stronger muscles. They also typically have lower body fat and stronger bones. Physical activity also has brain health benefits for school-aged children, including improved cognition and reduced symptoms of depression. Evidence indicates that both acute bouts and regular moderate-to-vigorous physical activity improve

the cognitive functions of memory, executive function, processing speed, attention, and academic performance for these children. (p. 47)

The recommendation for children ages 3 years to 5 years is that they should be "physically active throughout the day" (p. 47), and children and youth ages 6 years to 17 years should do "moderate and vigorous-intensity physical activity for periods of time that add up to 60 minutes or more each day" (p. 48). Especially for students who live in families where adults are not available for supervision of outside play or who live in neighborhoods or housing situations without nearby parks or where it is not safe to be outside, it is critical that schools provide daily opportunities for physical movement.

Exercise is important for learning because of its effect on students' brains. Doyle and Zakrajsek (2019) explained:

Exercise increases the production of three particularly important neurochemicals involved in learning: serotonin, dopamine, and norepinephrine. These three neurochemicals help your brain to be alert, attentive, motivated for learning, and positive toward learning (because they improve mood). . . . By increasing your levels of these three neurochemicals, exercise gives you the tools you need to make any learning situation highly productive. (p. 55)

Activity classes like physical education and dance may have been sacrificed in some schools to an emphasis on test preparation, but, in the end, without this vital movement, student learning and health will be diminished. Free body movement increases psychological and physical well-being and helps students recover the bandwidth they need to learn and grow. Movement time is also a wonderful belonging experience, especially for children who might struggle in other areas. Friendships formed in enjoyable physical games transfer into a sense of belonging in other learning settings. In Box 11.1, Chuck Pearson, who now works with high school students, describes his earlier work in a midwestern urban elementary school.

There are state regulations in some states related to physical activity. Five states require recess; three of those specify at least 20 minutes a day. Eight more states require physical activity for students, from 90 minutes per week to 30 minutes per day. In all, 39 states have some formal law about physical activity in elementary schools (Whitehouse & Shafer, 2017).

BOX 11.1.
Ideas in Practice: Walking, Free Play, and Safe Football

We prioritized play and exercise. We established a walking club at lunch for all ages. Students could choose to walk with friends or a playground staff person; they collected a popsicle stick for each lap. Students kept track of their laps on a chart. Monthly recognition was announced for top walkers at each grade level. Participation was high.

Seemingly, an easy and small thing was making sure basic play equipment was readily available. We used a small portion of the school budget to ensure that a soccer ball, playground balls (used for kickball and four square), long clothesline used as double-dutch jump ropes, and a football were all available every day, even in the winter.

A note about football: Mostly played by upper-grade boys and a long-standing tradition at this school, it was frequently rough and turned into full-contact tackle football and the playground staff person would take the football away. Students would frequently choose less desirable activities or even be more likely to fight because they were not engaged productively in an activity of their choosing. We implemented a two-hand touch rule and made sure an adult was assigned to loosely monitor the games. During my 11 years at the school, tackling during games was rare. This kept students literally in the game and having fun with peers during their free time.

These requirements are backed by sound scientific research, as stated by Wichita State University education professor Rick Pappas: "Kids behave better, they listen better, they're more focused (after recess), and all that goes toward learning" (quoted in Whitehouse & Shafer, 2017, para. 9).

Finally, some teachers and schools withdraw physical activity as a way to punish and isolate students for "bad" behavior or failure to meet some expectation. Sandy Kent, who was a fifth- and sixth-grade teacher for 8 years and a school principal for 14 years in Oklahoma, describes in Box 11.2 how she, as a principal, ensured that all of her students got the benefits of exercise even if it was not with other students at recess.

I appreciate how Sandy referred to this as the students' "time of need," recognizing that no matter why the student could not be included with others at recess, they still had needs she could address. In addition, she preserved the aspect of decision-making in this context, which, I suspect, is often the first thing that is taken away from students who are struggling, therefore nurturing their autonomy even in a somewhat restricted situation.

BOX 11.2.
Ideas in Practice: Movement for "No Recess" Students

There were times when students were not safe to be on the playground with others, whether it was for their own safety or for the safety of others. In those times, I recognized that it also was of no benefit for them to just sit while others were getting physical movement and release. Instead, I would "supervise" these students myself during their normal playtime and give them opportunity for activity. It might be in my office or the gym, if it was empty, or another classroom that was vacant. Movement could have been turning on music and dancing (something like the cha-cha slide) or making up their own movements. We would sometimes run laps or sometimes do an exercise rotation like push-ups, sit-ups, jumping jacks, and so on. I always tried to incorporate some choice in the movement routine for them so it was not me just telling them to move, but them deciding what they wanted to do within certain parameters. We found that these students were able to return to class in much more calm ways and have better days when they were still engaging in movement and decision-making in a safer environment in their time of need, rather than just "missing recess."

Margaret Martelle shares in Box 11.3 about the recess strategy used at her school in California.

BOX 11.3.
Ideas in Practice: Positive Playground Atmosphere

Our school has participated in Playworks (www.playworks.org), a Chicago-based company. They help schools create a more positive atmosphere on the playground, which translates into the classroom. Fifth- and sixth-graders take on junior coach leadership roles to help solve problems. Positive talk is taught and encouraged—"Good job, nice try" is the playground mantra. Easy-to-learn games are taught and always available so kids have lots of choices. Rock, paper, scissors is the alternative to fighting about who's out. I think we've had Playworks for 3 years, and the staff has seen a marked change in negative behaviors, arguments between students, and kids feeling inadequate.

Physical and Emotional Safety

According to the Center on the Developing Child (n.d.),

> In early childhood, research on the biology of stress shows how major adversity, such as extreme poverty, abuse, or neglect can weaken developing brain architecture and permanently set the body's stress response system on high alert. Science also shows that providing stable, responsive, nurturing relationships in the earliest years of life can prevent or even reverse the damaging effects of early life stress, with lifelong benefits for learning, behavior, and health. (para. 1)

For children and youth at school, physical and emotional safety are as important as food, water, and exercise. Fear is a major bandwidth stealer. When a student is constantly on the alert for danger, whether from the admonishments of a teacher or from a bullying classmate, he has diminished bandwidth for learning. Much of stress is about uncertainty. "Will I be in trouble today?" "Is there anyone here who will stand up for me?" "Will the bullies choose me as a target today?" However, if students are fairly sure that teachers will be kind with their feedback, that they will have an advocate if they need one, and that adults will protect them from a bully, they can use their attentional resources on schoolwork and on positive social interactions.

Consistency and routine for young children is an accepted best practice at school and at home and, as stated previously, is critical to the development of brain architecture. What might be less often emphasized is the importance of these same environmental factors for the brain development of youth.

> Teens *need* a predictable and stable environment at home, at school, and in their communities. Like younger children, they *need* to feel safe and nurtured. Teens growing up in fear and chaos tend to spend more time in the "survival brain," trying to feel okay, rather than in activities that develop their pre-frontal cortex. (Chamberlain, 2018, p. 9)

The adults in school can themselves be intentional about the way they treat students. The more insecure home is for children and youth, the more they need a school environment where they can find kindness, calmness, and reasonable limits. In addition to providing food and water to meet physical needs, teachers and other school staff can ensure the psychological safety of every student. Central to that are consistent and public messages that, without exception, every student is equally welcome in the school, including each student's unique expressions of self. Today, ideas about gender roles—and even about the gender binary of girl/boy—are not as clear-cut as they once were. Some children, as young as early primary grades, are expressing their transgenderness. Some youth are rejecting the notion that they need to identify with a gender at all. For these children and youth, life is full of uncertainty. In addition to the feeling that there is a "mix up" in their body/identity alignment, they have to worry about the responses of others. "Will I be accepted for who I am?" "Can't I just be *me* without a label or category?" "Will I be safe?"

To make school a welcoming place for all students, beginning in early learning settings, we can attempt to ungender the organization of our classrooms and routines. We can monitor our language so we no longer refer to certain categories of play or toys as "girl" or "boy." We can banish practices like the "girl line" and the "boy line." We can make sure all children have access to all play areas and choices of activities and that they are encouraged—or at least allowed—to express themselves freely related to dress, voice, level of activity, friend-connections, and preferences. The concept of unconditional positive regard (Rossen, n.d.) suggests that we, as the adult role models, treat every child and youth as an individual who is unquestioningly deserving of our respect and consideration. The tone we set will affect everything that happens in our classroom and school.

In addition to specific actions and attitudes of the adults, schools need to be attentive to the way students treat each other. Although antibullying programs have proliferated in the United States over the past 25 years, some children are still the targets of physical and emotional abuse by their peers, other children still seem to have a need to dominate and hurt others, and others continue to be traumatized by watching helplessly while a classmate is bullied. According to the U.S. Department of Education (2017b), in 2016, one in five children reported being bullied at school, with 25% noting name-calling, rumor-spreading, or being made fun of. Other actions included property damage, physical pushing and tripping, and exclusion; 10% was related to cyberbullying. Of middle and high school students, sixth-graders were most likely to be bullied and seniors the least. Girls were more likely than boys to report being bullied. By race/ethnicity, Black students were most likely to report being bullied (25%), followed by White (22%), Hispanic (17%), and Asian (15%) students. Victims of bullying had increased risk of loneliness, sadness, depression, anxiety, and suicide, and behavioral indicators included isolation, changes in eating habits, sleep disturbance, and alcohol and drug use. In the 2017 Youth Risk Behavior Survey (U.S. Department of Education, 2017a), 33% of lesbian, gay, or bisexual students reported being bullied at school, and another 27% reported being cyberbullied over the past year (compared to 17% and 13% of their non-LGB peers, respectively).

There are strategies that have been shown to decrease bullying and other negative behaviors in schools. The website stopbullying.gov offers a wealth of information about bullying and its consequences for victims, bullies, and witnesses, and the practices found to be the most effective in decreasing bullying (U.S. Department of Health and Human Services, 2017). Communicated clearly through the information and guidance on this site is the idea that bullying should be viewed and treated holistically, considering the motivations, concerns, and needs of all children and youth. Cook et al. (2010) analyzed 153 studies on bullying and found that both bullies and victims of bullying lacked social problem-solving skills, and bullies were often struggling academically. They suggest that "the most promising programs are those that focus on intervening at the levels of the individual, the peer ecology, and the broader contexts in which children and youth are nested" (p. 80).

The stopbullying website reflects this holistic focus on the school environment and on students, helping us to understand that bullies, bully-victims, and bystanders all have different experiences and need different kinds of attention and resources to improve the situation for the entire school community. Guidance is presented in four areas: "Help kids understand bullying . . . keep lines of communication open . . . encourage kids to do what they love . . . [and] model how to treat others with kindness and respect" (Stopbullying, n.d., para. 1). I return to these themes in chapter 12 about building community in schools.

On stopbullying.gov, there is a brief discussion of bullying as an *adverse childhood experience (ACE)*, defined as

a potentially traumatic event that can have negative, lasting effects on a person. . . . The impact can affect their development, the way they interact with others, and how they perform in school. It may also affect mental and physical health. (U.S. Department of Health and Human Services, 2017, para. 1)

In a major public health study in the late 1990s (Felitti et al., 1998), over 17,000 adults completed a 10-item survey about things that had happened to them when they were children. Researchers found high correlations between what happened to people when they were children (under 18 years old) and negative outcomes for adult health and well-being, including alcoholism and drug abuse, depression, smoking, high numbers of sexual partners, sexually transmitted diseases, physical inactivity, severe obesity, heart disease, and cancer. The original survey included, in the household of a child, physical and sexual abuse, physical and emotional neglect, domestic violence, mental illness and substance abuse in the adults, separation or divorce, and incarceration of adults in the family. Based on the number of reported ACEs, respondents had an ACE score of between 0 and 10; the risk for negative outcomes in adulthood increased with the ACE score.

How does understanding the impact of ACEs on long-term health and well-being affect our work with children in schools? Research indicates that the presence of a caring adult in the life of a child who is experiencing childhood trauma can considerably mitigate the negative effects of ACEs into adulthood.

> New and evolving brain science reveals that a child's positive and negative experiences can literally shape, and reshape, the brain. One of the most significant predictors of a child's resiliency in the face of trauma is consistent interaction with a caring and supportive adult. (National Criminal Justice Reference Service, n. d., paras. 2, 4)

Many children are living in families that are characterized by economic insecurity and other forms of uncertainty, violence, and dysfunction, and they need to be able to count on school as a place where they can experience consistent support from adults. Laura Pappano, writing for the *Harvard Education Letter*, explained what happens to traumatized children in school:

> Children who experience trauma struggle with interpersonal relationships, face cognitive deficits (including memory and language development), and overreact to everyday stress. In school, because traumatized students view the world as dangerous and misread social cues, minor events may trigger defiant, disruptive, or aggressive behavior. (Preston, 2018, para. 3)

It can be easy for those of us who have not experienced childhood trauma to think that children should be able to come to school and set those experiences aside while they are in what we think of as a safe, affirming environment that is dedicated to learning. That, however, is not the reality for many children.

> Traumatized children cannot simply remove their "trauma glasses" as they go between home and school, from dangerous place to safe place. They may anticipate that the school environment will be threatening and constantly scrutinize it for any signs of danger. Their mission is to avoid this perceived danger and pain. Sadly, this mission often sabotages their ability to hear and understand a teacher's positive messages, to perform well academically, and to behave appropriately. (Cole et al., 2005, p. 17)

A project funded by the U.S. Department of Justice, "Changing Minds" (*Witnessing Violence,* n.d.), suggests the following five gestures that can "make a world of difference" (para. 1) in the life of a child:

1. Celebrate—use "put-ups," not "put-downs"
2. Comfort—stay calm and patient
3. Collaborate—ask for their opinion
4. Listen—show an interest in their passions
5. Inspire—expose them to new ideas

When one student had an outburst at school from frustration about life, she said that a security person saw what happened and she remembered his response years later: "I felt that I was seen. I wasn't invisible anymore. I was supposed to be here" ("Unique's Story," n.d., 2:24). About this same student, a teacher reflected:

> If you can get to that pain . . . A lot of these children . . . My goodness. They just have something to say. They're not being listened to. They're crying out. They're acting out as their way of saying, "I'm in the room. I have something to say." ("Unique's Story," n.d., 3:16)

In *Building Equity* (Smith et al., 2017), the authors emphasized that it is critical to

> make the classroom as predictable as possible. For many students who have experienced trauma, unpredictable events are a trigger. They typically appreciate routines that they can count on and tend to do better when informed in advance that routines need to be changed. (p. 57)

It is important to understand that ACEs are not destiny, and the presence of even one caring adult can make a significant difference in outcomes. Additionally, people who study and apply the science of ACEs have taught me that when working with people who are acting out or who are struggling, the question has changed from "What is wrong with you?" (unmotivated, lazy, bad) to "What happened to you?" Or, in the case of children, "What is happening to you?" Changing the question can strongly influence our responses, from judgment, impatience, and anger to compassion, caring, and an impulse to want to help, described as "trauma-informed practice" (Udesky, 2019, para. 3).

Massachusetts Advocates for Children published a report and policy agenda called *Helping Traumatized Children Learn* (Cole et al., 2005), in which they focused on creating school environments that are supportive of children who have experienced family violence. The report recommended that schools "partner with parents and guardians—who may themselves be struggling with symptoms of trauma—and give teachers the support they need to teach children how to regulate or calm their emotions and behavior" (p. 5). I like the acknowledgment of the possibility of trauma in both children and their parents and the need to provide support for teachers as they work to help their students learn. Sections on academic performance, classroom behavior, and relationships offer understanding and practical strategies to make school environments "trauma-sensitive" (p. 42) so students can be nurtured and provided with the tools they need to succeed in school. Trauma-informed practice in schools "has educators checking raised voices, putting away detention slips, and looking not at bad behavior but at what triggered it" (Preston, 2018, para. 4). See Box 11.4 for some further strategies for trauma-informed practice.

BOX 11.4.
Ideas in Practice: Strategies Related to Trauma-Informed School Practices

From the Brockton, Massachusetts, school district:

> If a student is sent to the principal, rather than simply ordering a child down to the office (where they may wander the halls feeling angry), a counselor will walk to the office with the child and along the way discuss what's going on. (Preston, 2018, para. 17)

In two high schools in New Haven, Connecticut, "Miss Kendra's List" (see Box 11.5) is

> posted right at the high school entrance with trained psychologists standing by to help if a student indicates a need to talk, even with just a subtle nod at the list. They also distribute the list on cards with a number to call or text. Just a few minutes of talk and support . . . can allow a student to calm down and participate in school. (para. 14)

In Brockton, some classrooms have "cool-off areas" where there are headphones, classical music, playdough, and toys. A student who is worried about something that was happening at home is allowed to call home any time and check with a parent. If kids need a break, they can grab a pass and go to the counselors' office. The availability of these options, even if they are not used, gives students the feeling of security that allows them to stay engaged even in the midst of trauma-induced anxiety.

For LGBTQ youth, a sense of certainty and safety are especially precarious in middle and high school as they are in a sensitive developmental stage of identity formation and a social environment within which peer approval seems critical. According to the Centers for Disease Control and Prevention (2017), the following are policies and practices that schools can implement to help promote health and safety:

- Encourage respect for all students and prohibit bullying, harassment, and violence against all students.
- Identify "safe spaces."
- Encourage student-led and student-organized school clubs that promote a safe, welcoming, and accepting school environment.
- Ensure that health curricula or educational materials include HIV, other STD, or pregnancy prevention information that is relevant to LGBTQ youth.
- Encourage school district and school staff to develop and publicize trainings on how to create safe and supportive school environments for all students, regardless of sexual orientation or gender identity, and encourage staff to attend these trainings.
- Facilitate access to community-based providers who have experience providing health services, including HIV/STD testing and counseling, to LGBTQ youth.
- Facilitate access to community-based providers who have experience in providing social and psychological services to LGBTQ youth. (para. 9)

Landsman emphasized the critical role of all school staff to watch for signs that students might be distressed:

> It takes adult staff and teachers, teacher aides and secretaries to create such a safe space. Vigilance on the part of hall monitors, teachers, and principals is essential in spotting a student who is afraid, stays home, sneaks out to beat the rush home, disappears. (personal communication, November 6, 2019)

For all students, "Miss Kendra's List" (Box 11.5) can be posted in schools and shared with students in classrooms to give them the invitation and the language they need to tell a teacher or other adult at school what is going on in their lives (Miss Kendra, n.d.). This is an excellent example of universal design related to the needs of all children to feel safe and secure. Children who are experiencing these negative things in their lives have a place to report them and get support, and all children get the consistent message about the kinds of things that are hurtful to others and that help explain why a classmate

BOX 11.5.
Ideas in Practice: Miss Kendra's List

The Miss Kendra program aims to help schools face life together.
Miss Kendra's List (For Elementary)

- No child should be punched or kicked.
- No child should be left alone for a long time.
- No child should be hungry for a long time.
- No child should be bullied or told they are no good.
- No child should be touched in their private parts.
- No child should be scared by gun violence at home or in school.
- No child should have to see other people hurt each other.

BECAUSE

- It makes a child not care about school.
- It makes a child feel sad or scared or lonely.
- It makes a child feel angry and want to fight too much.
- It makes a child feel like not trying hard or giving up.
- It makes a child worry a lot about their family.

This Is What Miss Kendra Says . . . "What Do You Say?"

Note. From Miss Kendra (n.d., para. 3).

might behave in unexpected ways and that a compassionate response is more helpful than judgment or criticism.

Reliable Routines

Early childhood educators understand the importance of consistency for toddlers and preschool children. According to John Shonkoff, director of Harvard's Center on the Developing Child, in talking about the effects of poverty on infant development, "What science says is you need someone who will create an environment that's well-regulated and protective and predictable" (Economic Mobility Pathways, 2019, para. 6). It is reassuring to young students to know that their coat is hung in the same place every time they come to school and there is a cubby for their lunchbox and other things they bring. Children can relax when they know the schedule, that there is circle time at the beginning and end of each day, that there is a time to have food and a time for rest, and that these are the same every day. According to Brock et al. (2018),

> In order to promote positive developmental trajectories, children need predictable teacher-child social interactions that are consistently sensitive and responsive. In environments where children are surrounded by warm, supportive, nurturing adults whose behaviors, actions, and emotions are relatively consistent, children cultivate the confidence to explore their surroundings in ways that facilitate development across multiple domains. (p. 59)

This predictability and consistency continue to be critical, especially in the lives of children who often experience trauma in their lives outside of school. These authors summarize the research that links consistency of emotional support to "behavioral and academic gains from preschool through elementary grades" (Brock et al., 2018, p. 59). When children know what to expect at school, they are not using any bandwidth wondering what will happen next. In a study in which they observed 694 pre-K classrooms, Curby et al. (2013) found that when children can count on consistent emotional support from their teachers, they are more likely to do better academically and in interaction with peers, which is what the ACEs research indicates about the presence of a caring adult.

Especially for children whose basic needs are not consistently met at home, the school environment can offer enough stability for them to turn off their stress reflex at least part of the time during the school day. In Box 11.6, Pearson describes the careful structure of daily breakfast for kindergarten and first-grade students at a high-poverty school.

When a child or young person lives with adults who struggle with mental illness or substance abuse and where there might be intermittent violence, home might be a place where little is predictable, making it even more important that school is a place where things happen in patterns that are reliable (e.g., schedules, recess or breaks, trustworthy adults, places for safe refuge). Landsman suggests, "One way to relieve anxiety of students who are fearful or nervous in general is to write up on the board a list of activities for the day. Then check them off as you do them. Students seem to settle down as they feel you are in control to a degree and will keep the class going in a respectful way" (personal communication, November 6, 2019).

BOX 11.6.
Ideas in Practice: Calmness and Care to Start the Day

One way we brought certainty to our high-poverty, majority-minority, midsized midwestern city elementary school was the way we structured daily breakfast. We fed the kindergartners and first-graders separately from the older students. We kept the gymnasium lights low. Our literacy tutors, who the students knew and worked with daily, were part of the breakfast team. Each student was greeted as they came off their bus. Staff assisted them in getting their choice of breakfast food and established a Montessori-like routine: put your winter hat and mittens in your coat sleeve, place your coat on your seat, spread out your napkin and place your food on the napkin. The routine seemed to be comforting and the same every morning . . . the same adults, speaking individually with students, often on social topics and frequently offering them help with the choice of a breakfast, and always in a calming atmosphere.

LoCasale-Crouch et al. (2018) found that supportive and caring teacher-student relationships are important for positive student outcomes at any age, but they may be particularly important during early adolescence. If we think about the physical and emotional changes that are happening to youth in middle school and high school, it makes sense that all students at those ages would benefit from knowing that school is a place of security and some sense of normalcy. Talking about a school in New York (featured in Part Five), Eddie Blanding Jr., a social worker at East Lower School, said that, "Kids rebel against structure but they only feel safe with it" (University of Rochester Center for Urban Education Success, n.d.b). This relates back to the discussions of both belonging and safety; students will have more cognitive resources available for learning if they can consistently count on positive answers to their questions. "Will I be loved?" "Will I be safe?" "Will I be seen?" "Will I know what to do?" Uncertainty is a major bandwidth stealer and to the extent that we provide certainty during the school day, students can recover bandwidth at least while they are at school.

12

CLASSROOM AND
SCHOOL COMMUNITY

Restorative Practice

I n the past three chapters, I have described ways that teachers and schools
create communities with and for students and their families within
which everyone feels valued and safe and has opportunities to benefit
from public education. In effect, knowing that they are part of a community
that will stick by them no matter what can remove uncertainty and help
students recover bandwidth. When communities are functioning well, there
is mutual support, exchange of resources and knowledge, and opportunities for everyone to get a perspective from outside their home and family by
interacting with a variety of people in a trusting social environment. By being
in community, students, parents, teachers, and school staff can all contribute
to the educational enterprise for the benefit of all. I learned about "mirror
books" and "window books," concepts developed by Rudine Sims Bishop
(1990), from a colleague in early childhood development. The idea is that
children need to have books in which they see themselves reflected in terms
of age, race/ethnicity, culture, ability, gender, and so on, and they need to
have books that show and tell about people and places very unlike what they
know. According to Style (1996), school curriculum should

> function both as window and as mirror, in order to reflect and reveal most
> accurately both a multicultural world and the student herself or himself.
> If the student is understood as occupying a dwelling of self, education
> needs to enable the student to look through window frames in order to see
> the realities of others and into mirrors in order to see her/his own reality
> reflected. (para. 1)

Making a commitment to community is a serious undertaking. If schools aspire to be truly viable communities for children and families, practices need to be put in place that reflect the goal of creating learning environments in which all students (and families and teachers) can both see and be seen, respect and be respected.

As I discussed in chapter 2, "zero tolerance" policies have resulted in the disproportionate suspension and expulsion of students of color, removing from the learning environment students who, arguably, most need to be in school. Some schools have recognized that removing students from school isolates them from social interaction and disrupts the class group. These schools have decided to adopt "restorative practices" through which they commit to keeping the school community intact instead of excluding students who break the rules. I will explain the premises of what you might have heard called *restorative justice*, which is the basis for restorative practice. I have chosen to use the term *practice* because it seems more inclusive of everyday behavior and choices rather than something that involves courts or hearings or disciplinary procedures that are suggested by the word *justice*. Practices are behaviors and attitudes to which we can commit, similar to what Pranis (2012) called the "restorative impulse" (para. 3) to stay connected.

Restorative justice has a long history in certain faith communities, like the Mennonites, and in many Native American tribes and First Nations people in Canada. In 1989, New Zealand passed national legislation called the Children, Young Persons and Their Families Act, introducing family group conferencing, based on restorative justice, which comes from the traditions of the Māori, the indigenous people of New Zealand. Australia soon followed suit, and restorative justice programs were begun in prisons in Canada several years later. Since that time, communities and organizations around the world have used restorative justice principles to resolve conflict and maintain community instead of the more common practices that focus on retribution and punishment (Leung, 1999). My interest here is in the application of restorative justice principles in public schools to replace punishment, isolation, suspension, and expulsion.

Fundamental to the idea of restorative practice is the commitment to the restoration of relationships after harm has been done. A commitment to restorative practice means that all parties agree that there is no "getting rid of," "kicking out," or "excluding" people. Everyone agrees that staying connected is the only option. "From this worldview, 'getting rid of' is never a solution because we are never really rid of anything—we are always connected" (Winn, 2018, p. 8). In schools, this means that although a student may be removed in extreme circumstances, it is a last resort. Even then, efforts are made to reintegrate that student back into the school community.

When it is applied effectively in a learning environment, restorative practice can help students and teachers "feel safe and successful together" (Richards, 2018, para. 1).

The basic principles of restorative practice include addressing the following questions in response to a wrong behavior or incident of conflict:

- What happened?
- Who was harmed?
- What is necessary to make amends or "make things right"?
- What are the needs of the victim, the offender, and others in the community?
- What needs to happen to maintain and strengthen the community?

The question of harm is an interesting one. Where do we start to answer? Going back to the discussion of ACEs, many schoolchildren and youth are experiencing harm every day as a result of poverty, abuse, neglect, and family dysfunction. Schools that have employed what Duncan (2000) termed *urban pedagogies* that focus not so much on teaching but on controlling students, especially those from Black, Hispanic, and indigenous communities, have done harm to generations of children. This is not to make excuses for acting-out behavior, but it does suggest that the question of "who was harmed" is potentially more complex than it might look if we confine our analysis to a discrete incident.

Making amends is a positive, growth-oriented approach and has the potential to allow both the offender and the victim to come to some sense of peace about the harm that was done. Amends could include returning something that was stolen, fixing something that was damaged, doing a service for someone as a way to make up for the harm done, engaging in a learning opportunity that addresses a bad choice or decision, or reflecting in writing on what was learned and what might be a better course of action in the future.

A key aspect of restorative practice is the consideration of the needs of everyone involved in the wrongdoing. It is sometimes easiest to acknowledge the needs of the victims because they have been hurt or have had something taken from them and the harm is very clear. However, as experienced educators well know, the child or youth who is acting out is sometimes just as "in need" as the victim. Emma Mercier is a lead teacher in a Māori-philosophy early learning center in New Zealand where she teaches 2- to 4-year-olds. Box 12.1 explains how she is working on restorative practices with her students.

BOX 12.1.
Ideas in Practice: No More "Sorry"

In early childhood education, we are moving away from the word "sorry," which can too easily become just a throw-away word for children and doesn't teach them proactive social skills. We also understand that the instigator might actually be the more upset of the two children, as lashing out is often a result of intense emotions that affect young children in ways that are hard for them to understand and cope with. The first step, therefore, is to support both children in returning to a calmer state by reassuring them that we empathize with their emotions (if not their behavior) and that we can solve this problem peacefully together. When appropriate, once both children are calm enough to process and learn, we encourage (and prompt) the following conversation between the two children:

"Are you okay?"

"Yes/No."

"Do you need a hug?"

"Yes/No." (Many children say yes, but it's also perfectly fine to say no. Sometimes children don't want a hug from the instigator, which is reasonable, and in that case an additional hug from the teacher is often an acceptable substitution.)

"How can I help you feel better?" (Usually they say "Nothing," and often we suggest something. With practice, children get better at identifying what might help, which is an important skill in self-regulation.)

We then have a conversation geared toward addressing whatever happened that initiated the conflict. We might ask what the instigator was feeling and reassure them that it's okay to feel that way, but it's not okay to hurt someone else (verbally or physically). We then suggest a more positive way to resolve the situation. The goal is for both children to leave the interaction feeling supported and empowered in the knowledge that they can handle similar situations more positively in the future. It's okay for the instigator to also feel some guilt, but we want to ensure that they don't feel rejected or ashamed.

Until the needs of all parties are discovered and addressed, the community will likely continue to face difficult behavior that is disruptive to learning. If maintenance of healthy relationships is the consistent goal, everyone's needs are equally important. Teachers, especially those working in low-resourced schools with students experiencing many ACEs, may have ongoing needs for caring support if they are to participate genuinely and effectively in restorative practice in their classrooms and schools.

The Chicago Public Schools' (n.d.) *Restorative Practices Guide and Toolkit* described a restorative mind-set as follows:

> A restorative mindset describes how a person understands community and one's role in the community. The values and concepts that underlie a restorative mindset include: Relationships and trust are at the center of community.
>
> - All members of the community are responsible to and for each other.
> - Multiple perspectives are welcomed and all voices are equally important.
> - Healing is a process essential to restoring community.
> - Harm-doers should be held accountable for and take an active role in repairing harm.
> - Conflict is resolved through honest dialogue and collaborative problem-solving that addresses the root cause and the needs of those involved. (p. 4)

Discussion circles are important in many restorative practice processes because they set up an environment of equality and democracy in which everyone has a voice. Sometimes a *talking piece* is used as a way to ensure that everyone is heard. A talking piece could be any object that can be passed from one person to another in a circle (I use a talking stick). Participants agree to the following "rules":

- Only the person who is holding the talking piece is talking.
- All the others in the circle are listening and supporting the speaker.
- As the talking piece gets passed from one person to the next, each person may speak or pass.
- Discussion continues until everyone has had input (or not if they continually choose to pass).

In the circle, there is usually a *circle keeper*, as described by Bintliff (2014) in *Teaching Tolerance*:

> The Circle Keeper facilitates the Talking Circle by selecting the time and place, inviting members and preparing introductory remarks. Once the group reviews its established norms, the Circle Keeper can read a short piece of text to set the tone or just dive into the first question or reflection. Although the Circle Keeper is the facilitator, she participates as an equal member of the group. Once students learn the process, they can be invited to be Circle Keepers—an empowering process. (para. 3)

In restorative practice, the discussion is focused on who was harmed and what is needed to mend the harm so the community can remain intact.

In *Justice on Both Sides*, Maisha Winn (2018) described her work as a year-long participant observer in a high school where student circle keepers lead restorative justice processes. These student leaders were instrumental in helping resolve conflicts and develop and maintain healthy relationships at the school. They also learned a great deal and gained self-confidence and a sense of self-efficacy. The voices of the students are poignant. Here, one student talks about what he learned about the usefulness of punishment:

> You knew yourself punishment didn't really work, but, like, you didn't really think about it. Then, when we talk about it in training for restorative justice, then you realize why it doesn't work and how often it doesn't work. It's not [that it just doesn't] work for you. [Punishment] doesn't work for anybody. And that kind of like opened your eyes to it, and it makes me not want to just punish or just snap back for things, because the other person never really learns anything from it. (p. 76)

Another student described what it was like to combine accountability with support:

> So it's like you tap them on the hand because they did something wrong, but at the same time you're rubbing on their back to let them know you're there for them. . . . We can help you get through whatever you're trying to get through. We can help you kind of move, take those steps to move forward. (p. 71)

In my view, restorative practices are essential if we want to have equitable access to educational opportunities for all children and youth. In a society where economic and social inequities have such devastating negative effects on millions of students, public schools must be places of refuge and potential for students who live on the losing side of the inequality. It seems to me that we must choose restorative practices as the approach, reflecting an absolute commitment to community and to access to opportunity for all students. Winn asserts that without this commitment, it will be the default to go back to punishment and exclusion.

> If suspension and expulsion are an option, they will be exercised, because they do not require anyone to change or challenge established views or practices. No one is required to sit in the difficult space of revisiting something that they have always seen done. (p. 16)

For teachers who grew up in punitive systems in which harm was answered by more harm, adopting a restorative impulse may be a struggle, but it seems like one worth making. There is some evidence that teachers can and do change their perspectives in ways that work to preserve community in classrooms and schools. In a research project focused on decreasing student suspensions, Okonofua et al. (2016) found that a brief, online intervention encouraging an empathic (rather than a punitive) mind-set among teachers resulted in 50% fewer suspensions across five middle schools in three districts. Especially in underresourced schools, interventions like this, which are virtually no-cost, could significantly contribute to restoring healthy and effective relationships. Shalaby (2017) suggested that, instead of responding to misbehavior by "punishing or pathologizing" an individual child, we ask as a classroom community:

- Is there a kind of suffering that might show itself in behaviors like this?
- Are there things people need that they aren't getting in our classroom?
- What kinds of feelings might be behind these behaviors? (p. 176)

Restorative practice and student involvement as circle keepers are ideas that can be adapted for high school students, and younger students can work alongside teachers and other school staff to organize themselves around restorative practice principles. I suggest that even children in early learning settings can be engaged around conversations about justice and fairness, how we want to be treated, taking responsibility for behavior that hurts someone, and other restorative practice ideas. For instance, the early childhood curriculum in New Zealand, called *Te Whariki*,

> is underpinned by a vision for children who are competent and confident learners and communicators, healthy in mind, body, and spirit, secure in their sense of belonging and in the knowledge that they make a valued contribution to society. (Educa, n.d., para. 1)

When Emma Mercier worked at Whare Kakapo (not the real name of the school), an early learning center in Wellington, New Zealand, she created, with her students, the Treaty of Whare Kakapo, modeled after the Treaty of Waitangi, which was the 1840 treaty between the British government and the indigenous Māori people (NZ History, n.d.). Through this project, which Mercier describes in Box 12.2, she and the children in her class were proactively practicing a restorative impulse by agreeing on a set of behaviors that established a sense of community from which they could build ongoing relationships and make corrections when things did not go as planned.

BOX 12.2.
Ideas in Practice: Treaty of Whare Kakapo

We began by talking about the Treaty of Waitangi and how it helped people who had really different ideas about the world to know how to treat each other with kindness. As with many colonization stories, I had to tread somewhat carefully because so many awful things happened. I wanted to be honest with the children without misleading them. I think we can honestly say that the treaty was an effort to share New Zealand between Māori and non-Māori in a way that respected everyone. (We didn't get into how well that was enacted.) We had also talked about ANZAC Day (a national day of remembrance for New Zealanders and Australians who have died in war) a few months before, and we learned the National Anthem as part of our Waitangi Day celebrations. Out of this came a discussion about how lucky we are that there is not war in New Zealand, and how we can help everyone to continue to have a peaceful country by being kind to each other.

We celebrated that even though we all live in different houses, we all live in New Zealand, and that's something we share. Then we went on to celebrate that we all come to Whare Kakapo together, and that it is our special place. I said that I'd like for us to make a Treaty of Whare Kakapo to help us all understand how we live together in our community (at the time, we were also doing an exploration of the word *community* and what it meant to the children). I invited children to share their ideas of "what we should remember to do" to make sure Whare Kakapo was a wonderful community for us all.

Of course, as I have found to be typical of children, many things came in the form of negative statements (no hitting, no pushing, no breaking people's creations, no kicking, no throwing toys). I tried my best to honor the children's contributions and to change them as little as possible, while also promoting positive language. I put all the violence-related "no's" together and asked, "Could we call this, 'Keep our bodies safe?'" The children agreed, so that became the heading, but we still kept their specific language under it. The children wanted very specific prohibitions on war in the treaty (from previous discussions, of course), but they were willing to accept that war is the opposite of kindness, so putting "Be kind to each other" was an acceptable alternative. I tried to support them in coming up with lots of examples of what kindness looks like (helping a friend find their shoes, taking turns, reading together, checking on a friend who

(Continues)

BOX 12.2 (*Continued*)

is sad, etc.), but they struggled with that. I ended up providing some positive and negative examples myself and having them let me know if they were kind or not.

Once the treaty was finished, each child signed their name to it (to whatever degree they were able to do so). Then it was very important to refer to it often in discussions about choices and consequences throughout the days, or the children would forget about it.

I think a really big part of how this affirms community is empowering the children in their knowledge that they know how things work here. From an adult perspective, it can almost feel trite, because it's not as if I'm actually letting the children decide on rules or how we choose to teach them. A unanimous child vote that it's now okay to run inside would not make it on the treaty. But constructing the process so that (as much as possible) the words that are written down come from the students shows them that they don't actually need teachers hovering over them making sure they make the right choice. They already know how to be kind and safe, which is inherent to a sense of belonging and security. And then going a step further past belonging to ownership, they then feel that these rules are personally important to them because they were part of making them.

At Playa, a bilingual school in California, teachers hold their students to high expectations and offer the support they need to achieve them. The school expects teachers to "never give up on [students], no matter how challenging they might be" (Stillman & Anderson, 2017, p. 72); teachers are expected to provide whatever support is necessary to help students succeed. In this case, at least part of the context for this ethic is *familia*, which includes the concept of family, but is deeper and speaks to a connection with common cultural values and with each other. Culturally, these family values emphasize "interdependence, respect for tradition, loyalty, and impassioned hard work on one another's behalf" (Stillman & Anderson, 2017, p. 59).

As children get older, they also need to have a chance to "talk out" what they are feeling in a culturally responsive, safe space. Strazzabosco (2018), writing about the effects of poverty on children and youth, advocated that schools, with the help of trained facilitators (who might be teachers), build weekly, *mandatory*, group meetings into the schedule, where all students who live in poverty can discuss what's on their minds. Speaking out about issues that trouble them is crucial for kids who live in poverty, and is possibly more important than *any* curriculum item; coursework seldom seems to matter if one is angry, shamed, or afraid. (pp. 172–173)

I wonder if the effect of talking about life challenges helps to keep them, at least temporarily, from taking up so much bandwidth so there is more available for paying attention in class and learning. Such sharing does not change the conditions of life for students, but there might be some easing of tension from knowing that someone listens and understands. (And there are times when something is revealed that the teacher can help correct, like "My mom doesn't know my brother takes my lunch every day.")

Efforts toward restorative practices are consistent with best practices in learning approaches and have positive benefits beyond resolving behavior issues and nurturing a sense of community. According to Richards (2018), the process "fortifies compassion and empathy for others and humanizes the experience of mistake-making" (para. 10), which leads nicely into the next chapter on growth mind-set.

13

GROWTH MIND-SET

When she was working with children in her research as a professor at Stanford, Carol Dweck (2006) identified two distinct mind-sets about learning. A person with a growth mind-set about something they are trying to learn believes that, if they work on it long enough and get help when they need it, they can master the subject or skill. However, if a person with a fixed mind-set fails in the beginning of a task, they may give up, believing their brain is just not good at that thing. Students might have a fixed mind-set that says, "I can't do math" or "I'm just not good at music" or "I tried that once and just couldn't do it." A growth mind-set says that we can grow our brain, which has been shown to be true. Every time we learn something, new neural pathways are created in our brain; we actually get smarter and better able to learn the next new thing. In Table 13.1, I summarize some of the important distinctions between growth and fixed mind-set beliefs. It is pretty clear that, as a teacher or a classmate, it is much more productive to be working with a student who has a growth mind-set. A student might have a growth mind-set about some subjects and a fixed mind-set about others. They may be willing to revise their writing to learn and improve but claim that "I just don't get science!"

Another critical thing to know is that mind-sets are not set for life. By creating learning environments in which students have their full bandwidth, we can help them develop a growth mind-set. One of the key lessons from Dweck's mind-set work is that mistakes provide the best opportunities for growing our brains. The past four chapters tie together the absolutely critical area of "mistake-making." Only when students feel that their funds of knowledge and identity are acknowledged and valued and that they belong, and experience a reasonable degree of certainty, will they have the necessary bandwidth to learn from mistakes and thrive in spite of setbacks.

TABLE 13.1
Growth Mind-Set Beliefs and Fixed Mind-Set Beliefs

Growth Mind-Set Beliefs	Fixed Mind-Set Beliefs
People can change how "smart" they are by learning new things and growing their brains.	People are born as smart as they'll ever be; intelligence is a fixed quality.
With hard work and effort, anyone can learn and do just about anything.	Hard work and effort are futile; if a person is not good at something, that's just the way it is.
No matter how smart people seem, they can still learn and improve their knowledge and skills.	Even really smart people can't get any smarter; it's just the way they were born.
People may seem to have certain characteristics, but they can change them with hard work and effort.	You're a certain kind of person and you can't change that.
The smartest people work really hard, studying and practicing, so they can grow their brains and improve their skills.	Only people who aren't very smart or skilled have to work really hard, like doing homework or practicing music or sports.
It's in facing new challenges and learning new things that the most growth happens in our brains.	Challenges are just frustrating and defeating; it's better to stick with the things for which you have natural talent.
The most important thing is to learn and grow; mistakes are just part of the process.	If a person tries something new and fails, people will know they are not smart.
Only if people give each other constructive feedback about their work can we know where we need to improve and work to do it.	People shouldn't criticize others; it just makes them feel bad about themselves and, anyway, they can't help it if they make mistakes.

Note. Adapted from Dweck (2006).

When mistakes lead to feedback and assistance, then learning can happen, so it is critical that students are willing to take risks, try things, and ask for help. Students with fixed mind-sets tend to avoid challenge and give up easily. They focus on *performance* goals in order to get affirmation for the intelligence they have. When students have a growth mind-set about a subject or task, they have *learning* goals because they see their intelligence as malleable, something that they can improve with effort and persistence (Moore & Shaughnessy, 2012). Nine years after the publication of her book *Mindset*, Dweck (2015) reflected that some people had overstated the importance of effort. She had advised parents and teachers to praise effort rather than ability to encourage a growth mind-set in children. She wrote:

> *A growth mindset isn't just about effort.* Perhaps the most common misconception is simply equating the growth mind-set with effort. Certainly, effort is key for students' achievement, but it's not the only thing. Students need to try new strategies and seek input from others when they're stuck. They need this repertoire of approaches—not just sheer effort—to learn and improve. (para. 5)

For students to develop the repertoire Dweck described, they need to know that mistakes are okay and that asking for help is a good thing. When students fail to achieve a learning goal, like on a writing assignment or an exam, they often just try harder, spending more time and energy doing the same things they did to prepare in the first place. If they are not confident that they will get help if they ask, they will not seek input and will not learn the new strategy that might help them improve both learning and performance. It is important that teachers create growth mind-set classrooms so students are affirmed in mistake-making, asking for help, and learning new ways to approach problems.

When the focus is on learning, the inculcation of a growth mind-set is a natural part of the school day. An emphasis on collaborative learning communicates to students that knowledge and skills are sharable commodities and that we all benefit from supporting each other's growth and development. In *Building Equity* (Smith et al., 2017), part of instructional excellence is a focus on collaborative learning, based on Vygotsky's idea that learning is social.

> We strive for collaborative learning to consume about 50 percent of instructional class time. That's a goal, not a mandate, but we feel that collaborative learning is the centerpiece of instruction and that it builds the kind of skills students need to function in their adult lives. (p. 115)

Student bandwidth is enhanced when learning is seen as a shared project. Collaborative projects and study, when done well, invite participation by all students and leverage the various strengths of the members of the group. Again, students need to feel safe and secure if they are going to open themselves to close collaboration with peers.

Once students learn about having a growth mind-set and the fact that they can grow their brains by trying new things, making mistakes, and trying again, they need to experience the kinds of challenges that push them to brain-growing efforts. With college students, I have used an assignment, called *Neurobics*, which was developed by James Watson for his design students (Verschelden, 2017). For this assignment, students, outside of class, try something new—and at least slightly uncomfortable—for them, like eating alone in a restaurant, talking to three people they do not know, going to the opera, or not looking at social media for a whole day. Then they write a short reflection about why that activity was a neurobic for them and what they learned from the experience. I have modified the college assignment a bit in Figure 13.1 to be more appropriate for adolescents.

A growth mind-set in teachers and students and in classroom and school environments is necessary for everyone to be able to thrive. Combined with collaborative learning and a restorative impulse, it creates a learning space within which students feel confident to say, "I don't know," "I need help," or "I'm afraid or uncertain," and adults and peers can say, "I don't know either, but I think we can figure it out together" and "Let's talk about what's worrying you and figure out a way for you to feel safe." Mercier suggests ways that teachers of young children can model a growth mind-set in the classroom in Box 13.1.

Going forward, having the confidence to make and correct mistakes is a critical life skill. In discussing the presence of a caring adult in the life of every child as that child grows into adolescence and then adulthood, Roche (2015) emphasized the importance of being able to learn from mistakes as part of exploring the world. "Becoming an adult requires that we take risks and make mistakes. It is only by making mistakes that we learn to assume responsibility for our actions, to ask forgiveness and begin to understand our relationship to others" (para. 4). At San Diego's Thrive Public Schools, there is an intentional focus on incorporating social-emotional learning in a way that encourages a growth mind-set. Principal Nicole Assisi described how they "emphasize self-regulation and good decision-making in the pursuit of ambitious goals, helping students understand that some of the greatest learning can come from reflection on 'failures'" (quoted in Vander Ark & Ryerse, 2017, para. 10).

BOX 13.1.

Ideas in Practice: Teacher Modeling of Growth Mind-Set in the Early Childhood Classroom

I encourage my teachers to engage with children in activities in which they're not very confident and let the children know that they're just learning but will keep practicing and getting better. I also role model use of various growth mind-set strategies such as asking aloud, "I wonder what I did that didn't work?" or saying, "I don't know, but I could ask ____ or look it up in our book on ____." It's a pretty powerful thought for children that even their teachers' brains are still growing.

Figure 13.1. Neurobics for middle and high school students.

Neurobics Assignment

Neurobics (neuron + aerobics) are stretching exercises to increase oxygen and give our brain's neurons more life by experiencing or participating in some new activity, situation, or event. When we stretch our mind, it never returns to its previous shape. Making our brain work with unfamiliar exercises can improve our ability to learn, remember, and solve problems.

For this assignment, do something that you don't ordinarily do. It is best if you do something that makes you feel just a bit uncomfortable. That discomfort is the feeling of your brain growing! Here are some ideas:

- Go to a public art event
- Try playing a new sport
- Change your diet (like no sweet drinks for a week)
- Break a bad habit (like biting your fingernailsor gossiping)
- Visit a new place
- Do a kind thing for someone
- Learn a new word everyday
- Walk backward at school all day
- Learn how to play chess
- Start a conversation with one new person every day for a week
- Volunteer at school or in the community
- Write in a journal every day for a week
- Dont TV for a whole week
- Get up early and watch the sun rise

Neurobics Report

Print name   The *neurobic* event or activity

Place of event or activity   Date(s) of event or activity

Describe the event or activity and why it was a *neurobic* for you?

How did you grow or change through this experience? What did you see or learn about yourself or someone else that will stay with you and help you in school or life?

Note. The word *neurobics* was created by James Robert Watson, http://www.jamesrobertwatson.com/neurobics.html

When Sonya Hernandez was the principal at an elementary school in Muskegon Heights, Michigan, the students created a pledge (Box 13.2) that was posted around the school. I like the growth mind-set expressed in "Today is a new day." The message is a powerful one about starting each day with a clean slate, ready to learn as an "intelligent," "valuable" "somebody."

Snipes et al. (2012) reviewed many promising research findings on mind-set. The concept is actually quite straightforward and has been approached in a variety of ways with students in educational settings from elementary schools to colleges and universities. They assert that much of the research is

BOX 13.2.
Ideas in Practice: Student Pledge

_____ ELEMENTARY
STUDENT PLEDGE
TODAY IS A NEW DAY
TO LEARN SOMETHING NEW
TO HAVE A POSITIVE ATTITUDE
TO BE PERSISTENT

RIGHT NOW
AT THIS VERY MOMENT
I RECOMMIT MYSELF
TO HONOR AND RESPECT
MYSELF
TEACHERS AND STAFF
MY SCHOOLMATES
AND TO GIVE
NOTHING BUT THE BEST
AT ALL TIMES

I AM
INTELLIGENT
VALUABLE
AND I AM
SOMEBODY

WRITTEN BY: (list of student names)

WRITTEN
February 10, 2012

based on the hypothesis that when students feel that their academic abilities are fixed, they are less likely to be motivated to persist at tasks or to take on new academic challenges. Instead, they are likely to focus on others' perceptions of their abilities and trying to avoid "failing" in front of others. By contrast, when students believe that their intelligence "grows like a muscle" over time as they put in effort, they are more likely to work hard and have positive outcomes. (p. 10)

Williams et al. (2013) found that giving a specific growth mind-set message (e.g., "Remember, the more you practice, the smarter you become" to students in an online course) resulted in more attempts at problems and more progress compared to students who got nongrowth mind-set messages. It is a fundamental task of teachers and schools—and a task that appears to be ultimately doable and scalable—to find and light up that place in each student in which the belief in their own potential for learning and growth is sometimes very well hidden.

Individual potential is central to the concept of "least restrictive environment" (p. 26, this volume) for students with disabilities for whom a growth mind-set on the part of the school and the teacher is probably more important than for any other students. Through a survey of educational experts, Ryndak et al. (2000) identified five components of inclusion for students with moderate to severe disabilities in a general education context:

1. Placement in natural general education settings
2. All students together for instruction and learning
3. Supports and modifications within general education to meet appropriate learner outcomes
4. Belongingness, equal membership, acceptance, and being valued
5. Collaborative integrated services by education teams (p. 108)

In an article from New Brunswick, Canada (New Brunswick Association for Community Living, n.d.) about the benefits of inclusive education, the first of their "Beliefs and Principles" is "all children can learn" (para. 5), which is the foundational belief of having a growth mind-set. Key features of inclusive education include the following growth mind-set practices:

- Providing as much support to children, teachers and classrooms as necessary to ensure that all children can participate in their schools and classes.
- Looking at all children at what they can do rather than what they cannot do.

- Teachers and parents have high expectations of all children.
- Developing education goals according to each child's abilities. This means that children do not need to have the same education goals in order to learn together in regular classes.
- Designing schools and classes in ways that help children learn and achieve to their fullest potential. (para. 7)

14

COMMUNICATION

Humans are social creatures, a fact that, as is evident in all of the underminers, is both a blessing and a curse. We need each other for affirmation and support, and we can absolutely devastate each other with our words and behaviors. Maybe this should have been the first chapter in the bandwidth recovery section because the quality of the communication among children and youth, teachers, parents, school staff, and the community will determine the success of recovery efforts for all involved. There are many facets of communication that affect how public schools support the development of the human potential of children, youth, families, and communities. In all of those, it seems to me that if there is any chance of creating equity of educational opportunity in public schools, one of the principles should be that everyone's voice needs to be heard. For bandwidth recovery, I see the importance of effective communication in three major areas:

1. Communication for understanding and connection
2. Communication for information and engagement
3. Communication for collaboration

Communication for Understanding and Connection

In chapter 9, we learned about recognizing and acknowledging funds of knowledge and identity of students and their families. This is about understanding, about trying to connect on a personal level so that schools can better respond with viable and relevant education. We know that culture and background affect many issues such as views on education, family roles, how children should be treated and behave, ideas about school readiness, family boundaries, and communication styles and preferences (National Center on

Parent, Family and Community Engagement, n.d.). Understanding is critical in the development and maintenance of any healthy relationship and it is what is needed between and among teachers and students, teachers and families, and schools and communities. As teachers, we can intentionally strive to learn about our students and families and find ways to connect and communicate with them in their context, rather than expecting them to accommodate ours.

In Head Start, the idea of "positive goal-oriented relationships" National Center on Parent, Family and Community Engagement, n.d., p. 2) incorporates many of the most important foundations for effective communication.

These relationships

- are fueled by families' passion for their children,
- are based on mutual respect and trust,
- affirm and celebrate families' culture and languages,
- provide opportunities for two-way communications,
- include authentic interactions that are meaningful to those who participate in them,
- and often require an awareness of one's personal biases and how those biases can affect mutual respect and trust.

Positive, goal-oriented relationships improve wellness by reducing isolation and stress for both families and staff. (National Center on Parent, Family and Community Engagement, n.d., p. 3)

Written for early childhood programs, these principles of relationships seem to me to be applicable to schools at all levels, as they start with the acknowledgment that parents care about their children and there is a common goal that is focused on child well-being. Everything else can grow from that point.

Students who have experienced trauma have a special need for communication and connection with a trusted adult. Students who have been traumatized, often by an adult, may have trouble developing trusting relationships with the adults at school. If a teacher or staff person can communicate with and truly connect with a student, they can be in a position to help them heal (Smith et al., 2017) and, thus, have a chance to thrive at school. Schickedanz and Marchant's (2018) work in pre-K classrooms affirms the importance of the relationship between the teacher and a child, emphasizing the one-on-one conversation.

One-on-one conversations . . . allow teachers to show genuine interest in children's ideas and their experiences outside of school. Responsive and sensitive interactions between teachers and children in the pre-K classroom are correlated with a better emotional climate in the classroom, which is a good predictor of better outcomes for children's language, literacy, and social development (Mashburn et al., 2008). One-on-one conversations with caring adults also reduce cortisol levels in children who are under stress. This effect is very consequential today, with so many children experiencing stress and research findings indicating that high cortisol levels have serious negative consequences for the developing brain (Hatfield & Williford, 2017). (p. 118)

Although one-on-one conversations with teachers are critical to child development both intellectually and socially, play with peers might ultimately be even more important to a child's ability to get along in the world. When children play together, they are practicing relationship-building and mutual learning. When they are allowed to play freely, with minimal adult interference, they learn to communicate with each other. Hanscom (2016) reminded us that children learn important skills in free play: "Waiting your turn. Following the rules. Dealing with feelings of frustration and anger in a healthy way. Sharing toys. Making new friends" (p. 56).

In fact, play can provide the primary avenue for communication among young children and among them and adults. Through play, children get to explore things, face and overcome fears, learn to figure things out with others, resolve conflicts, stand up for themselves, make decisions, move at their own pace, lead and follow, create, and move their bodies freely. When adults join in child-driven play, they get to see the world from a child's viewpoint, pay close attention to children to build relationships, communicate in supportive ways, offer guidance only when needed or requested, and engage fully with children. Especially for less verbal children, play may be one of the primary sources of insight into a child's views, experiences, and frustrations (Ginsburg et al., 2007). Play is the opportunity for children to practice communication, learning from the responses of peers and adults what works to make the play fun for everyone.

Understanding and connecting with students are critical for all teachers and school staff. When students are truly known, educators can attempt to maximize their strengths, increase their funds of knowledge and identity, and help mitigate the negative effects of the conditions of their lives that might involve persistent economic insecurity, trauma, mental health struggles, and other challenges they bring with them to the classroom. Connecting with students through understanding is a prerequisite for being "let in" to their lives. Many students who live in difficult circumstances at home are unlikely to think the adults at school will understand, sympathize, and help them

BOX 14.1.
Ideas in Practice: Daily Check-In and Community Mentors

To support students with anxiety and other needs we put several practices into place. At our urban elementary school, we used the practices that best fit the child, including an adult check-in buddy. Each morning the student would start the day by checking in with the adult. That person might be another teacher besides their own, a social worker, an office secretary, or other support staff. Some students had a goal sheet and they briefly discussed the day and what to look forward to. They checked in at the end of the day as well. This ensured the student was seeing a caring adult in addition to their own teacher.

Another practice was assigning a community mentor for students who were really struggling socially or academically in the school. A nearby church sent regular mentors; a local high school did as well. The mentor would work with the student, take them out of the classroom for tutoring, to the Dairy Queen across from the school, to shoot baskets or some other one-on-one activity that provided individual attention. Mentoring occurred for a month or even all year if that was what the student wanted and needed.

with their needs for support, both physical and emotional. They and their families may have encountered less-than-positive people and institutions who mostly blamed and shamed them for their inadequacies. Milner (2015) advised that "conversations about meeting the needs of school-dependent students (1) acknowledge the fact that some students' needs are being met at home and others may not be and (2) take place within a space of possibility, optimism, and hope" (p. 50). Although most schools routinely provide assistance in the form of free and reduced-price meals, for instance, the manner in which these provisions are made can communicate volumes to students and families, reflecting generosity or judgment. Communication that expands bandwidth for students and families is characterized by empathy, kindness, and messages of encouragement. In Box 14.1, Pearson describes a system of daily check-ins and community mentoring that was used at his urban elementary school.

Communication for Information and Engagement

Effective communication is at the heart of all teaching and learning. If information and lessons are not moving from teacher to student and back, and between students, learning is not happening. In order for information to "get through," everyone in the process needs to be engaged at some level. The fundamental national principle of education for all rests on the premise that all students in public school have access to learning. In her discussion of using transformative justice teacher education for preservice teachers, Winn (2018) asserted that the ideas of restorative practice require communication and open exchange of perspectives and ideas. This model of teacher education views teaching as "a justice-seeking endeavor and learning as both a civil and human right for all students" (p. 145). Meira Levinson (2012), in *No Citizen Left Behind*, described her ideas about school environments that support the civic learning development of all students:

> I want to look at pedagogies that support an "open classroom climate" for real, engaging discussions in which students feel comfortable and supported taking on controversial points of view and listening to others' perspectives. The positive association between an open classroom climate and desirable civic outcomes is probably the most robust finding in the civic education research literature. (p. 192)

She reminded us that research has consistently indicated that

> low-income students of color and immigrant students are less likely to experience rich discussions within an open classroom climate than wealthier, White, and native-born students—even though the benefits of such experiences for their civic knowledge and engagement are disproportionately positive when they do. (pp. 193–194)

There are strategies teachers can use to create an open classroom climate in which students can share ideas, hear alternative perspectives, challenge one another, change their minds, investigate issues together, and learn to listen to everyone. Levinson (2012) talked about the effectiveness of "wait time" (p. 191), where the teacher waits for a few beats before calling on a student who is volunteering to talk or answering the question herself. This simple tactic can give verbal space to slower-to-volunteer, more reflective students who may often be excluded from the conversation. This climate of openness is critical for not only teaching and learning in the present but also giving every student the opportunity to contribute and learn.

> Schools inherently shape young people's civic experiences. Both students and adults learn "their place" and what's expected of them in the broader public sphere by observing and participating in the limited public space we call schools. (p. 174)

BOX 14.2.
Ideas in Practice: Collaborative Final Exam

For the final exam, students were divided into two groups. Each group wrote the final exam collaboratively. In each group, two students were designated as "envoys" who could be sent to the other group to consult on an answer and report back to the group. Two students in each group were given access to a dictionary and only they could look up words and meanings. Other students had different roles. This method brought out the knowledge and skills of each student while encouraging group cooperation. (The fact that his students did not have to be silent—that their voices were heard—was very important to Edminster, even though he was sometimes criticized for his classroom being "too noisy.")

Classrooms can be arranged to encourage communication between and among students so that all of them are included and valued. Hinchey and Konkol (2018) discussed how the way students are seated can impact their sense of community and belonging. When students sit in rows and are discouraged from talking with each other or getting help from a peer it teaches them that they are on their own. "In contrast, allowing students to sit at tables teaches them they are community members, while seating them in a circle for a conversation teaches them their voices are legitimate—and expected in the work of the classroom" (p. 55).

Jim Edminster, who taught high school English in Chicago for 50 years, told me how he designed his final exam to encourage collaboration and so that all voices were included and valued (Box 14.2).

When Levinson taught eighth grade, she wanted to teach her students how to have productive classroom discussions by learning the skills of listening, asking for clarification, building on the ideas of others, and respectfully disagreeing or offering another perspective. She offered a set of sentence stems; for the first few months of the year, she required them to begin with one of the stems when they wanted to talk. She also gave students a set of questions to help them develop active listening skills; both of these lists are in Figure 14.1. (Notice in the active listening questions the application of the concepts of funds of knowledge and connecting the known to the unknown.)

The ability to ask questions effectively begins in early childhood. Even though some early child development theorists, like Piaget, suggested that we should not answer children's questions so they will figure out things for themselves, Harris's (2012) research suggests that we encourage children to ask questions by answering theirs. He found that children

Figure 14.1.   Sentence stems and active listening questions.

Sentence Stems
• I agree with her because . . .
• One question I have is . . .
• I don't understand why/how . . .
• This example may help . . .
• In order to make your argument, you are assuming that . . .
• What I hear you saying is . . .
• To answer this question, we need to know . . .
• The main issue seems to be . . .
• Something that people haven't brought up yet is . . .
Active Listening Questions
• Is this person making an argument or just talking for the sake of talking?
• What is the main point of disagreement?
• Are people supporting their arguments with facts, opinions, or assertions?
• Could this question be answered if we did some research? What would we have to learn?
• Why do people care about this topic?
• How does this issue affect my own life, or how might it affect my own life?
• Have I experienced anything personally that relates to this issue?

Note. Reprinted from Levinson (2012, p. 198).

respond with the cautious reflection and the persistent curiosity of good scientists. By implication, rather than leaving children to their own devices, we should encourage them to join the community of inquiry that is characteristic of science. (p. 44)

Teaching children how to ask questions and come to conclusions is of critical importance in this age of information. Adults are daily role models for the way to make decisions based on facts and investigations. When pre-K teachers give explanations of their reasoning, they are showing their students a valuable skill. When teachers provide evidence for the conclusions they make, children begin to do the same (Schickedanz & Marchant, 2018). See Box 14.3 for ideas from Mercier about how to engage young children in conversations about knowing and wondering.

In order for students to learn to communicate effectively both inside and outside of school, we need to pay attention to the extent to which we are all "speaking the same language." Strazzabosco (2018), in discussing the

BOX 14.3.
Ideas in Practice: Supporting Children's Knowing and Wondering

I think there is substantial and valuable middle ground between refusing to answer children's questions and always answering them. I think it refers back to understanding and connecting, because if you know a child well, you can make an informed decision about what response will best scaffold their learning. Is this an opportunity to challenge them to draw their own conclusions and feel empowered by their ability to think logically or an opportunity to engage in a collaborative exchange of ideas that increases their curiosity? Could you refer them to a peer, or acknowledge that you don't know either but we could learn together?

No matter which one, I think the part that encourages them to join the community of inquiry is that you take their question seriously and engage in an authentic exchange about it. One response I often use is "What do you think?" I listen to their response and then, if appropriate, add, "Well, I think . . ." This communicates several helpful things: (a) I care what and how you think (not just that you have the right answer), (b) I believe you have valuable thoughts and reasoning abilities, (c) it's okay for us to think different things and still respect each other.

needs of students who grow up in poverty, emphasized the importance of teaching students to speak in the "formal register" as opposed to the "casual register" that they might use at home or in their neighborhood and among their friends. He explained that people in the middle and upper classes speak differently than those who live in poverty, the formal and casual register, respectively. The formal register is the language of school and business and the focus is on getting things done. People who live with persistent economic insecurity use the casual register, which is about developing and maintaining relationships, which makes sense, because, "in poverty your friends help you stay alive" (p. 131). Although one language model is not necessarily better, per se, than the other, the reality is that if one wants to succeed in school and economic life, one must be able to use the formal register. Instruction and practice in the formal register is one of the important dynamics that happens in a mentoring relationship between a middle- or upper-class mentor and a young person who lives in poverty. In addition to its importance for communication at school and work, Strazzabosco asserted that learning to speak in the formal register encourages youth in "if-then" discourse, reasoning, and thinking. This kind of thinking is essential to making good choices, especially for children and youth who have grown up in poverty,

BOX 14.4.
Ideas in Practice: Modern-Day Rapunzel

A little girl, who was in a wheelchair, lived in the projects, in a second-floor room that had a window that opened onto a ventilation shaft. Her mom worked a couple of jobs and so didn't have the time or the resources to take her daughter out into the fresh air and sunshine. The girl was lonely and bored in her apartment day after day.

One summer day, a vagrant moved into the ventilation shaft. The girl heard him and called out. They began to talk and, for the first time, the girl had some company and didn't feel quite so lonely. As the months went by and the temperature began to drop, the vagrant said he would have to move out and find a warmer place to stay. The little girl didn't want him to go, so she decided to throw her blankets down to him. She gathered up the blankets and leaned out the window to drop them down, but she leaned too far out and fell out the window and down onto the vagrant. They both died.

whose brain development might already have left them deficit in executive function (Center on the Developing Child, n.d.).

In Jim Edminster's English classes, he helped students in his majority-Black classrooms realize that they needed to translate their words and sentences from their perfectly functional casual register to Standard English. One of the strategies he used to affirm the richness of their culture and language was having them write fairy tales or fables from within the context of their lived reality. He related his memory of a student's rendition of the Rapunzel story in Box 14.4.

I can imagine that this assignment gave students many opportunities to express their thoughts and feelings about their lives and gave Edminster critical insight into the worries, joys, and imaginings of his students. Fundamentally, he was honoring their funds of knowledge and affirming that their lives had meaning and worth by casting their experiences and creativity within the time-honored realm of storytelling.

Children, especially those who grow up in families that lack the resources to provide educationally enriching experiences, need the input of adults outside the family to learn, grow, and find out things. Even though young children may get the majority of their information from people in their families, as children get older, they count on other adults and peers for information and perspectives. One of the ways they decide on who to believe is by paying attention to whose information has been reliable in the past. According to Harris (2012), children learn about their culture by looking "vertically" up to their primary caregivers: their mother and father, and others within their immediate family circle. However, children can also profit by looking "horizontally." Family members are not omniscient—neighbors, elders, and playmates likely know things that family members do not. Not surprisingly, children are willing to optimize their acquisition of skills and information by looking outside the circle of familiar caregivers—especially if the outsiders prove more reliable in the information they offer. (p. 97)

This is why having teachers and other school staff as role models and confidants and givers-of-information is critical to many students. In addition, mentors and elders from the community can play important roles when invited into the school life of students. The way teachers talk with students can communicate their expectations and bolster (or crush) hope. Christopher Alas, who teaches psychology at Houston Community College, said that he had not been

> aware of the effect of my word choices until one of my high school students met with me and said "thank you" for always saying "when you go to college" not "if you go to college." The student was being genuine; his entire academic system had been against him due to an environment of low expectations. (personal communication, K. Sáenz, October 9, 2019)

Communication for Collaboration

Most parents and teachers would say they see the education of children and youth as, ideally, a collaborative process between families and schools. When the school environment mirrors that in the home—for instance, when middle-class children go to schools where the teachers and staff come from similar backgroundscollaboration may feel like it happens naturally with minimal effort. For children and youth who grow up with persistent economic insecurity in severely underresourced homes with parents who themselves are undereducated, communication and collaboration between school and home needs to be much more intentional.

> To connect with parents, teachers should consider (1) developing explicit suggestions for how they can support their children at home (this can be essential for early childhood and elementary school teachers as they develop tools to help parents support their children's learning and development); (2) explicitly sharing in writing four or five things they expect or need from parents . . . [and] parents should express to teachers their expectations and

needs as well, and teachers should listen. Keeping these lines of communication open can be an essential element in supporting students. (Milner, 2015, p. 101)

Although it may sometimes seem as if parents are not interested in the education of their children because they do not attend meetings or respond to requests from the school, I suspect it is often the case that the realities of their lives keep them away from school appointments and they may, literally and figuratively, speak a different language than teachers and school staff. They may not feel like they belong at the school or feel confident in their ability to communicate effectively and may have had negative experiences with school when they were children. As described earlier in this chapter, schools should focus on building positive goal-oriented relationships with families. They should assume that parents love their children and want them to succeed at school. If a partnership attitude is demonstrated by teachers and school staff, parents are more likely to respond in kind and be open to ideas about helping their child learn.

In addition to collaborations between schools and families, schools can set the stage for students to learn to collaborate effectively with teachers and other adults inside and outside the school. The authors of *Building Equity* (Smith et al., 2017) referenced the work of Costello et al. (2009), who told us that one of the most important outcomes of inclusive and democratic processes is that schoolteachers and staff are doing things *with* students rather than *to* them and that this increases the likelihood that students will choose to make positive changes. Learning how to collaborate this way for the benefit of everyone in the school community is not only productive in the present but also a valuable skill to have for life and work.

School is important for students for many reasons, including academic knowledge and subject matter competence, as well as the development of life skills. These are the skills that we all need to interact with other people at work and at home and in the community in a way that can be positive, growthful, and satisfying for everyone. In *Building Equity*, Smith et al. (2017) suggested that the following prosocial skills should be inculcated in our schools:

- Communicating, verbally and nonverbally, with others
- Demonstrating commitment and perseverance
- Flexibility and adaptability, especially to stressful situations and changing demands
- Time management and task monitoring
- Leadership, taking responsibility for tasks, and motivating others

- Creativity and problem-solving skills
- Teamwork and collaborative efforts (pp. 102–103)

It is interesting that the list starts with communication and ends with collaboration. This organization makes sense to me as it is hard to imagine true and effective collaboration without open and honest communication as both a foundation and a strategy. Students need to be taught these skills and abilities through explanation, modeling, and many chances to practice.

PART FOUR

BANDWIDTH RECOVERY— PARENTS AND TEACHERS

15

PARENTS

The default impulse is to blame parents and families for what teachers, administrators, and the public tend to view as deficits rather than focusing on how the school community can build capacity.

—M. T. Winn (2018, p. 21)

R emember the discussion in chapter 7 on all the things that steal bandwidth from parents? In addition to constant worry about money for those living in poverty or near-poverty, parents, like their children, often experience microaggressions based on perceived social class, race, gender, sexual orientation, mental illness, or some other kind of difference. In addition, increasing economic inequality in the United States leaves more and more people out of the experience of full participation in the life of the country that is, theoretically, the "land of opportunity," making them feel like they have little value. All of this weighs on parents, and they do their best to hide the stress from their children so they can have a chance to grow and develop without sharing the serious pressures of adulthood. Life can seem overwhelming to many parents, leaving them with depleted bandwidth, resulting in behaviors that may look like they do not care about the education of their children. What they need is understanding and support.

What can schools and communities do to help parents recover bandwidth so they can support their children's learning? Most importantly, we can recognize and acknowledge that parents have multiple demands on their bandwidth, especially those who are living in poverty or near-poverty and who experience the effects of racism, classism, and other kinds of marginalization. When parents have depleted bandwidth, even though we realize they are the experts about their own children, they might appreciate concrete support from teachers and school leaders that will help them be effective collaborative partners in the education of their children. This might be especially important for single parents, those who are living far away from extended family, and those who are coming from other countries and trying to acclimate to life in the United States.

Schools can support parents by sharing information on child development at each age and grade level so they can better understand their children. School staff can work with parents to help them create and maintain regular routines at home and emphasize the importance of consistent expectations and consequences for their child's development and sense of security. Teachers and other school staff can consult often with parents about their child's behavior and development to identify concerns early so they can work on them together. Teachers can affirm parents' funds of knowledge by asking them to be involved in the classroom by coming to read or tell a story, teach a unique skill, provide a special food, go on a field trip, or volunteer to help with a project.

Schools can help families with basic needs by referring them to services in the community like food and housing programs, mental and physical health services, classes for English language learners, legal assistance, and recreation programs for adults and children. They can help parents find books for their children through community organizations and referrals to the public library and help them understand the importance of reading to children and listening to them read when they are ready. As children get older, teachers can talk with parents about providing a quiet place for homework and how to best support learning at home.

For the parents of middle and high school youth, schools could provide information on key developmental tasks of adolescence. They could work with parents to help them understand the importance of keeping open lines of communication with their children about difficult issues, such as sex and sexuality, identity, racism, violence, and other interpersonal relationship challenges. They could talk with parents about how to maintain high expectations for their adolescents and provide or, when needed, connect them with support services for academic achievement. A study of parent needs conducted by the United Negro College Fund in 2012 found that low-income parents needed help with academic support for their children at home (95%), information about grade-level expectations (93%), and support for their children beyond academics (91%) (Bridges et al., 2012).

If we sincerely wanted to help parents support the education of their children, we could decide to do the things that we know work. We know, for instance, the strategies that are effective in keeping students on track in middle and high school because they have worked in isolated projects around the country. "Diplomas Now," a program involving more than 30,000 students in middle and high schools (Balfanz, 2014), applied support strategies, including teams of teachers connected with common groups of students, more time for math and English, coaching for teachers and principals, welcoming students to school and calling them if they were absent or did not turn in homework, and early interventions when students were struggling with behavior or performance. After just the first few years, the results were encouraging: "44% reduction in absenteeism, 59% reduction in suspensions, 57% reduction in students failing English, 58% reduction in students failing math" (Healthy People 2020, n.d., para. 13). Since the start of the project, four of the high schools have reported increases in graduation rates ranging from 8.5% to 23%. We know the things that need to be done to increase positive educational outcomes for children and youth. Parents of middle and high school students would be best served if we made a collective commitment to actually do them.

When teachers and school leaders connect with parents outside of school, it might help them feel they are on an equal footing in this collaborative process. How might this happen without adding more demands outside of the school day? If teachers do not live in the neighborhood of the school, they could choose to frequent a grocery store near the school or use the nearest public library or the hardware store down the street. Casual encounters between parents and school personnel in these nonschool places might provide chances to relate as equals and help make more formal collaborations more effective.

16

TEACHERS

A growing body of research indicates that schools and classrooms are more important in shaping students' desired academic behaviors than the personal qualities they bring with them to school.

—*L. Farnham et al. (2015, para. 32)*

To teachers reading this: I know teaching is hard work on the best days. I do not think that a few ideas (things you probably already do) will relieve your bandwidth depletion and save the day. As you know, the goal is, on average, to have the rewards of teaching outweigh the frustrations of social and educational systems that can seem to work in opposition to the best interests of children. You stay in the business because of the gifts of life and hope your students give you daily and because you believe your work makes a difference. Having said that . . . .

In chapter 8, I wrote about several things that rob teachers of bandwidth, including underresourced schools, overemphasis on high-stakes testing, low salaries compared to professional peers, and more students per classroom in schools with the largest number of children from poor and near-poor families. In an ideal world (or one closer to ideal than we have), teachers would get paid like their professional peers in other fields, they would have regular and affordable access to high-quality professional development opportunities including further higher education, there would be reasonable student:teacher ratios in all schools along with adequate paraprofessional assistance, supportive and capable school leadership, and competent and active school boards. I wish I could say I think the political process will make these things happen in the near future. Unfortunately, I suspect these issues will be with us—and may even deteriorate further—for the foreseeable future, so public school teachers are likely to continue to have bandwidth challenges that keep them from doing their best for students.

Students and their development suffer when teachers have depleted bandwidth for life and work. What can schools and parents (and teachers themselves) do to help teachers recover bandwidth so they can better help students learn and thrive? Teachers can understand major bandwidth stealers and work together as school teams to try to mitigate the negative effects of the pressure. In Winn's (2018) discussion of restorative practices in schools, she talked about one of the major principles, which is looking at who has been harmed by a person's actions. In regard to the historic realities of racism, she reminds us that,

> as a group, teachers and other educational professionals have, in many cases, also experienced harm (many feel devalued, most receive low pay, many experience strained relationships with administrators, etc.) and have needs that must be considered. (p. 20)

Similar to Strazzabosco's (2018) idea of a weekly group meeting for students living in poverty, Santoro (2018) advocated for a chance for teachers to talk about how they are feeling: "I suggest that engaging in, rather than ignoring or silencing, discussions about professional moral concerns may prevent demoralization" (p. 33). Schools need to be intentional about listening to the voices of teachers and other school staff and ensuring that there are opportunities to express both the joys and pains of this difficult and critical work. Landsman told me about a practice called "Good Friday"—teachers are invited to stop by a location (maybe the school library) on Friday afternoons to share what went right during the week so they leave for the weekend on a positive note. Finding time for productive and healthy conversations for mutual support can be challenging in itself in environments under constant pressure, but it seems to me the time would be well spent both for individual teachers and staff and, ultimately, for students.

One of the most negative effects of the emphasis on test preparation and testing is that teachers feel constrained to focus on that one thing—performance on high-stakes tests. People have chosen teaching as their life profession because they love children and young people, they are creative thinkers and want to contribute to the development of young minds, and they want to invest their energies into making a better future for the country and world. Many teachers enter their first years feeling excited about the potential for doing good and then quickly realize all the limitations put on them by the regulatory culture of public school education today. They may soon feel stymied and discouraged.

"Teachers work best when they feel free to make 'errors of enthusiasm'" (Jensen, 2009, p. 100). It needs to be okay for school staff to try new things with students, to take risks and make mistakes. One critical way to model a growth mind-set for students is to let them see that the adults make mistakes, too, and that the response is not censure or punishment, but reflection and conversations about how we can do better next time. One of the most critical aspects of teacher development is effective supervision that is focused on improvement and support.

Effective supervision from school staff and lead teachers can contribute significantly to the bandwidth recovery of classroom teachers. The idea that someone is on your side in your efforts to do the best work you can strengthens a teacher's self-confidence and sense that there is support even in difficult times. In addition, the process of supervision can act as a model for relationships (e.g., model how a teacher could relate to students' families). How supervisors behave toward teachers can demonstrate important aspects of productive relationship-building with families. As I discussed in chapter 9 related to a strengths-based approach in interactions with children and their parents, a similar attitude will result in effective supervision of teachers, giving them useful feedback so they feel like they have expanded bandwidth for their work. The following are strengths-based attitudes for supervision for teachers in early childhood education, which seem relevant to teachers at any level. Teachers and staff

- deserve the same support and respect we are asking them to give families;
- are our partners with a crucial role in achieving outcomes;
- have expertise about their own fields of practice; and
- contribute in ways that are valuable and important. (National Center on Parent, Family and Community Engagement, n.d., p. 28)

When teachers and school staff feel validated in their work, some of their bandwidth is freed up for their actual work. Professional development and ongoing support help teachers to have a long list of strategies they can employ to help their students and to make their classrooms places where students can access all their bandwidth. When teachers have many options for effective interventions and approaches, they can be calmer and use less bandwidth on anxiety because they know they can reach for a second or third or fourth idea to help a student who is struggling. Because most of us realize—and the research shows—that we have implicit biases that play out to the detriment of some students, professional development should include interventions that have been shown to reduce bias (Gilliam et al., 2016).

Another key area of professional development that is needed for the establishment and maintenance of inclusive schools where all students are together in the general education classroom is how to support students with disabilities to reach their highest potential. Classroom teachers, special education experts, school leaders, parents, and students need to collaborate consistently to maximize the learning of each student. Ideally, preservice teachers receive training in this area, and ongoing professional development is needed to both inform teachers about the latest knowledge about specific disabilities and guide them in effective approaches and the most productive ways to work with colleagues to make the classroom and playground positive learning environments for all children. Students will do better to the extent that general education teachers and special education teachers share information and expertise and both have input into the instructional activities and content of lessons (Kimbrough & Mellen, 2012).

Riester-Wood (2015) suggested that the use of peer support for students with disabilities might be effective in enhancing their learning. Without adding more instructional positions, this might be a way for teachers to increase individual attention to students who are most in need of it. Riester-Wood described the following peer support strategies:

- Collaborative Learning—An instructional strategy used to reinforce skills taught by the teacher. This teaching method allows time for practice, review, and opportunities for students to use higher-level thinking skills.
- Cross-Age Peer Support—[This] approach typically involves older students, usually high school age, who provide instructional support for elementary or secondary students.
- Peer Modeling—[This approach] can be used to help students learn academic processes and classroom routines. It also provides the classroom teacher opportunities to use peers to assist with instruction, clarifying directions and giving social reminders with little or no disruption to the lesson cycle. It is an excellent way for peers to provide appropriate behavioral models for students who need to improve their social skills. (para. 6)

I know from my own work the bandwidth recovery value of affirming students for their knowledge and skill by asking them to share them with other students. It is good for both the helper and the helped and is effective in leveraging finite teacher resources for students who need extra support.

Because life in underresourced schools can be especially challenging to everyone's bandwidth, public school administrators, staff, and teachers can think about ways to help themselves and their students recover bandwidth that do not cost very much money. Affirmations and expressions of appreciation are free. Short bits of communication to parents and families from the school can make a big difference to their feeling of being connected and part of a common effort on behalf of students. Movement in the classroom is free and has wonderful advantages for learning. Greetings at the beginning and the end of the school day that communicate welcome and good wishes can set the tone for positive interaction in the school and classroom. Celebrations with stories and songs of important cultural holidays and customs can be done with little cost. Finding a way each day to compliment each child can build up self-confidence in everyone. When consistent and intentional support for students is seen as a core function of specific personnel in a school, working collaboratively with teachers, teachers are able to free up some of their bandwidth to focus on their core goals of teaching and learning (Walsh et al., 2014).

Santoro (2018) suggested that professional teacher organizations could help teachers organize around issues that affect the moral core of their work. Although labor unions are often seen as self-serving groups that are only looking out for the best interest of their members, teacher unions can and do use their power to advocate for the improvement of school environments for the good of students and the community as well. Building on Kenneth S. Goodman's (1990) "A Declaration of Professional Conscience for Teachers," New York City public school teacher Colin Schumacher (2015) has put forward "An Ethic for Teachers of Conscience in Public Schools" (para. 12). I have included it in full in Figure 16.1 as a clear and forthright statement of principles for public school teachers.

One way for teachers to recharge and recover bandwidth is to reap what Santoro (2018) has called the *moral rewards* of teaching, defining them as "renewable resources that teachers can access when doing good work" (p. 176). She defined *good work* as work that has a positive social purpose that contributes to the well-being of others. To do good work, school environments have to develop habits that "cultivate respect for others and for learning" (p. 177). Although individual teachers bring to the work their own expertise, motivation, and skill, the overall school culture is paramount in creating the conditions under which teachers can do the good work from which they reap moral rewards, which brings us back to the importance of community-building and mutual support. In addition, when teachers feel like they are teaching in culturally relevant ways and, thereby, affirming and encouraging all of their students, they are more likely to be energized. Carmen Tisdale described her journey back to life as a teacher: "Culturally relevant teaching gave meaning and joy to learning for my students, so it gave meaning and joy back to me" (in Baines et al., 2018, p. 4). The education of our children must be seen as a shared responsibility of schools, families, and communities if we want a future in which democracy can truly thrive in the hands of capable, thoughtful citizens.

Figure 16.1. An Ethic for Teachers of Conscience in Public Education.

A Moral Imperative to Attend to the Development and Well-Being of Our Students

- We develop strong relationships with students and their families, built on mutual respect and trust. We respect the abilities, cultural identities, languages, and values that our students come to us with.
- We devote ourselves to fostering the cognitive, academic, social, emotional, and physical development of our students.
- We foster students' inherent desire to learn and help to develop the skills and dispositions necessary for lifelong learning and effective community and civic engagement.
- We support students in developing their creative potential and offer robust experiences with the arts.
- The welfare of students in our schools is paramount. We protect students from violence and all forms of mistreatment, abuse, and exploitation.
- We work against discrimination and injustices that affect students and that are present within our educational institutions.

A Moral Imperative to Know Our Students Well and Understand Their Learning

- We give our students opportunities to present and reflect on their learning through multiple modalities.
- We use multiple methods of assessment to know students well and to understand their learning.
- We are discerning when considering the biases, reliability, and validity of assessment methods and in evaluating the information that those methods reveal.
- We require assessments to be transparent and to have a direct application to teaching and curriculum development.
- We do not generalize or make high-stakes decisions based on a single method of assessment.
- We do not define students, or encourage students to define themselves, by their assessment results.
- We do not carry out assessments with the primary purpose of ranking and sorting students or bestowing statuses upon students.

(Continues)

Figure 16.1. (*Continued*)

A Moral Imperative to Serve Our Communities

- We will welcome and teach all children without prejudice—regardless of race, ethnicity, religion, language, national origin, gender, disability, sexual orientation, or citizenship.
- We value diversity in our public school communities and believe that integrated schools are fundamental to an integrated society.
- We believe that teaching students to understand and value diversity contributes to a viable democracy.
- We consider public schools to be a part of the commons. We will work to make our schools spaces that support the learning, health, and the democratic participation of our local communities.

A Moral Imperative to Promote Learning in Service of the Public Good

- We teach students literacy and the fundamental skills necessary to advance learning and pursue their full potentials.
- We teach students to think critically and problem-solve.
- We teach students to apply their learning to issues of social justice.
- We teach students to work collaboratively toward a common purpose.
- We teach students to be stewards of the natural world around them.
- We teach students civic engagement and democratic values.
- We teach students social ethics and how to work through conflict constructively.
- We are committed to our own development as teachers, including but not limited to trainings, coursework, observations and exchanges, descriptive reviews, and teacher-led inquiry and research.

A Moral Imperative to Preserve Public Education

- We believe that students have the right to equitable resources through public funding.
- We believe that public education must remain democratically governed and in service of the public good, not private interests or for-profit businesses.
- We believe that policies that divert public funding to privatized alternatives to public schools undermine the purpose and potential of public education.

(*Continues*)

Figure 16.1. (*Continued*)

- We believe that public schools must remain accountable to institutions that are publicly controlled and democratically governed, including parent associations, school leadership teams, school boards, and local, state, and federal governments.
- We believe that public agencies and governing bodies must conduct their business transparently, maintain public records, and seek ways to involve the public in decision-making processes.
- We believe that the implementation of standards, assessment systems, curriculum materials, and teaching programs must be done in consultation with teachers and democratic governing bodies. Implementation must not be driven by private profit or through the decision-making processes of private entities.

Note. From Schumacher (2015, para. 11–15). Reprinted with permission.

Bettina Love (2019), in her advocacy for schools where Black and Brown children can not only survive but also thrive, emphasized the importance of the overall health of the entire school, beginning with the teachers:

> For schools to be well, educators need to be well. Educators need free therapy, love, compassion, and healing, and to embrace theories that explain why getting well is so hard. Teacher wellness is critical to creating schools that protect students' potential and function as their homeplace. Educators, students, and parents need to be on a path to wellness together for schools to be sites of healing. Schools cannot be doing just alright; they have to be well by putting everyone's mental health as the first priority. (p. 161)

PART FIVE

SYSTEMS VIEW

PART FIVE

SYSTEMS VIEW

17

CASE STUDY

Rochester, New York

While doing research for this book, I continued to conduct workshops around the United States related to my first book about bandwidth recovery for college students. I began to have conversations with colleagues who had experience in pre-K–12 environments and my ears were always open to the wisdom of those who knew the realities of work in underresourced and troubled schools. After giving a talk at Finger Lakes Community College in Canandaigua, New York, I visited Rochester, New York, which is located about 30 miles northwest of Canandaigua. During a casual exchange with a couple of people who worked in the Rochester Public Schools system, I learned that the system was struggling mightily. On that same trip, I was introduced to the work of John Strazzabosco (2018), the author of *Ninety Feet Under*. Strazzabosco lives in Rochester and wrote about his work there. I read more about Rochester and decided to focus on the city and the schools as a case study related to bandwidth recovery.

Rochester was a familiar name to me as a child because my cousins lived there. One of five children, my Uncle Joe grew up with my Mom in Nebraska, then moved to Rochester and worked for Kodak for 37 years. He and Aunt Helen raised eight children in Rochester. Kodak, the film processing giant, opened in Rochester in 1892 (Sparkes, 2012). In 1982, it employed one quarter of the metro area (more than 60,000 people at its peak) and accounted for half of the economic activity there (Ryssdal, n.d.). Rochester, like many medium-sized northeast cities that thrived in manufacturing, was a place where people could live a decent lifestyle, work for the same company for decades, and earn a pension that guaranteed them a secure retirement. As those industries declined, like film processing, or moved overseas, like many segments of the auto industry, these communities began to deteriorate, affecting most severely people with little education past high school who could not easily move into other occupations. People in the service sectors saw their jobs disappear while middle- and upper-management layoffs resulted in outmigration from city centers.

Rochester, a once vibrant company city, now ranks at the top of the bottom. According to a report from the Rochester-Monroe Anti-Poverty Initiative (2018), 2017 census data indicate that Rochester's child poverty rate was just under 52%, the rate of extreme poverty (below half of federal poverty line) had increased from 16.3% in 2013 to 16.8% in 2017, and the city ranked third in overall poverty among the 75 largest U.S. metropolitan areas (behind Detroit and Cleveland). In the Rochester Public Schools system in 2018, 94% of students were poor, 21% had disabilities, and 88% were non-White. The differences in household wealth across school districts in the area is one of the largest in the country.

A 2014 report showed segregation in New York schools to be severe and increasing. In the Rochester metro area, White students made up 70% of public school enrollment but were only 15% of enrollment in urban schools (Kucsera, 2014). The high school graduation rate in June 2017 was 52% (57% if you count the students who finished in August). This rate was the lowest among urban districts in the area and one of the lowest in the United States; in June 2016, fewer than 48% of students graduated on time (Spector & Murphy, 2018), so the 2017 metrics were actually encouraging. Today, the Rochester City School District (RCSD) continues to be characterized by the negative effects of decades of neglect and deterioration. Murphy (2018) summarized some of the "features and flaws" of RCSD:

- A student body that is overwhelmingly poor and segregated by race, with massive concentrations of homelessness, disability, trauma and lack of English skills.
- A tottering, ever-changing district bureaucracy unable to serve them.
- A mostly white teaching corps, in many cases unequipped to connect with children from a very different background.
- A city government by turns supportive, combative and complicit.
- A surrounding suburban core that has kept its distance from the troubled district they share borders with. (para. 6)

Although it seems as though there is only bad news to report about RCSD, there are people in Rochester who are not giving up on the schools or the kids. There are some amazing turnarounds happening, giving hope to the entire system that things can improve and the children and youth of Rochester do not need to be forever deprived of the opportunity to learn and thrive.

In July of 2019, I met with Shaun Nelms, a faculty member at the University of Rochester's Warner School of Education and also the superintendent of East Lower and Upper Schools, which entered into an educational partnership organization (UR-EPO) with the university's Center for Urban Education Success (CUES) in fall 2015. Previously, Superintendent Nelms had described the goal

> to create systems and structures that: address and improve attendance, academic achievement, and family and community engagement; build capacity among staff; and promote a positive culture and climate.(Nelms, n.d., para. 1)

We talked about the transformation that was happening at the school and the strategies and practices that have been adopted to, in my words, help "scholars" (East's word for its students) recover bandwidth so education can be the focus. After 3 years, there are many hopeful indications that the changes are having the desired results in improved outcomes. The high school graduation rate has increased from 40% in 2016 to 61% in 2018. Average daily attendance went from 77% in 2014–2015 to 91% in 2018 for the Lower School and 85% in the Upper School in fall 2018 (University of Rochester–East High School Educational Partnership Organization, 2019). According to Nelms, suspensions have decreased by nearly 85% over 3 years, and the number of fights and altercations fell from 230 in 2014–2015 to just 68 in 2016–2017 (University of Rochester Center for Urban Education Success, n.d.c). In Box 17.1, I have included a section of the CUES's (n.d.c) plan for the UR-EPO because it so clearly describes the radical commitment to making sure this effort works for everyone.

Nelms, like many effective leaders, has been quick to point out that the successes at East have been the result of team effort. His assertion is far more than modesty or the desire to share credit. It reflects a very specific management approach they call "distributed leadership," which is described on the UR-EPO website (University of Rochester Center for Urban Education Success, n.d.b):

> At East, leadership emerges from whomever is most knowledgeable for a given situation. Staff and administrators have learned to rely on each other to address critical problems as they emerge in the community. Distributed leadership expands accountability and voice to teachers, staff, students and families. (University of Rochester Center for Urban Education Success, n.d.b, para. 1)

BOX 17.1.
Ideas in Practice: UR-EPO Plan "All In . . . All the Time"

- *School family groups.* Each grade is organized into small "family groups" (about 10 students each) that meet daily with a mentor (faculty, staff, or administrator) to work on student interests and needs, such as leadership development, attendance, study skills, academic performance, community service projects, restorative justice practice, and other topics that support students' development and achievement. School family group time is augmented by community advocate support to engage students and their parents and families on a daily basis.
- *Engaged, active students.* The UR-East EPO plan places students squarely at the center of the schooling experience. Students are starting to take charge of their learning and are beginning to take on leadership roles both within the school and community. Students are being prepared through both family group work and student-driven pedagogy in all classes to be active citizens in their community.
- *Expanded social and emotional support.* We are promoting and implementing a vision for social and emotional health that supports a safe and healthy school environment for teachers, students, and their families, using a restorative justice approach with systematic support of counselors, social workers, and comprehensive health services.
- *Deep recognition of families as true partners.* East uses a model of engagement and relationship building that focuses on the strengths of students and families, creating meaningful opportunities for shared decision-making with youth, families, and other partners in the Rochester community. East will be open evenings and weekends to serve as a focal point for the community and to provide academic and other support services to families.
- *Better support for English language learners.* East offers a full continuum of programs for English language learners, including integrated supports throughout the school program, as well as an enhanced dual language program for students whose home language is Spanish. Professional learning for content teachers strives to better serve English language learning students, and efforts are being made to attract school personnel who can speak languages other than English.

(Continues)

BOX 17.1 (*Continued*)

> - *Professional learning.* Transformation of the East culture requires ongoing, embedded, and intensive professional learning for all school staff, and includes extensive summer work that continues through the academic year. All teachers have daily collaborative planning time to work on curriculum design, assessment, and data analysis to inform instruction, planning, and professional learning.

Note. From *Key Elements of UR-EPO* from the University of Rochester Center for Urban Education Success (2017), https://www.rochester.edu/warner/cues/home/east-epo/key-elements-of-ur-epo-plan/

About this new kind of organization, Assistant Superintendent Lorna Washington explained,

> I think that how we were able to transition and be comfortable with the distributive leadership model is just trust. As we learned to trust each other, we were able to get a better understanding of the strength of each of our colleagues and where we may have been weak we could tap into someone else who was stronger in that area. (University of Rochester Center for Urban Education Success, n.d.a, 4:38)

Within this model, "teacher leaders" are a critical part of the leadership structure, planning and implementing instructional initiatives.

> Teacher leaders are responsible for coaching content area teachers, coordinating curriculum development, facilitating daily collaborative planning time (CPT), and leading "learning labs." The teacher leaders ensure that the time, space, and collaborative practice is in place for effective peer-to-peer learning. (University of Rochester Center for Urban Education Success, n.d.e, para. 9)

Clearly, the concept of teacher leaders is a manifestation of the "all in" philosophy that was described in Box 17.1.

To support scholars' social-emotional well-being, each scholar at East is a member of a family group (about 10 scholars) led by two teachers or other staff persons, called "carents" (University of Rochester, n.d., para. 32). Family groups meet for 30 minutes every day during all the years of a scholar's attendance at East. Scholars and the adults talk together about academic and personal issues, get to know each other, and provide mutual support.

Groups operate with restorative practices, honestly talking out disagreements or conflicts. Daily lessons are coconstructed between the scholars and the adults. One of the scholars explained that whereas previously, there may have been scholars no one knew, that has now changed; now at least 10 people in the school know each scholar, and they notice when somebody is missing. Family groups help scholars who might have been lost in the school and in the classroom, who were not likely to speak. They use a talking piece that is passed around the circle so everyone has a chance to be heard and others are invited to listen.

Community-building, problem-solving, and conflict resolution are done using restorative practices, as I described in chapter 12. Michelle Garcia, social worker at East Lower School, explained, "When we talk about restorative practices in schools, we talk about doing things *with* people instead of *to* them. Because once we get to know each other and learn from each other the likelihood of conflict is lessened" (University of Rochester, n.d.c). When students have conflicts, they come together and "circle about it," but that is just one kind of circle. Other times the circles are about community-building or celebrations or giving support to a classmate who has experienced a loss of a family member. When a conflict arises between students, they are likely to come to an adult and ask for a circle; they want to avoid a fight. Both family groups and restorative practice are about reliable structures that students can count on for support. Marlene Blocker, principal at East Upper School, said,

> I think the greatest role that restorative practices have played here is in repairing relationships. I think in the past it was easy to dole out consequences and think that that was going to change things around, but in reality, after the consequence ended, there was no repair to relationships and if you don't have the relationships that are strong and respectful in place, then it really diminishes some of the other opportunities for growth that are available. (University of Rochester, n.d.d, 3:40)

The turnaround of East Lower and Upper Schools in Rochester is an illustration of the power of school leadership, teachers, scholars, parents, and communities to use evidence-based practices to change the trajectory of a failing school. The emphasis on building and maintaining relationships built on caring and trust is infused in every part of the project. Scholars, teachers, administrators, parents, and community allies are "all in." Individual and collective bandwidth has been recovered within this learning context even as the struggles of Rochester as a city continue. There is hope in this transformation as these young people are the future leaders of this city and cities like it all over the country. Their educational and personal transformations hold promise for all of our futures.

Before we leave Rochester, I want to touch on one other wonderful thing that is going on in Rochester that relates to health and, ultimately, to bandwidth for children and youth. There appears to be a "play revolution." Rochester is home to the Strong National Museum of Play. Rochester native Margaret Woodbury Strong, born in 1859, was a collector who left over 27,000 dolls and 100 dollhouses, and other toys, to the city; the museum in her name opened in 1982. Today, the Strong National Museum of Play is the home to Halls of Fame for Toys and Video Games and rich archives of research on play in many forms. So it is fitting that there is a play movement in Rochester.

Nora Doebrich, a Rochester art therapist, works at the Family Trauma Intervention Program at the Society for the Protection and Care of Children. She has written about the importance of play and movement for children to express themselves, especially young children whose verbal skills are still developing. Doebrich (n.d.) said, "Movement and play allow all of us to express the link between our minds and bodies" (para. 4). Children who live in poverty and who experience adversity need ways to give expression to what are sometimes high levels of stress. Doebrich explained,

> One expectation that I frequently witness is the idea that children will sit still and if they are not able to be still, this communicates some level of dysfunction. Children need to move and we need to allow them the space and freedom to do so in a healthy manner. Through movement, children improve focus, self-regulation, body awareness, coping and relaxation skills. In providing our children with opportunities to develop these skills and express themselves within healthy limits, we are increasing their capacity to better understand themselves and the world in which they live. (para. 5)

In some areas of Rochester, it is the children most needing to play and move freely who have the least opportunity to do so because of unsafe neighborhoods. Children, with their adult allies, are leading the movement to demand safe play spaces. On May 30, 2019, children from the after-school program of Cameron Community Ministries marched for "peace and their right to play in safe neighborhoods" (Common Ground Health, 2019, para. 1). These children, who live in one of the most violent neighborhoods in the city, marched with signs that read, "Keep us safe, let us play" (para. 4) and wore shirts with a quote from Frederick Douglass that said, "It is easier to build strong children than to repair broken men" (para. 2).

An initiative of Common Ground Health, Healthi Kids launched a project called "The Power of Play," which asserts, "Play is foundational to whole child health. Kids who play every day are healthier, do better in school and have reduced feelings of anxiety" (Healthi Kids, n.d., para. 1). The Healthi Kids Coalition stated:

> Our advocacy agenda brings back the importance of play for whole child health and moves to advance solutions in schools and neighborhoods that safeguard play. We do this by advocating for change that:
>
> - Invests in safe, accessible infrastructure that supports every child's right to play in school and in their neighborhood
> - Promotes playful neighborhoods by advocating for youth and resident driven play in communities across the region
> - Safeguards play as a cornerstone of school learning for Pre-Kindergarten through 2nd grade and
> - Ensures that every child has access to unstructured play in early childcare settings and at school. (Healthi Kids, n.d., para. 3)

Free body movement during play without adult interference provides children and youth with opportunities for physical expression of feelings, working out rules and relationships, and bandwidth-expanding affirmation of self-sufficiency and health. Bringing play back to neighborhoods and schools seems critical in a city in which so many children are living with adversity.

18

WISDOM FOR PRINCIPALS AND SUPERINTENDENTS

A s we know, from early learning settings to high school classrooms, teachers are the heart of the educational endeavor and, for children and youth, the most critical factor in the day-to-day experience of school. We also know that, for a variety of reasons related to legislation, funding, regulation, and the practical realities of managing complex systems, the options that teachers have are prescribed by school leaders at the building and district levels. How can principals and superintendents help to create learning environments where students, teachers, and parents can recover mental bandwidth lost to poverty, racism, and other "differentisms?"

With direction from the school board and regulations and laws from local, state, and federal government, school leaders may themselves sometimes feel like they have very little control over what happens in their buildings or district. What they can always work to affect, however, is the atmosphere of their school. When a child or parent walks through the doors of a school, is there a message of welcome and affirmation, of acceptance and hope, of invitation to all? Although the conditions and adequacy of the physical facility is important to learning, what is more vital are the human connections that happen within an invitational environment in which every person is valued for the unique set of gifts and challenges they bring and the potential contribution they can make to the school.

Behind the scenes, outside of direct contact with students, parents, and the community, school leaders need to build their teams in ways that maximize the effectiveness of each individual and of the collective. Leaders could do the personal values exercise from chapter 10 (see Figure 10.1) with all school employees and have discussions about how each of their values guides their work in the school. When the staff come from a variety of backgrounds and when they are working under pressure, it is easy to think they have little in common. However, talking about basic values tends to help people realize we have more that unites than divides us and that we can work from shared values for the betterment of our own well-being and in the service of students and families.

In addition, when school staff recognize and acknowledge their own bandwidth challenges and those of their colleagues, responses can be transformed from blame and shame to understanding and support. Most people, even those who are White and relatively healthy and economically secure, face challenges in their lives related to family, relationships, illness, financial crises, and other unexpected bumps in the road. If staff can understand that these things deplete bandwidth, they can respond with compassion and caring; support each other; and, in the process, help everyone regain bandwidth.

Belonging

In chapter 10, the focus was on the importance of a sense of belonging for all students. Ensuring that students, parents, teachers, and community members feel like they belong in the school may be the most critical aspect of a learning environment. Without a sense of belonging, so much bandwidth can be used up worrying about everything from whether or not you will find a friend to knowing who to ask for help to basic physical and psychological safety. Parents who feel they belong are more likely to be involved in their children's education to the extent they are able, to work in partnership with teachers and school leaders in the best interest of their children, and to contribute positively to the life of the school. Teachers who feel like they belong will be able to do their best work and thrive within the school environment, asking for and giving support when needed.

An important aspect of belonging is identity safety. Each person—child, parent, teacher, school leader, community member—must be able to see themselves reflected in the life of the school. Leaders can be intentional about examining the public art displayed in the school, pictures of people on the walls in halls and classrooms, and signage and other messaging in public spaces for the extent to which they represent the population of the school. Are the cultural traditions, histories, and current realities of students a vital part of the school? Do students see significant parts of their identity reflected in the identities of teachers, staff, and school leaders? Are the contributions of community members embraced in the school; for instance, are cultural elders asked to come into the school and interact with the students, telling stories and demonstrating their knowledge and skills and sharing their wisdom?

One feature of identity that is seldom discussed as such, I think, is the concept of variation in ability in so many areas of living and learning. When we take into account ideas about varying abilities related to cognitive functioning, physical health and mobility, mental health challenges, and communication differences, it is clear that we must be very intentional about the way we design our learning environments so that everyone can thrive. The New Zealand Ministry of Social Development's Office of Disability Issues (2001) has defined *disability* as "the process which happens when one group of people create barriers by designing a world only for their way of living, taking no account of the impairments other people have" (para. 2). I like that the statement clearly puts the problem where it belongs—not with people who are differently abled, but with "normally abled" people who have created situations that result in the exclusion or disadvantage of others.

Emma Mercier, who teaches preschool-age children in New Zealand, wanted to communicate to the parents of the children in her school the educationally sound reasons why inclusivity is in the best interest of all children. Her explanation, which I have included in its entirety in the Appendix, is titled "Benefits to Typically Developing Children of Learning Alongside Children With Disabilities." Even though written for the parents of young children, the concepts are equally valid for students of any age. This statement is a helpful summary of the many more specific points in the explanation:

> Learning alongside children who are different in the fundamental ways they process and interact with the world provides a wide range of benefits to typically developing children and helps us guide them toward being ethical, capable, and mentally healthy human beings. (p. 174, this volume)

So many important messages for all of us! Schools would be lovely places if we all lived within these guidelines—for instance, "It's a good idea to give people a chance to try things" reminds me of the wish of teachers to be granted the grace to make "errors of enthusiasm" (Jensen, 2009, p. 10). And would we not all do better if we learned to accept that "sometimes even when you do your part, life throws you a curve ball" (p. 203, this volume)? And when we recognize that curve balls happen in everyone's life, we can embody that "everyone is entitled to respect, no matter what" (p. 204, this volume).

For the establishment of an inclusive school environment, the role of school leaders is critical in creating learning environments that authentically nurture and value every student, teacher, and parent. Leadership is essential in providing ongoing professional development for teachers on how to help every student reach their full potential and the time to collaborate with each other to make classrooms as effective as possible for students at all levels and abilities.

Similarly, children and youth who are lesbian or gay or transgender or who do not fit into a strict girl/boy binary need to be able to bring those unique parts of their identities safely and comfortingly into the classroom and the school. Some students have parents or other family members who identify in one of those ways, and they need to feel like the people they love and who care for them are also welcome at school as their authentic selves. All people need to feel that they are accepted and welcomed as valuable and important parts of the school community. School leaders can help create this nurturing environment by supporting policies and practices that allow people to identify themselves and their names and pronouns as they wish and that respect each person's right to their own definitions of themselves. As long as the needs of children are met in the interest of their learning and growth, family members and other support people should be treated as critical parts of a collaborative team, with respect and inclusion.

Practically, school leaders can be intentional about the information they ask of parents. For instance, a form could ask for the name of "parents/legal guardians" rather than "father" and "mother." Forms might ask for "preferred name" for both the student and the adults connected with the student so that each person could be addressed by the name with which they are most comfortable. Dress codes should be reviewed to make sure the standards are not arbitrarily gendered and that there are sound, education-related reasons for the rules that we impose on students. Sometimes unexamined rules reflect someone's idea of what is "proper" for a girl or boy to wear in a strictly gendered world but that are not relevant to the educational endeavor for individuals or groups of students. Schools can have gender-neutral restrooms so that students and visiting adults do not have to make uncomfortable choices. Signage and other visuals can be made inclusive by considering the languages that are spoken by students and their families and that some people are differently abled relative to the written word. The concepts of universal design can help school leaders to monitor the environment so that everyone can feel welcome and be informed about the location of resources and key facilities (e.g., restrooms, office, library, gym). What works for the people who have some barriers of mobility or understanding will often be better for everyone.

Funds of Knowledge

All students and their families bring valuable information, knowledge, skills, and values to the school community. These funds of knowledge, when acknowledged and affirmed, can be leveraged to increase the richness and vitality of a school. There is almost unlimited opportunity for cross-cultural sharing of experiences, multigenerational interactions, collaborations between school and community, inclusion of diverse perspectives and ideas, and the embracing of the wisdom that exists in every community. Many adults, especially those who attended the school as children, are honored to be asked to share their expertise with children, from an artistic ability to storytelling to professional mentoring to helping coach a sports team. Many people appreciate the importance of a good school to the overall health of a community and are willing to invest time and talent when asked. It is easy to assume that family members who have few material resources and who have many demands on their bandwidth will not have the time or energy to contribute to the school (and many do not), but school leaders should ask and be open to the many varied ways people can be helpful. Most people want to feel like they have something to offer and that their willingness is recognized and appreciated.

The funds of knowledge of teachers are some of the most valuable resources in a school. Jenny Bronski, a longtime teacher from metropolitan Chicago suggested that, because it has often been many years since school leaders have been in a classroom full-time, they should remember to look to teachers for input and expertise. Like in Rochester, New York, school leaders can practice "distributed leadership" (University of Rochester Center for Urban Education Success, n.d.b, para. 1), inviting teachers to propose and take the lead on school enhancement projects in which they have interest and expertise. Teachers' bandwidth can be recovered when they have ownership over a project through which they are contributing to the well-being of students and their learning. The ability to retain a bit of control over a small but promising project can make a big difference for a teacher, especially those teachers who are buffeted about by persistent pressures in underresourced and struggling schools.

Certainty

School leaders can support the bandwidth recovery of all members of the school community by creating, to the extent possible, an environment characterized by certainty. Many children and families experience high levels of chaos in their lives due to poverty or persistent economic insecurity, unemployment, mental and physical illness, dangerous neighborhoods with frequent violence, unsafe or insecure housing, food insecurity, and the negative effects of racism, classism, and other forms of "differentism." For all children, but especially for these, school must be a place of certainty, where they can count on the adults to be reliable and supportive, where routines are followed, where their needs for food and drink are met, and where they feel safe and secure.

BOX 18.1.
Ideas in Practice: Breakfast in the Classroom

> To address food insecurity, we instituted a Breakfast in the Classroom program that gave all students access to breakfast with no questions asked; 100% of the students were allowed to have breakfast regardless of their SES status. Breakfast was delivered to rooms each morning and students simply took what they wanted and as much as they wanted. This also helped with behavior in the mornings. Many students come to school with a lot of stress from home and what may have happened the night before or that morning. Going to a large cafeteria filled with noise and a lot of stimulation often resulted in arguments, meltdowns, and general bad starts to the day for many students. Once we went to Breakfast in the Classroom, students reported directly to the safety of their own classroom, their own teacher, their own space (their table or desk), and so on, which provided a much calmer and peaceful start with a sense of belonging.

Sandy Kent, a principal in Oklahoma, began a practice in her school called "Breakfast in the Classroom" (Box 18.1), through which all children were nourished each morning, contributing to a sense of certainty, care, and belonging.

Sometimes outside forces set schools on paths they do not anticipate. Karen Sáenz, a psychology faculty member at Houston Community College, told me that after Hurricane Harvey's devastating floods, the Houston Independent School District eliminated the stigma of free and reduced lunch and provided no-cost meals for breakfast and lunch at all schools. In 2019, the practice is continuing (HISD News Blog, 2019–2020).

Parents also need to be able to count on the school as a place where their children are nurtured and loved and where their needs are recognized and addressed. Parents want to be informed of how their children are doing and treated as vital partners in their education. Even when parents are low on bandwidth themselves, most want to be informed and involved to the best of their ability. They need to know when changes are going to happen so they can ask questions, understand, and help prepare their children. When life is full of uncertainty, it is very counterproductive for the school to add to that uncertainty for students and families. Transparency about policies, practices, rules, and routines is critical to effective communication with students and their families. Parents and families cannot be supportive of students if they are not fully aware of school practices and the specific and developing needs of their children. When parents are kept informed and involved, they do not need to spend their own limited bandwidth on wondering what will happen next or what is going on with their child at school. In schools with large numbers of families whose home language is not English, employing reception desk staff who are fluent in the predominant language of families, where practical, could help both students and parents feel welcomed, valued, and understood. The community, too, needs to be able to count on the school as a place that is open to them, where positive and growth-enhancing activities happen. A school where certainty is consistently present can be a safe haven for students, their families, and the community.

School leaders can create environments of certainty by communicating openly and honestly, reaching out to engage families and communities, and supporting the development of teachers and other staff so that they can be consistently effective in teaching and supporting students.

CONCLUSION

Integral to a true sense of safety and security is the assurance of the freedom to be a fully independent being as a student and person in school. This is especially true when children and youth are at the crucial developmental stages in which their identities are taking shape. If "fitting in" comes at the cost of pieces of identity, then students have not found a place where they can be genuinely themselves, including all the aspects of who they are. Beginning in early learning settings, children thrive when they have reasonable freedom of movement, the choice about what and with whom to play, the choice to be quiet and still or vocal and active, permission and opportunity to take risks and problem-solve on their own, and the knowledge that they are fully affirmed and loved. As students enter elementary school and proceed through high school, they continue to need these same things at each developmental level. In her book *Troublemakers*, Shalaby (2017) suggests that children and youth who act up and act out at school may be the "canaries in the mine" (p. xv), indicating that some of the ways we have structured school and our expectations of children are fundamentally destructive. Landers (2018) observed, "School is a place that prioritizes the group at the cost of the individual" (p. 27). For children who live in economically secure, two-parent families in which they receive ample individual attention and affirmation of their autonomy and capabilities, this group-focused quality of school might be fine. For children and youth who live with persistent economic insecurity, family instability, racism, classism, ableism, homophobia, and pervasive negativity related to other "differentisms," school needs to be a place where they get daily assurances of the value of their personhood, that they are important "somebodies" with potential to learn and thrive.

EPILOGUE

A New Normal

It is May of 2020, and it is difficult to have a conversation about anything significant related to education without including the impacts of the COVID-19 pandemic. As I read the final draft of this book, I cannot count how many times I thought about adding a sentence along the lines of, "And let me tell you the ways that this situation has been exposed by the pandemic." The gross inequities of life in the United States have been spotlighted and publicly analyzed in a way unimaginable before this critical threat to global health. The disproportionate effects of the pandemic on poor and low-income families and on Black and Brown people, in terms of both the illness itself and the negative outcomes of the shutdown of major parts of the economy, have brought to painful light the ubiquitous inequality that has been and continues to be the reality for millions of citizens. The ever-present and widening divide between the rich and the poor has been starkly revealed in the unfolding of the pandemic. Uncertainty, which steals bandwidth from all of us, has been distributed among the population in direct proportion to their position on the scales of income, wealth, and health. People who live on the periphery of access to opportunity are now experiencing the worst of the effects of the pandemic, including job loss, employment in high-risk "essential" service sectors, food and housing insecurity, loss of resources provided by public schools, lack of access to technology for school and work, and unsafe homes and neighborhoods where they are now "sheltered." Stay-at-home orders bring certainty only to those of us who have safe homes, have reliable salaries, and live in neighborhoods where it's safe to walk. This pandemic has caused us to reexamine the concept of home as a place of shelter and safety in ways that we as a society have mostly chosen to ignore until now.

The uncertainty that has been added to the lives of people who live precariously in the best of times is stacked on top of the longstanding bandwidth depletion caused by poverty, racism, classism, xenophobia, and all the other "differentisms." I suspect it is true in any crisis—public health, economic, natural disaster—that the people who are already struggling take the brunt of the negative impact. The stresses of day-to-day living are exacerbated by yet more challenges related to job security, education of children, and safety and security.

It is far beyond the scope of this book (and my expertise) to present a thorough analysis of the relative illness and death rates from COVID-19, although the daily news brings frequent reports that Black and Brown people are dying in disproportionate numbers compared to White people. The fact that there is a great deal of variance in the ways states are counting and documenting death rates and reporting age and race and ethnicity demographics further complicates the matter (and is a subject for close scrutiny in itself). In this book, I have discussed the cost to overall health and well-being and the resultant bandwidth tax of being poor and a person of color in the United States. During the global pandemic, these factors have contributed to higher mortality rates for people whose health was compromised from the start. In addition, the closing of schools at all levels has brought to light the extent of the "digital divide," as students in poor and near-poor families lack the resources in computers and internet connection to transition from in-person to remote learning. Even if families have a computer, it might need to be shared by several people, and finding a quiet time and place for study is an additional challenge. The difference in access to effective learning is further exacerbated by the level of education and availability of parents to support their children's learning. Situations involving child abuse, substance addictions, and domestic violence are inevitably worsened in this environment of added stress and confined living. So many challenges for so many families, distributed unevenly across lines of income and race and ethnicity, will surely result in increased inequality in educational and health outcomes.

Given the realities of inequality and the disproportionate burden of societal upheaval on the most vulnerable of us, what can we learn from this pandemic and how do we use that learning to close equity gaps in pre-K-12 public education going forward? Most importantly, let us acknowledge what we can no longer deny, that the "normal" state of affairs in this country was not working well for millions of children and youth. Over the past few months, I have heard educators resist the idea of getting "back to normal." Why would we want to get back to a normal that undermines the basic education and, therefore, the life chances of millions of children? What we need is a new normal that we create from the lessons of the pandemic. I suggest the following principles:

- Recognize and act on the fact that to educate children and youth in public school, more resources (not less) are required to buttress the well-being and academic achievement of students who live in poor and near-poor families and who belong to marginalized groups.

- Eliminate the digital divide. As a country, we could decide that access to computer technology and the required internet connection are public utilities, like water, gas, and electricity, and make them available to everyone.
- Acknowledge that food insecurity negatively affects learning and implement healthy nutrition programs in all public schools for all children (as the Houston Independent School District did in Texas after Hurricane Harvey; see chapter 18, this volume).
- Ensure that all voices are part of the conversation. In some cases, as teaching moved online, children's voices were heard in the classroom where they had not been heard before. Others were even more seriously silenced. After the pandemic, we must continue to listen to all voices so we can learn from each other and give everyone's brain a chance to grow. On Zoom, teachers might have done a roll call to see that everyone was there; the same idea could be implemented in a classroom with a policy of "every voice, every day." It is also important to remember that voices can be heard in writing and art and song and story, not just in recitation and discussion.
- Find out what "funds of knowledge" were tapped by children, youth, and their parents during these trying times and leverage those to help everyone thrive at school in the new normal. Work with students and their families to systematically gather and record these funds so we all recognize their importance in skill-building. Do not simply write them off as, "We just did what needed to be done, and now that's over." Consider mutual support in neighborhoods; extended family assistance with child care and schooling; intentional relationships developed between children and their teachers as all tried to stay connected; teaching innovations that sprang from necessity that turned out to be very effective; and the many ways children, youth, and adults stepped up to support each other day-to-day.

Let us remember what it felt like to have our school communities disrupted by physical distance and never again underestimate the power of close communities of respect and mutual support to help students overcome adversity and survive and thrive in school. Let us not go back to the old normal. Let us maintain and strengthen the communities of support around student learning that have been developed, through necessity, during this pandemic. The critical groups include teachers and school leaders, of course, but also include our information technology personnel; food service staff (who packaged millions of meals for students staying at home); and especially parents, who had to balance the uncertainty in their lives with trying to support learning at home. Parents have always been essential players in their children's education. This pandemic has shone a light on what we already knew, that parents in some families have way more bandwidth, knowledge, and time for that work. What parents need today, and will always need in direct proportion to their level of resources, are respect and inclusion, not judgment and blame.

COVID-19 may return in waves even as we reopen schools, and there may be other viruses, and there will surely be other natural and human-made disasters. Schools that have developed ongoing relationships and support for families will be poised to continue during these times. Families who are struggling with all the things that steal bandwidth and compromise education for children need well-resourced public schools that can consistently fill in the gaps left by economic insecurity and all the underminers, giving all children a chance to achieve their potential in school and life.

Benefits to Typically Developing Children of Learning Alongside Children With Disabilities

The choice to be an inclusive learning setting is not one made lightly.

- A great deal of research and reflection has gone into models of learning, and inclusiveness in early childhood has consistently proven to be in everyone's best interest.
- Including children with unique/challenging needs does not mean we are putting their needs above those of typically developing children.
- Learning alongside children who are different in the fundamental ways they process and interact with the world provides a wide range of benefits to typically developing children and helps us guide them toward being ethical, capable, and mentally healthy human beings.

When your child finds a way to communicate with someone who communicates differently, your child is learning

- that communication doesn't just mean talking, and is, at its foundation, about making connections with other people;
- that innovation is an intrinsic part of interacting with others; and
- to take pride in their ability to be kind and understanding.

Note: We all value people in our lives who go the extra mile to figure out how to speak to us in ways that make us feel valued as individuals. Our children can be practicing this amazing skill from a young age.

When your child sees another child engaging in inappropriate behavior, your child is learning that

- there are many choices available;
- they know what is right and wrong for them, and can make their own choices, even if other people make different ones; and

This appendix is reprinted from Emma Mercier (personal communication, October 19, 2019). It is reprinted with permission.

- everyone makes mistakes, and we can forgive them and help them make positive choices in the future.

Note: Your child might try out some behavior they've witnessed. This is perfectly normal and even healthy. We would like children to choose positive behavior because they are developing a sense of right and wrong, not because they don't know that inappropriate choices are available.

When your child notices that the consequences and/or expectations for another child are different than they are for them, your child is learning that

- appropriate expectations are based on ability as well as effort;
- not everyone has the capabilities, privileges, experiences, and means to make the most helpful choice at any given moment;
- supporting progress is often more important than adhering to strict expectations; and
- "fair" is not everyone getting the same of everything all the time, but rather each person getting what they need to grow, learn, and thrive.

Note: We would like to support children in learning about the prosocial, empowering motivations behind positive behavior, as well as the harmful effects of negative behavior on the people around them. We would like them to choose positive behavior because they know it is right, not because they are afraid of the consequences of negative behavior. Children are astute observers and researchers, and can from an early age understand that it is inappropriate to break something or hurt someone even if they'd "get away with it." This moral compass that they are developing is refined through seeing a variety of behavior responded to in a variety of ways, within the context of supportive relationships.

When your child sees another child achieve something they could never do before, your child is learning

- to be proud of someone else;
- to celebrate individual progress, rather than comparing one person's success with their own or others';
- everyone can learn and that learning just looks different for each person; and
- to avoid limiting people with our expectations.

Note: Children are naturally inclined to be inclusive, and if they understand that the adults around them value another child's contributions to the learning environment, they are ready to do so as well.

When your child sees a child with a delay in some area demonstrating strength in a different area, your child is learning

- everyone is better at some things than other things;
- it is a good idea to give people a chance to try things (and to give things a try ourselves), because you never know what they could achieve; and
- we can all learn from each other's strengths and support each other's areas of difficulty.

Note: No one is the expert at everything, and no one has nothing to offer, so tuakana-teina (older children supporting younger children's learning) applies in different ways in each relationship. And it's good for all of us to remember that people can surprise us if we give them a chance.

When your child tries all their usual conflict resolution skills and they're just not working with a particular child, your child is learning that

- sometimes even when you do your part, life throws you a curve ball;
- it's okay to seek help when you feel confused, nervous, or overwhelmed;
- the same strategies don't work with everyone, so we need to be able to get to know individuals and work within a positive relationship; and
- if you don't feel comfortable with a particular interaction, it is always your right to move away or find support that helps you feel comfortable.

Note: A huge part of what children are learning during the first years of life is how to be a social being within a social group. We all work hard to teach them appropriate skills and want them to be positively reinforced through their interactions. It can seem that when they interact with children who react differently or unpredictably these skills might be being undermined, but in fact, they are learning very valuable lessons that will serve them well throughout their lives.

Your children will interact with many different people throughout their life, and some of them will challenge them or even try to take advantage of them. The previously described skills are very important for your child to be able to navigate the increasingly complex social situations they will face, and it is far healthier to learn them in the safe environment of an early childhood center than when they're older and the stakes are higher.

When your child gets hurt by another child, your child is learning

- how to cope with their own feelings (hurt, worry, confusion, uncertainty) and what to do (internally and externally) to return to a more positive state;
- that sometimes other people do inappropriate things, and we can't control that, but we can control how we react;
- how to be resilient in the face of difficulty;
- that when things go wrong, it can be really hard for a little while, but it will get better again; and
- that there are always people around you (teachers or other children) who will help you, whether that is tending a *mamae* (injury), giving a hug, or just being together until you feel better.

Note: Research indicates that avoiding small injuries (both physical and emotional) in early childhood hinders the development of resilience and decreases children's faith in themselves. We cannot create a world in which children will not grow up to face challenges of all kinds, but we can help them to develop resilience, confidence, and problem-solving skills in the hope that when the big challenges come, they will be ready to overcome them. The best way to do this is to be there to help them process and learn from upsetting things throughout their childhoods, not to shelter them from them. Each small injury, problem, confusion, and disagreement provides another opportunity to learn that things going wrong is a part of life, and the happiest people are those who know how to deal with them and move on.

When your child chooses to be kind or helpful to a child who has hurt them in the past, your child is learning

- empathy;
- forgiveness;
- that everyone is entitled to respect, no matter what;
- how good it feels to be generous and kind; and
- that they can make a positive difference in someone else's life.

Note: We would like to raise children to be people who will help make our world a better place for us all, and what better way than show them that they can start right now?

REFERENCES

Alsubaie, M. A. (2015). Hidden curriculum as one of current issue of curriculum. *Journal of Education and Practice, 6*(33), 125–128.

Ambady, N., Shih, M., Kim, A., & Pittinsky, T. L. (2001). Stereotype susceptibility in children: Effects of identity activation on quantitative performance. *Psychological Science, 12*(5), 385–390. https://doi.org/10.1111/1467-9280.00371

Aronson, J., Fried, C. B., & Good, C. (2001). Reducing the effects of stereotype threat on African American college students by shaping theories of intelligence. *Journal of Experimental Social Psychology, 38*(2), 113–125. https://doi.org/10.1006/jesp.2001.1491

Aronson, J., Lustina, M. J., Good, C., Keough, K., Steele, C. M., & Brown, J. (1998). When White men can't do math: Necessary and sufficient factors in stereotype threat. *Journal of Experimental Social Psychology, 35*(1), 29–46. https://doi.org/10.1006/jesp.1998.1371

Association for Psychological Science. (2007, September 24). Racism's cognitive toll: Subtle discrimination is more taxing on the brain. *Science Daily.* https://www.sciencedaily.com/releases/2007/09/070919093316.htm

Babcock, E. (2018, March). *Using brain science to transform human services and increase person mobility from poverty.* US Partnership on Mobility from Poverty. https://www.mobilitypartnership.org/using-brain-science-transform-human-services-and-increase-personal-mobility-poverty

Baddeley, A., & Hitch, G. (1974). Working memory. In G. Bower (Ed.), *The psychology of learning and motivation* (pp. 47–89). Academic Press.

Badger, E., Miller, C. C., Pearce, A., & Quealy, K. (2018, March 19). Extensive data show punishing reach of racism for Black boys. *New York Times.* https://www.nytimes.com/interactive/2018/03/19/upshot/race-class-white-and-black-men.html

Baines, J., Tisdale, C., & Long, S. (2018). *"We've been doing it your way long enough": Choosing the culturally relevant classroom.* Teachers College Press.

Baker, D. B., Farrie, D., & Sciarra, D. (2018, February). *Is school funding fair? A national report card* (7th ed.). Rutgers Graduate School of Education–Education Law Center.

Baldwin, D. A., & Moses, L. J. (1996). The ontogeny of social information gathering. *Child Development, 67*(5), 1915–1939. https://doi.org/10.1111/j.1467-8624.1996.tb01835.x

Balfanz, R. (2014, June 7). Stop holding us back. *New York Times.* https://opinionator.blogs.nytimes.com/2014/06/07/stop-holding-us-back/

Barr, D. A. (2014). *Health disparities in the United States: Social class, race, ethnicity, and health* (2nd ed.). Johns Hopkins University Press.

Barratt, W. (2011). *Social class on campus: Theories and manifestations.* Stylus.

Becerra-Culqui, T. A., Liu, Y., Nash, R., Cromwell, L., Flanders, W. D., Getahun, D., Giammattei, S. V., Hunkeler, E. M., Lash, T. L., Millman, A., Quinn, V. P., Robinson, B., Roblin, D., Sandberg, D. E., Silverberg, M. J., Tangpricha, V., & Goodman, M. (2018). Mental health of transgender and gender nonconforming youth compared with their peers. *Pediatrics, 141*(5). https://doi.org/10.1542/peds.2017-3845

Bell, R. (2017, September/October). How poverty kills wonder and what we can do about it. *The Humanist,* 16–19.

Bem, S. L. (1989). Genital knowledge and gender constancy in preschool children. *Child Development, 60*(3), 649–662. http://doi.org/10.2307/1130730

Bintliff, A. (2014, July 22). *Talking circles: For restorative justice and beyond.* Teaching Tolerance. https://www.tolerance.org/magazine/talking-circles-for-restorative-justice-and-beyond

Bishop, R. S. (1990). Mirrors, windows, and sliding glass doors. *Perspective, 6*(3), ix–xi.

Bitsko R. H., Holbrook J. R., Robinson L. R., Kaminski, J. W., Ghandour, R., Smith, C., & Peacock, G. (2016). Health care, family, and community factors associated with mental, behavioral, and developmental disorders in early childhood—United States, 2011–2012. *Morbidity and Mortality Weekly Report, 65*(9), 221–226. http://dx.doi.org/10.15585/mmwr.mm6509a1

Boustan, L. P. (2013). *Racial residential segregation in American cities* (Working Paper Series No. 19045).National Bureau of Economic Research (NBER).

Boyce, W. T. (2012, Spring/Summer). A biology of misfortune. *Focus, 29*(1), 1–6. https://www.irp.wisc.edu/publications/focus/pdfs/foc291a.pdf

Brammer, J. P. (2018, January 3). *None of America's 100 largest churches are LGBTQ-affirming, new report says.* NBC News. https://www.nbcnews.com/feature/nbc-out/none-america-s-100-largest-churches-are-lgbtq-affirming-new-n834266

Bridges, B. K., Awokoya, J. T., & Messano, F. (2012). *Done to us, not with us: African American parent perceptions of K–12 education.* Frederick D. Patterson Research Institute, UNCF.

Brock, L. L., Curby, T. W., & Cannell-Cordier, A. L. (2018, June 10). Consistency in children's classroom experiences and implication for early childhood development. In A. Mashburn, J. LoCasale-Crouch, & K. Pears (Eds.), *Kindergarten transition and readiness* (pp. 59–83). Springer.

Brown v. Board of Education, 347 U.S. 483 (1954).

Bureau of Labor Statistics. (2019, August 16). *Employment and unemployment among youth summary.* https://www.bls.gov/news.release/youth.nr0.htm

California Newsreel. (2008a). Income and wealth [Suppl.] *Unnatural causes . . . is inequality making us sick?* [Documentary series]. https://unnaturalcauses.org/resources.php?topic_id=7

California Newsreel. (2008b). 10 things to know about health. [Suppl.] *Unnatural causes . . . is inequality making us sick?* [Documentary series]. https://unnatural causes.org/ten_things.php

Carroll, G. (1998). Mundane extreme environmental stress and African American families: A case for recognizing different realities. *Journal of Comparative Family Studies, 2*(2), 271–284. https://www.jstor.org/stable/41603564

Carter, E. R., Peery, D., Richeson, J. A., & Murphy, M. C. (2015). Does cognitive depletion shape bias detection for minority group members? *Social Cognition, 33*(3), 241–254. https://doi.org/10.1521/soco.2015.33.3.241

Carter, K., Sugimoto, A., Stoehr, K., & Carter, G. (2018). Under the school roof, inside the classroom walls: The power of place-based plot patterns to shape school stories of happiness and glee or humiliation and shame for elementary students. In S. P. Jones & E. C. Sheffield (Eds.), *Why kids love (and hate) school: Reflections on difference* (pp. 93–112). Myers University Press.

Causton-Theoharis, J., & Theoharis, G. (2008). Creating inclusive schools for all students. *The School Administrator, 65*(8), 24–28, 30–31.

Cauthen, N. K., & Fass, S. (2008). *Measuring poverty in the United States*. National Center for Children in Poverty, Columbia University, Mailman School of Public Health. http://www.nccp.org/publications/pub_825.html

Centre for Excellence in Universal Design & National Disability Authority. (n.d.). *The 7 principles*. http://universaldesign.ie/What-is-Universal-Design/The-7-Principles/

Center on the Developing Child. (n.d.). The impact of early adversity on children's development. *InBrief*. https://developingchild.harvard.edu/resources/inbrief-the-impact-of-early-adversity-on-childrens-development/

Centers for Disease Control and Prevention. (2017, June 21). *LGBT youth*. https://www.cdc.gov/lgbthealth/youth.htm

Chaiken, S., & Trope, Y. (1999). *Dual-process theories in social psychology*. Guilford Press.

Challis, R. (2004). Maternal corticotropin-releasing hormones, fetal growth, and preterm birth. *American Journal of Obstetrics and Gynecology, 191*(4), 1059–1060. https://doi.org/10.1016/j.ajog.2004.06.071

Chamberlain, L. B. (2018). *The amazing adolescent brain: What every educator, youth serving professional, and healthcare provider needs to know*. Multiplying Connections. http://www.multiplyingconnections.org/become-trauma-informed/amazing-adolescent-brain

Cherry, K. (2020, April 28). *The zone of proximal development as defined by Vygotsky*. Verywell Mind. https://www.verywellmind.com/what-is-the-zone-of-proximal-development-2796034

Chicago Public Schools. (n.d.). *Restorative practices guide and toolkit*. https://blog.cps.edu/wp-content/uploads/2017/08/CPS_RP_Booklet.pdf

Child Trends. (n.d.). *Low and very low birthweight infants*. https://www.childtrends.org/indicators/low-and-very-low-birthweight-infants

Chrishti, M., & Hipsman, F. (2015, May 21). *In historic shift, new migration flows from Mexico fall below those from China and India.* Migration Policy Institute. https://www.migrationpolicy.org/article/historic-shift-new-migration-flows-mexico-fall-below-those-china-and-india

Christian, L. M., Glaser, R., Porter, K., & Iams, J. D. (2013). Stress-induced inflammatory responses in women: Effects of race and pregnancy. *Psychosomatic Medicine, 75*(7), 658–669. http://doi.org/10.1097/PSY.0b013e31829bbc89

Cohen, G. L., Garcia, J., Apful, N., & Master, A. (2006). Reducing the racial achievement gap: A social-psychological intervention. *Science, 313*(5791), 1307–1310. http://doi.org/10.1126/science.1128317

Cohen, G. L., Garcia, J., Purdie-Vaughns, V., Apfel, N., & Brzustoski, P. (2009). Recursive processes in self-affirmation: Intervening to close minority achievement gap. *Science, 324*(5925), 400–403. http://doi.org/10.1126/science.1170769

Cohn-Vargas, B. (2015, April 20). Identity safe classrooms and schools: As an antidote to implicit bias and stereotype threat, educators can build identity-safe classrooms and schools. *Teaching Tolerance.* https://www.tolerance.org/magazine/identity-safe-classrooms-and-schools

Cole, S. F., O'Brien, J. G., Gadd, M. G., Ristuccia, J., Wallace, D. L., & Gregory, M. (2005). *Helping traumatized children learn: Supportive school environments for children traumatized by family violence.* Massachusetts Advocates for Children: Trauma and Learning Policy Initiative (in collaboration with Harvard Law School and The Task Force on Children Affected by Domestic Violence).

Coleman-Jensen, A., Rabbitt, M. P., Gregory, C. A., & Singh, A. (2017, September). *Household food security in the United States in 2016.* (Economic Research Report No. ERR-237). United States Department of Agriculture. https://www.ers.usda.gov/webdocs/publications/84973/err-237.pdf?v=0

Common Ground Health. (2019, May 29). *Kids walk for the right to play in safe neighborhoods.* https://www.commongroundhealth.org/kids-walk-for-the-right-to-play-in-a-safe-neighborhood-2

Cook, C. R., Williams, K. R., Guerra, N. G., Kim, T. E., & Sadek, S. (2010). Predictors of bullying and victimization in childhood and adolescence: A meta-analytic investigation. *School Psychology Quarterly, 25*(2), 65–83. https://doi.org/10.1037/a0020149

Costello, B., Wachtel, J., & Wachtel, T. (2009). *The restorative practices handbook for teachers, disciplinarians, and administrators.* International Institute for Restorative Practices.

Creswell, J. D., Welch, W. T., Taylor, S, Sherman, D. K., Gruenewald, T. L., & Mann, T. (2005). Affirmation of personal values buffers neuroendocrine and psychological stress. *Psychological Science, 16*(11), 846–851. http://doi.org/10.1111/j.1467-9280.2005.01624.x

Curby, T. W., Brock, L. L., & Hamre, B. K. (2013, March). Teachers' emotional support consistency predicts children's achievement gains and social skills. *Early Education and Development, 24*(3), 292–309. https://doi.org/10.1080/10409289.2012.665760

Cutts, D. B., Meyers, A. F., Black, M. M., Casey, P. H., Chilton, M., Cook, J. T. Geppert, J., Ettinger de Cuba, S., Heeren, T., Coleman, S., Rose-Jacobs, R., & Frank, D. A. (2011). US housing insecurity and the health of very young children. *American Journal of Public Health, 101*(8), 1508–1514. http://doi.org/10.2105/AJPH.2011.300139

Daley, A., Phipps, S., & Branscombe, N. R. (2018). The social complexities of disability: Discrimination, belonging and life satisfaction among Canadian youth. *Population Health, 5,* 55–63. https://doi.org/10.1016/j.ssmph.2018.05.003

DeAngelis, T. (2009, February). Unmasking "racial microaggressions." *American Psychological Association Monitor on Psychology, 40*(2). http://www.apa.org/monitor/2009/02/microaggression.aspx

Delva, J., Horner, P., Martinez, R., Sanders, L., Lopez, W. D., & Doering-White, J. (2013). Mental health problems of children of undocumented parents in the United States: A hidden crisis. *Journal of Community Positive Practices, 13*(3), 25–35.

Desilver, D. (2018, August 7). For most U.S. workers, real wages have barely budged in decades. *Fact Tank.* www.pewresearch.org/fact-tank/2018/08/07/for-most-us-workers-real-wages-have-barely-budged-for-decades/

de Weerth, C., & Buitelaar, J. K. (2005). Cortisol awakening response in pregnant women. *Psychoneuroendocrinology, 30*(9), 902–907. https://doi.org/10.1016/j.psyneuen.2005.05.003

Doebrich, N. (n.d.). The art of play and movement. Society of the Protection and Care of Children. https://www.spcc-roch.org/the-art-of-play-and-movement/

Doyle, T., & Zakrajsek, T. (2019). *The new science of learning: How to learn in harmony with your brain* (2nd ed.). Stylus.

Drewnowski, A., Rehm, C. D., & Constant, F. (2013, June 19). Water and beverage consumption among children age 4–13y in the United States: Analyses of 2005–2010 NHANES data. *Nutrition Journal, 12,* 85. https://doi.org/10.1186/1475-2891-12-85

Du Bois, W. E. B. (1903). *The souls of black folk.* A. C. McClurg & Co.

Duncan, G. (2000). Urban pedagogies and the celling of adolescents of color. *Social Justice, 27*(3), 29–42.

Dweck, C. S. (2006). *Mindset: The new psychology of success.* Penguin Random House.

Dweck, C. S. (2015, September 22). Carol Dweck revisits the "growth mindset." *Education Week.* https://www.edweek.org/ew/articles/2015/09/23/carol-dweck-revisits-the-growth-mindset.html

Economic Mobility Pathways. (2019, December 10). *Harvard research: Impact of poverty begins in the womb, but it doesn't have to.* https://www.empathways.org/news/article/harvard-research-impact-of-poverty-begins-in-the-womb-but-it-doesnt-have-to

Edbuild. (n. d.). *Nonwhite school districts get $23 billion less than white districts despite serving the same number of students.* https://edbuild.org/content/23-billion

Educa. (n.d.). *Te Whāriki, early childhood education curriculum—New Zealand.* https://www.geteduca.com/frameworks/te-whariki-ece-curriculum-new-zealand/

Edwards, H. S. (2018, March 8). "No one is safe." How Trump's immigration policy is splitting families apart. *Time, 191*(11), 34–40.

Elliott, I. (2016, August). *Poverty and mental health: A review to inform the Joseph Rowntree Foundation's anti-poverty strategy.* Mental Health Foundation. https://time.com/longform/donald-trump-immigration-policy-splitting-families/

Ennis, D. (2017, June 30). Department of justice: Title IX protects trans students from discrimination. *Advocate.* https://www.advocate.com/politics/transgender/2015/06/30/department-justice-affirms-title-ix-protection-trans-studdents

Esteban-Guitart, M., & Moll, L. C. (2014). Lived experience, funds of identity and education. *Culture and Psychology, 20*(1), 70–81. https://doi.org/10.1177/1354067X13515940

Farnham, L., Fernando, G., Perigo, M., & Brosman, C. (2015, February 17). Rethinking how students succeed. *Stanford Social Innovation Review.* https://ssir.org/up_for_debate/article/rethinking_how_students_succeed#

Felitti, V. J., Andra, R. F., Nordenberg, D., Williamson, D. F., Spitz, A. M., Edwards, V., Koss, M. P., & Marks, J. S. (1998, May). Relationship of childhood abuse and household dysfunction to many of the leading causes of death in adults: The Adverse Childhood Experiences (ACE) Study. *American Journal of Preventive Medicine, 14*(4), 245–258. https://doi.org/10.1016/S0749-3797(98)00017-81

Foley, K. R., Blackmore, A. M., Girdler, S., O'Donnell, M., Glauert, R., Llewellyn, G., & Leonard, H. (2012). *To feel belonged:* The voices of children and youth with disabilities on the meaning of wellbeing. *Child Indicators Research, 5*, 375–391. https://doi.org/10.1007/s12187-011-9134-2

Geronimus, A. T., Hicken, M., Keene, D., & Bound, J. (2006). "Weathering" and age patterns of allostatic load scores among Blacks and Whites in the United States. *American Journal of Public Health, 96*(5), 826–833.

Gilliam, W. S., Maupin, A. N., Reyes, C. R., Accavitti, M., & Shic, F. (2016, September 28). *Do early educators' implicit biases regarding sex and race relate to behavior expectations and recommendations of preschool expulsions and suspensions?* Yale Child Study Center.

Ginsburg, K. R., Committee on Communications, & Committee on Psychological Aspects of Child and Family Health. (2007, January). The importance of play in promoting healthy child development and maintaining strong parent-child bonds. *Pediatrics, 119*(1), 182–191. https://doi.org/10.1542/peds.2006-2697

Glisczinski, D. (2011). Lighting up the mind: Transforming learning through the applied scholarship of cognitive neuroscience. *International Journal for the Scholarship of Teaching and Learning, 5*(1), 1–13. https://doi.org/10.20429/ijsotl.2011.050124

GLSEN (Gay, Lesbian, & Straight Education Network). (n.d.). *The 2017 school climate survey executive summary.* https://www.glsen.org/sites/default/files/2019-12/NSCS_Executive_Summary_English_2017.pdf

Goffman, E. (1959). *The presentation of the self in everyday life*. Doubleday.

González, N., Moll, L. C., & Amanti, C. (Eds.). (2005). *Funds of knowledge: Theorizing practices in households, communities, and classrooms*. Routledge.

Goodman, K. S. (1990). *A declaration of professional conscience for teachers*. https://www.rcowen.com/PDFs/A%20Declaration-KenRev-611x17.pdf

Grant, J. M., Mottet, L. A., Tanis, J., Harrison, J., Herman, J. L., & Keisling, M. (2011). *Injustice at every turn: A report of the National Transgender Discrimination Survey*. National Center for Transgender Equality and National Gay and Lesbian Task Force. https://www.thetaskforce.org/wp-content/uploads/2019/07/ntds_full.pdf

Greenfield, B. (2019, December 10). *Harvard research: Impact of poverty begins in the womb, but it doesn't have to*. Yahoo News. https://news.yahoo.com/how-breakthrough-science-can-change-the-lives-of-poor-families-starting-in-the-womb-100020836.html

Gross, E., Efetevbia, V., & Wilkins, A. (2019, April 18). *Racism and sexism against Black women may contribute to high rates of Black infant mortality*. Child Trends. https://www.childtrends.org/racism-sexism-against-black-women-may-contribute-high-rates-black-infant-mortality

Hanscom, A. J. (2016). *Balanced and barefoot: How unrestricted outdoor play makes for strong, confident, and capable children*. New Harbinger Publications.

Harris, P. L. (2012). *Trusting what you're told: How children learn from others*. The Belknap Press of Harvard University Press.

Harvard University Center on the Developing Child. (n.d.). *Executive function & self-regulation*. https://developingchild.harvard.edu/science/key-concepts/executive-function/

Hatfield, B. E., & Williford, A. P. (2017). Cortisol patterns for young children displaying disruptive behavior: Links to a teacher–child relationship-focused intervention. *Prevention Science, 18*(1), 40–49. https://doi.org/10.1007/s11121-016-0693-9

Healthi Kids. (n.d.). *The power of play*. https://www.healthikids.org/our-priorities/the-power-of-play

Healthy People 2020. (n.d.). *Increasing graduation rates in our nation's public high schools*. Office of Disease Prevention and Health Promotion. https://www.healthypeople.gov/2020/healthy-people-in-action/story/increasing-graduation-rates-in-our-nations-public-high-schools

Heard-Garris, N. J., Cale, M., Camaj, L., Hamati, M. C., & Dominguez, T. P. (2018). Transmitting trauma: A systematic review of vicarious racism and child health. *Social Science & Medicine, 199*, 230–240. https://doi.org/10.1016/j.socscimed.2017.04.018

Hecht, C. (2018, February 18). *Safe water in schools: What do we know? What can we do?* Green Schools National Network. https://greenschoolsnationalnetwork.org/safe-water-in-schools-what-do-we-know-what-can-we-do/

Hill, M. L. (2016). *Nobody: Casualties of America's war on the vulnerable, from Ferguson to Flint and beyond*. Atria.

Hinchey, P. H., & Konkol, P. J. (2018). *Getting to where we meant to be: Working toward the educational world we imagine/d*. Myers Education Press.

HISD News Blog. (2019–2020). *HISD students to eat all meals at no charge this school year*. https://blogs.houstonisd.org/news/2019/08/08/hisd-students-to-eat-all-meals-at-no-charge-this-school-year/

Hulleman, C. S., & Harackiewicz, J. M. (2009). Promoting interest and performance in high school science classes. *Science, 326*(5958), 1410–1412. http://doi.org/10.1126/science.1177067

Human Rights Campaign. (n.d.a). *Defining LGBTQ words for elementary school students*. https://assets2.hrc.org/welcoming-schools/documents/WS_LGBTQ_Definitions_for_Students.pdf

Human Rights Campaign. (n.d.b). *Growing up LGBT in America: HRC youth survey report key findings*. https://assets2.hrc.org/files/assets/resources/Growing-Up-LGBT-in-America_Report.pdf

Human Rights Watch. (2016, December 7). *"Like walking through a hailstorm": Discrimination against LGBT youth in US schools*. https://www.hrw.org/report/2016/12/07/walking-through-hailstorm/discrimination-against-lgbt-youth-us-schools

Inequality.org. (n.d.). *Wealth inequality in the United States: The United States exhibits wider disparities of wealth between rich and poor than any other major developed nation*. https://inequality.org/facts/wealth-inequality/

Jacobs, D. E. (2011). Environmental health disparities in housing. *American Journal of Public Health*, Suppl. 1, *101*(S1), S115–S122.

Jagannathan, M. (2019, October 23). 1 in 5 LGBTQ Americans lives in poverty—and some groups are particularly worse off. *MarketWatch*. https://www.marketwatch.com/story/1-in-5-lgbtq-americans-lives-in-poverty-and-some-groups-are-particularly-worse-off-2019-10-22

Jaime, E. (2015, March 27). *The personal is political . . . and educative*. To Breathe Is Political. https://tobreatheispolitical.wordpress.com/2015/03/27/the-personal-is-political-and-educative/

Jensen, E. (2009). *Teaching with poverty in mind: What being poor does to kids' brains and what schools can do about it*. ASCD.

Katz, C. (2012, November 1). People in poor, non-White, neighborhoods breathe more hazardous particles. *Scientific American*. https://www.scientificamerican.com/article/people-poor-neighborhoods-breate-more-hazardous-particles/

Kendi, I. X. (2016). *Stamped from the beginning: The definitive history of racist ideas in America*. Nation Books.

Kenney, E. L., Long, M. W., Cradock, A. L., & Gortmaker, S. L. (2015, August). Prevalence of inadequate hydration among US children and disparities by gender and race/ethnicity: National health and nutrition examination survey, 2009–2012. *American Journal of Public Health, 105*(8), 113–118. http://doi.org/10.2105/AJPH.2015.302572

Kids Count Data Center. (n.d.). *Infant mortality by race in the United States*. The Annie E. Casey Foundation. https://datacenter.kidscount.org/data/tables/21-infant-mortality-by-race

Kids Matter. (n.d.). *Belonging at schools makes a difference.* Australian Government Department of Health, beyondblue, & Early Childhood Australia. http://east maddingtonps.wa.edu.au/wp-content/uploads/2018/05/Belonging-at-School-Makes-a-Difference.pdf

Kimbrough, R., & Mellen, K. (2012). *Perceptions of inclusion of students with disabilities in the middle school. Research summary.* https://www.amle.org/BrowsebyTopic/WhatsNew/WNDet/TabId/270/ArtMID/888/ArticleID/308/Perceptions-of-Inclusion-of-Students-with-Disabilities-in-the-Middle-School.aspx

Klein Dytham Architecture. (2003). *PechaKucha.* http://www.klein-dytham.com/pechakucha

Koball, H., & Jiang, Y. (2018). *Basic facts about low-income children: Children under 18 years, 2016.* National Center for Children in Poverty. Columbia University Mailman School of Public Health, Health Policy & Management. http://www.nccp.org/publications/pub_1194.html

Kochhar, R., & Cilluffo, A. (2017, November 1). *How wealth inequality has changed in the U.S. since the Great Recession, by race, ethnicity and income.* Pew Research Center. https://www.pewresearch.org/fact-tank/2017/11/01/how-wealth-inequality-has-changed-in-the-u-s-since-the-great-recession-by-race-ethnicity-and-income/

Koenig, A. M., & Eagly, A. H. (2005). Stereotype threat in men on a test of social sensitivity. *Sex Roles, 52*(7), 489–496. https://doi.org/10.1007/s11199-005-3714-x

Kornbluth, J. (Director).(2013). *Inequality for all.* [Film]. 72 Productions.

Kosciw, J. G., Greytak, E. A., Giga, N. M., Villenas, C., & Danischewski, D. J. (2015). *The 2015 national school climate survey: The experiences of lesbian, gay, bisexual, transgender, and queer youth in our nation's schools.* GLSEN. www.glsen.org

Kosciw, J. G., Palmer, N. A., Kull, R. M., & Greytak, E. A. (2013, October 30). The effect of negative school climate on academic outcomes for LGBT youth and the role of in-school supports. *Journal of School Violence, 12*(1), 45–63. https://doi.org/10.1080/15388220.2012.732546

Kucsera, J. (2014, March 26). *New York State's extreme school segregation: Inequality, inaction and a damaged future.* The Civil Rights Project, University of California. https://www.civilrightsproject.ucla.edu/research/k-12-education/integration-and-diversity/ny-norflet-report-placeholder

Kuzawa, C. W., & Sweet, E. (2009). Epigenetics and the embodiment of race: Developmental origins of U.S. racial disparities in cardiovascular health. *American Journal of Human Biology, 21*(1), 2–15. https://doi.org/10.1002/ajhb.20822

Lambert, C. (2012, March–April). Twilight of the lecture. *Harvard Magazine.* https://harvardmagazine.com/2012/03/twilight-of-the-lecture

Landers, J. (2018). The troublemakers. *Harvard Ed. Magazine,* Winter, 20–27. https://www.gse.harvard.edu/news/ed/18/01/troublemakers

Leung, M. (1999). *The origins of restorative justice.* https://www.cfcj-fcjc.org/sites/default/files/docs/hosted/17445-restorative_justice.pdf

Levinson, M. (2012). *No citizen left behind.* Harvard University Press.

Lewis, E., & Cantor, N. (2016). *Our compelling interests: The value of diversity for democracy and a prosperous society.* Princeton University Press.

LoCasale-Crouch, J., Jamil, F., Pianta, R. C., Rudasill, K. M., & DeCoster, J. (2018, July–September). *Observed quality and consistency of fifth graders' teacher-student interactions: Associations with feelings, engagement, and performance in school* (Research Paper, pp. 1–11). SAGE. https://doi.org/10.1177/2158244018794774

Love, B. L. (2019). *We want to do more than survive: Abolitionist teaching and the pursuit of educational freedom.* Beacon Press.

Loveless, T. (2017, March 22). *2017 Brown Center report on American education: Race and school suspensions.* Brown Center on Educational Policy. https://www.brookings.edu/research/2017-brown-center-report-part-iii-race-and-school-suspensions/

Lutz, W., & Endale, K. (2018, April 14). Education and health: Redrawing the Preston curve. *Population and Development Review.* https://onlinelibrary.wiley.com/doi/full/10.1111/padr.12141

Martin, C. L., & Ruble, D. N. (2010). Patterns of gender development. *Annual Review of Psychology, 61,* 353–381. https://doi.org/10.1146/annurev.psych.093008.100511

Masci, D. (2014, September 25). *National congregations study finds more church acceptance of gays and lesbians.* Pew Research Center. http://www.pewresearch.org/fact-tank/2014/09/25/new-study-finds-a-greater-church-acceptance-of-gays-and-lesbians-2/

Mashburn, A. J., Pianta, R. C., Hamre, B. K., Downer, J. T., Barbarin, O. A., Bryant, D., Burchinal, M., Early, D. M, Howes, C. (2008). Measures of classroom quality in prekindergarten and children's development of academic, language, and social skills. *Child Development, 79*(3), 732–749. http://doi.org/10.1111/j.1467-8624.2008.01154.x

Maslow, A. H. (1943). A theory of human motivation. *Psychological Review, 50*(4), 370–396. https://doi.org/10.1037/h0054346

Masterpiece Cakeshop, LTD. v. Colorado Civil Rights Commission, 584 US (2018). https://www.supremecourt.gov/opinions/17pdf/16-111_j4el.pdf

Mathewson, T. G. (2017, April 19). How poverty changes the brain: The early results out of a Boston nonprofit are positive. *The Atlantic.* https://www.theatlantic.com/education/archive/2017/04/can-brain-science-pull-families-out-of-poverty/523479/

McFarland, J., Hussar, B., Zhang, J., Wang, X., Wang, K., Hein, S., Diliberti, M., Cataldi, E. F., Mann, F. B., & Barmer, A. (2019, May). *The condition of education 2019.* U.S. Department of Education National Center for Education Statistics.

McGuire, T. G., & Miranda, J. (2008, March/April). New evidence regarding racial and ethnic disparities in mental health: Policy implications. *Health Affairs, 27*(2), 393–403.

Medini, S. (2017, December 6). *Our children & microaggressions-5 ways we can help* [Blog]. Huffington Post. https://www.huffingtonpost.com/shari-medini/our-children-microaggress_b_9433452.html

Menjívar, C., & Cervantes, A. G. (2016, November). The effects of parental undocumented status on families and children. *American Psychological Association, Children, Youth and Families (CYF) News.* http://www.apa.org/pi/families/resources/newsletter/2016/11/undocumented-status.aspx

Migration Policy Institute. (n.d.). *Children in U.S. immigrant families, by age group and state, 1990–2016.* https://www.migrationpolicy.org/programs/data-hub/charts/children-immigrant-families

Milner, H. R. IV. (2015). *Rac(e)ing to class: Confronting poverty and race in schools and classrooms.* Harvard Education Press.

Miss Kendra. (n.d.). *Miss Kendra's List and "Child Safety" classroom activities.* https://misskendraprograms.org/miss-kendras-list-and-child-safety-classroom-activities/

Moll, L. C., Amanti, C., Neff, D., & González, N. (1992, Spring). Funds of knowledge for teaching: Using a qualitative approach to connect homes and classrooms. *Theory Into Practice, 31*(2), 132–141. https://doi.org/10.1080/00405849209543534

Moll, L. C., & Greenberg, J. B. (1990). Creating zones of possibilities: Combining social contexts for instruction. In L. C. Moll (Ed.), *Vygotsky and education* (pp. 319–348). Cambridge University Press. https://doi.org/10.1017/CBO9781139173674.016

Moll, L. C., Vélez-Ibáñez, C., Greenberg, J., Whitmore, K., Saavedra, E., Dworin, J., & Andrade, R. (1990). *Community knowledge and classroom practice: Combining resources for literacy instruction.* (OBEMLA Contract No. 300-87-0131). University of Arizona, College of Education and Bureau of Applied Research in Anthropology.

Moore, T.-L. M. B., & Shaughnessy, M. F. (2012). Carol Dweck's views on achievement and intelligence: Implications for education. *Research Journal in Organizational Psychology & Educational Studies, 1*(3), 174–184.

Morris, M. W. (2016). *Pushout: The criminalization of black girls in schools.* The New Press.

Mullainathan, S., & Shafir, E. (2013). *Scarcity: The new science of having less and how it defines our lives.* Picador/Henry Holt.

Murphy, J. (2018, June 8). Why are Rochester schools America's worst? Study Kodak Park School 41. *Democrat and Chronicle.* https://www.democratandchronicle.com/story/local/communities/time-to-educate/stories/2018/06/06/worst-public-schools-america-rochester-ny-rcsd-kodak-park-school-41/550929002/

Musu-Gillette, L., de Brey, C., McFarland, J., Hussar, W., Sonnenberg, W., & Wilkinson-Flicker, S. (2017, July). *Status and trends in the education of racial and ethnic groups 2017.* U.S. Department of Education National Center for Education Statistics. https://nces.ed.gov/pubs2017/2017051.pdf

National Alliance on Mental Illness. (n.d.). *The issue: Mental health in schools.* https://www.nami.org/Learn-More/Mental-Health-Public-Policy/Mental-Health-in-Schools

National Alliance to End Homelessness. (2018, June 4). *Racial inequalities in homelessness, by the numbers.* https://endhomelessness.org/resource/racial-inequalities-homelessness-numbers/

National Center for Children in Poverty. (2018). *About NCCP.* Columbia University Mailman School of Public Health, Health Policy & Management. http://www.nccp.org/about.html

National Center for Education Statistics. (2017). Table 211.50. Estimated average annual salary of teachers in public elementary and secondary schools: Selected years, 1959–60 through 2016–17. *Digest of Education Statistics: 2017.* https://nces.ed.gov/programs/digest/d17/tables/dt17_211.50.asp?referrer=report

National Center for Education Statistics. (2019a, May). *Concentration of public school students eligible for free and reduced-price lunch.* Institute of Education Sciences. https://nces.ed.gov/programs/coe/pdf/coe_clb.pdf

National Center for Education Statistics (2019b). *Indicator 7: Racial/ethnic concentration in public schools.* Status and Trends in Education of Racial and Ethnic Groups. https://nces.ed.gov/programs/raceindicators/indicator_RBE.asp

National Center on Parent, Family and Community Engagement. (n.d.). *Guide to developing relationships with families* (Building Partnerships Series for Early Childhood Professionals). https://eclkc.ohs.acf.hhs.gov/sites/default/files/pdf/building-partnerships-developing-relationships-families.pdf

National Criminal Justice Reference Service. (n.d.). *Special feature: Children exposed to violence.* https://www.ncjrs.gov/childrenexposedtoviolence/index.html

National Education Association. (2015, January). *ESEA reauthorization: Excessive high-stakes testing has negative effects on students, teachers.*

Nelms, S. (n.d.). *Superintendent's perspective.* University of Rochester Center for Urban Education Success. https://www.rochester.edu/warner/cues/home/east-epo/superintendents-perspective/

Nelson, S. (2018 May 29). *The story of access.* https://stories.starbucks.com/stories/2019/the-story-of-access/

New Brunswick Association for Community Living. (n.d.). *Inclusive education and its benefits.* https://nbacl.nb.ca/module-pages/inclusive-education-and-its-benefits/

New Zealand Ministry of Social Development's Office of Disability Issues. (2001). *NZ disability strategy – summary.* https://www.odi.govt.nz/nz-disability-strategy/about-the-strategy/new-zealand-disability-strategy-2001/2001-strategy-read-online/summary/

No Time for Flash Cards. (2018, February 11). *How to use funds of knowledge in your classroom and create better connections* [Blog]. https://www.notimeforflashcards.com/2018/02/funds-of-knowledge.html

Nunez, R. d. (2012, March 5). *Homelessness: It's about race, not just poverty.* City Limits. https://citylimits.org/2012/03/05/homelessness-its-about-race-not-just-poverty/

NZ History. (n.d.). *The treaty in brief.* https://nzhistory.govt.nz/politics/treaty/the-treaty-in-brief

Okonofua, J. A., Paunesku, D., & Walton, G. M. (2016, April 25). Brief intervention to encourage empathic discipline cuts suspension rates in half among adolescents. *Proceedings of the National Academy of Sciences of the United States of America.* https://doi.org/10.1073/pnas.1523698113

Orfield, G., Kucsera, J., & Siegel-Hawley, G. (2012, September 19). *E pluribus . . . separation: Deepening double segregation for more students.* The Civil Rights Project, University of California. https://civilrightsproject.ucla.edu/research/k-12-education/integration-and-diversity/mlk-national/e-pluribus...separation-deepening-double-segregation-for-more-students/

Orr, A., & Baum, J. (n.d.). *Schools in transition: A guide for supporting transgender students in K–12 schools.* American Civil Liberties Union, Gender Spectrum, Human Rights Campaign Foundation, National Center for Lesbian Rights, National Education Association. https://www.genderspectrum.org/staging/wp-content/uploads/2015/08/Schools-in-Transition-2015.pdf

Pascoe, M. J., Wood, D. L., Duffee, J. H., Kuo, A., Committee on Psychosocial Aspects of Child and Family Health, & Council on Community Pediatrics. (2016, March). Mediators and adverse effects on child poverty in the United States [from the American Academy of Pediatrics Technical Report]. *Pediatrics.* https://doi.org/10.1542/peds.2016-0340

Pierce, C., Carew, J., Pierce-Gonzalez, D., & Wills, D. (1978). An experiment in racism: TV commercials. *Education and Urban Society, 10*(1), 61–87. https://journals.sagepub.com/doi/10.1177/001312457701000105

Potter, G. (2008). Sociocultural diversity and literacy teaching in complex times the challenges for early childhood educators. *Childhood Education, 84*(2), 64–69. https://doi.org/10.1080/00094056.2008.10522975

Poverty Facts. (n.d.). *The population of poverty USA.* https://www.povertyusa.org/facts

Pranis, K. (2012, January 9). *The restorative impulse.* Tikkun: The Prophetic Jewish, Interfaith, & Secular Voice to Heal and Transform the World. https://www.tikkun.org/the-restorative-impulse

Preston, J. (2018, September 12). "Trauma-sensitive" schools: A new framework for reaching troubled students. *The Chronicle of Evidence-Based Mentoring.* https://www.evidencebasedmentoring.org/trauma-sensitive-schools-a-new-framework-for-reaching-troubled-students/

Quillian, L., Pager, D., Midtbøen, A. H., & Hexel, O. (2017, October 17). Hiring discrimination against Black Americans hasn't declined in 25 years. *Harvard Business Review.* https://hbr.org/2017/10/hiring-discrimination-against-black-americans-hasnt-declined-in-25-years

Richards, J. (2018, September 4). *How restorative justice helps students learn.* George Lucas Educational Foundation. https://www.edutopia.org/article/how-restorative-justice-helps-students-learn

Riester-Wood, T. (2015, September 9). *Peers supporting in inclusive school climate.* Inclusive Schools Network. https://inclusiveschools.org/peers-supporting-an-inclusive-school-climate/

Robinson, S., & Truscott, J. (2014). *Belonging and connection of school students with disability.* Children with Disability Australia.

Roche, J. (n. d.). *Children need caring adults, a chance to make mistakes to succeed in life.* ACES Too High News. https://acestoohigh.com/2015/04/28/children-need-caring-adults-a-chance-to-make-mistakes-to-succeed-in-life/

Rochester-Monroe Anti-Poverty Initiative. (2018, December 11). *U.S. census data show Rochester poverty rate and child poverty rate increases.* https://www.actrochester.org/tinymce/source//Census%20Update%202018.pdf

Rossen, E. (n.d.) Unconditional positive regard and effective school discipline. *Oxford Clinical Psychology.* https://www.oxfordclinicalpsych.com/page/effective-school-discipline/featured-article-unconditional-positive-regard-and-effective-school-discipline

Russell, S. T., & Fish, J. N. (2016, May 31). Mental health in lesbian, gay, bisexual, and transgender (LGBT) youth. *Annual Review of Clinical Psychology, 12,* 465–487. https://doi.org/10.1146/annurev-clinpsy-021815-093153

Russell, S. T., Ryan, C., Toomey, R. B., Diaz, R. M., & Sanchez, J. (2011). Lesbian, gay, bisexual, and transgender adolescent school victimization: Implications for young adult health and adjustment. *Journal of School Health, 81*(5), 223–230. https://doi.org/10.1111/j.1746-1561.2011.00583.x

Ryan, C. L. (2010). *"How do you spell family?": Literacy, heteronormativity, and young children of lesbian mothers.* (Doctoral dissertation, Ohio State University).

Ryan, C. L., & Hermann-Wilmarth, J. M. (2018). *Reading the rainbow: LGBTQ-inclusive literacy instruction in the elementary classroom.* Teachers College Press.

Ryndak, D. L., Jackson, L., & Billingsley, F. (2000, May). Defining school inclusion for students with moderate to severe disabilities: What do experts say? *Exceptionality, 8*(2), 101–116. http://doi.org/10.1207/S15327035EX0802_2

Ryscavage, P. (1995, August). A surge in growing income inequality? *Monthly Labor Review.* https://www.bls.gov/opub/mlr/1995/08/art5full.pdf

Ryssdal, K. (n.d.). Rochester looks to rebuild from the rubble: Can manufacturing save America? [Radio installment]. *How the Deck Is Stacked.* Reported in conjunction with Frontline and PBS NewsHours. http://longform.marketplace.org/can-manufacturing-save-america

Sahadi, J. (2016, August 18). *The richest 10% hold 76% of the wealth.* CNNMoney. https://money.cnn.com/2016/08/18/pf/wealth-inequality/

Santoro, D. A. (2018). *Demoralized: Why teachers leave the profession they love and how they can stay.* Harvard Education Press.

Schickedanz, J. A., & Marchant, C. (2018). *Inside preK classrooms: A school leader's guide to effective instruction.* Harvard Education Press.

Schumacher, C. (2015, June 26). *Re-claiming a moral profession in unethical times.* Huffington Post. https://www.huffpost.com/entry/re-claiming-a-moral-profession-in-unethical-times_b_7147126

Semega, J., Kollar, M., Creamer, J., & Mohanty, A. (2019, September). *Income and poverty in the United States: 2018.* United States Census Bureau. https://www.census.gov/content/dam/Census/library/publications/2019/demo/p60–266.pdf

Sentencing Project. (2017, December 12). *Black disparities in youth incarceration.* https://www.sentencingproject.org/publications/black-disparities-youth-incarceration/

Shalaby, C. (2017). *Troublemakers: Lessons in freedom from young children at school.* The New Press.

Shapiro, D., Dundar, A., Huie, F., Wakhungu, P., Yuan, X., Nathan, A., & Hwang, Y. A. (2017, April). *A national view of student attainment rates by race and ethnicity—Fall 2010 cohort* (Signature Report No. 12b). National Student Clearinghouse Research Center.

Sheats, K. J., Irving, S. M., Mercy, J. A., Simon, T. R., Crosby, A. E., Ford, D. C., Merrick, M. T., Annor, F. B., & Morgan, R. E. (2018). Violence-related disparities experienced by Black youth and young adults: Opportunities for prevention. *American Journal of Preventive Medicine, 55*(4), 462–469. https://doi.org/10.1016/j.amepre.2018.05.017

Sherman, D. K., Bunyan, D. P., Creswell, J. D., & Jaremka, L. M. (2009). Psychological vulnerability and stress: The effects of self-affirmation on sympathetic nervous system responses to naturalistic stressors. *Health Psychology, 28*(5), 554–562. http://doi.org/10.1037/a0014663

Sherman, D. K., Hartson, K. A., Binning, K. R., Prudie-Vaughns, V., Garcia, J., Taborsky-Barba, S., ...& Cohen, G. L. (2013). Deflecting the trajectory and changing the narrative: How self-affirmation affects academic performance and motivation under identity threat. *Journal of Personality and Social Psychology, 104*(4), 591–618. http://doi.org/10.1037/a0031495

Siciliano, C. (2013, March 28). *Christianity and the parental rejection of LGBT youth* [Blog]. Huffington Post. https://www.huffingtonpost.com/carl-siciliano/christianity-and-the-parental-rejection-of-lgbt-youth_b_2966849.html

Skiba, R. J., Chung, C.-G., Trachok, M., Baker, T. L., Sheya, A., & Hughes, R. L. (2014, August). Parsing disciplinary disproportionality: Contributions of infraction, student, and school characteristics to out-of-school suspension and expulsion. *American Education Research Journal, 51*(4), 640–670. https://doi.org/10.3102/0002831214541670

Skiba, R. J., & Rausch, M. K. (2006). Zero tolerance, suspension, and expulsion: Questions of equity and effectiveness. In C. M. Evertson & C. S. Weinstein (Eds.), *Handbook of classroom management: Research, practice, and contemporary issues* (pp. 1063–1089). Erlbaum.

Smith, D., Frey, N., Pumpian, I., & Fisher, D. (2017). *Building equity: Policies and practices to empower all learners.* ASCD.

Snipes, J., Fancsali, C., & Stoker, G. (2012, August). *Student academic mindset interventions: A review of the current landscape.* Impact International & the Stupski Foundation.

Southern Education Foundation. (2019). *A new majority report bulletin: Low income students now a majority in the nation's public schools.* New Majority Report. https://www.southerneducation.org/what%20we%20do/research/newmajorityreportseries/

Sparkes, M. (2012, January 19). Kodak: 130 years of history. *The Telegraph*. https://www.telegraph.co.uk/finance/newsbysector/retailandconsumer/9024539/Kodak-130-years-of-history.html

Spector, J., & Murphy, J. (2018, February 7). RCSD June graduation rate increases to 51.9 percent; still worst among Big 5. *Democrat and Chronicle*. https://www.democratandchronicle.com/story/news/2018/02/07/rcsd-graduation-rate-increases-51-9-percent-still-worst-among-big-5/315050002/

Spencer, S., Steele, C. M., & Quinn, D. (1999). Stereotype threat and women's math performance. *Journal of Experimental Social Psychology, 35*, 4–28. https://doi.org/10.1006/jesp.1998.1373

Steele, C. M. (1997). A threat in the air: How stereotypes shape intellectual identity and performance. *American Psychologist, 52*(6), 613–629. http://doi.org/10.1037//0003-066x.52.6.613

Steele, C. M. (2010). *Whistling Vivaldi: How stereotypes affect us and what we can do.* W. W. Norton.

Steele, C. M., & Aronson, J. (1995). Stereotype threat and intellectual test performance of African Americans. *Journal of Personality and Social Psychology, 69*(5), 797–811. http://doi.org/10.1037//0022-3514.69.5.797

Stillman, J., & Anderson, L. (2017). *Teaching for equity in complex times: Negotiating standards in a high-performing bilingual school.* Teachers College Press.

Stone, C., Trisi, D., Sherman, A., & Taylor, R. (2018, December 1). *A guide to statistics on historical trends in income inequality.* Center on Budget and Policy Priorities.

Stone, J. (2002). Battling doubt by avoiding practice: The effect of stereotype threat on self-handicapping in White athletes. *Personality and Social Psychology Bulletin, 28*, 1667–1678. https://doi.org/10.1177/014616702237648

Strazzabosco, J. (2018). *Ninety feet under: What poverty does to people.* Word & Deed Publishing.

Stopbullying. (n.d.). *How to prevent bullying.* https://www.stopbullying.gov/prevention/how-to-prevent-bullying

Style, E. (1996, Fall). Curriculum as window and mirror. *Social Science Record, 33*(2), 35–45. https://nationalseedproject.org/images/documents/Curriculum_As_Window_and_Mirror.pdf

Sue, D. W., Capodilupo, C. M., Torino, G. C., Bucceri, J. M., Holder, A. M. B., Nadal, K. L., & Esquilin, M. (2007). Racial microaggressions in everyday life: Implication for clinical practice. *American Psychologist, 62*(4), 271–286. https://doi.org/10.1037/0003-066X.62.4.271

TEAM. (n. d.). *How do mental health conditions affect the LGBTQ+ community?* https://www.myteam.org/lgbtq

Ternus-Bellamy, A. (2017, March 8). Gender-neutral bathrooms are more than symbolic to kids. *Enterprise*. https://www.davisenterprise.com/local-news/different-paths-growing-up-transgender-in-davis-part-2/

Tollenaar, M. S., Beijers, R., Jansen, J., Riksen-Walraven, J. M. A., & de Weerth, C. (2011). Maternal prenatal stress and cortisol reactivity to stressors in human infants. *Stress, 14*(1), 53–65. https://doi.org/10.3109/10253890.2010.499485

Tran, V. (2018, June 19). *Asian Americans are falling through the cracks in data representation and social services*. Urban Wire: Poverty, Vulnerability, and the Safety Net (Urban Institute). https://www.urban.org/urban-wire/asian-americans-are-falling-through-cracks-data-representation-and-social-services

Turner, E. (2019, May 24). *Carter explores what it means to be a community of belonging for people with disabilities*. Vanderbilt Kennedy Center Notables, Vanderbilt Kennedy Center. https://notables.vkcsites.org/2019/05/carter-explores-facets-of-true-belonging-inclusion-of-people-with-disabilities-in-our-communities/

Udesky, L. (2019, February 13). *Shifting the focus from trauma to compassion*. ACEs Too High News. https://acestoohigh.com/?s=shifting+the+focus&submit=Search

Unique's Story [Video]. (n.d.). *Childhood trauma: Changing minds*. U.S. Department of Justice Office of Justice Programs. https://changingmindsnow.org/stories

United Health Foundation. (2016). *America's health rankings annual report: A call to action for individuals and their communities, 2016182*. https://assets.americas healthrankings.org/app/uploads/ahr16-complete-v2.pdf

University of Rochester. (n.d.). *All in at East*. http://www.rochester.edu/news/east-high/

University of Rochester–East High School Educational Partnership Organization. (2019, February). *All in at East: A progress report from the University of Rochester-East High School Educational Partnership Organization*. Center for Urban Education Success. https://www.rochester.edu/warner/cues/wp-content/uploads/2019/02/2955-Warner_East-High-Report-v11.pdf

University of Rochester Center for Urban Education Success. (n.d.a). *Distributed leadership* [Video]. https://www.rochester.edu/warner/cues/videos/

University of Rochester Center for Urban Education Success. (n.d.b). *Distributed leadership* [Video]. https://www.rochester.edu/warner/cues/2018/11/07/video-distributed-leadership/

University of Rochester Center for Urban Education Success. (n.d.c). *Remaking East: The community school* [Video]. https://www.rochester.edu/warner/cues/videos/

University of Rochester Center for Urban Education Success. (n.d.d). *Restorative practices* [Video]. https://www.rochester.edu/warner/cues/videos/

University of Rochester Center for Urban Education Success. (n.d.e). *Teacher leaders*. https://www.rochester.edu/warner/cues/videos/

University of Rochester Center for Urban Education Success. (2017). *Key elements of UR-EPO plan*. https://www.rochester.edu/warner/cues/home/east-epo/key-elements-of-ur-epo-plan/

USDA Food and Nutrition Service. (2019, March 20). Tools for schools: *Focusing on smart snacks*. https://www.fns.usda.gov/school-meals/tools-schools-focusing-smart-snacks

U.S. Bureau of Labor Statistics. (2019, August 16). *Employment and unemployment among youth summary*. https://www.bls.gov/news.release/youth.nr0.htm

U.S. Department of Education. (n.d.). *About IDEA*. https://sites.ed.gov/idea/about-idea/#IDEA-History

U.S. Department of Education. (2016, February). *Racial and ethnic disparities in special education: A multi-year disproportionality analysis by state, analysis category, and race/ethnicity.* Office of Special Education and Rehabilitative Services. https://www2.ed.gov/programs/osepidea/618-data/LEA-racial-ethnic-disparities-tables/index.html

U.S. Department of Education. (2017a). *LGBTQ youth.* https://www.stopbullying.gov/at-risk/groups/lgbt/index.html

U.S. Department of Education. (2017b). *A snapshot on bullying in America.* https://www.stopbullying.gov/sites/default/files/2017-10/stop-bullying-infographic.pdf

U.S. Department of Education. (2018). *Digest of education statistics, 2016* (NCES 2017-094, chap. 2). National Center for Education Statistics.

U.S. Department of Education. (2019). *The condition of education 2019.* National Center for Education Statistics.

U.S. Department of Health and Human Services. (2017, August). *Bullying as an Adverse Childhood Experience (ACE).* https://www.stopbullying.gov/sites/default/files/2017-10/bullying-as-an-ace-fact-sheet.pdf

U.S. Department of Health and Human Services. (2018). *Physical activity guidelines for all Americans* (2nd ed). https://health.gov/sites/default/files/2019-09/Physical_Activity_Guidelines_2nd_edition.pdf

Vander Ark, T., & Ryerse, M. (2017, March 27). Embedding SEL across the curriculum. *Education Week.* https://blogs.edweek.org/edweek/on_innovation/2017/03/embedding_sel_across_the_curriculum.html

Vawter, E. (2016, February 17). *Microaggressions hurt young teens more than you realize* [Video]. sheknows. https://www.sheknows.com/parenting/articles/1072663/microaggressions-hurt-young-teens-more-than-you-realize-video

Verschelden, C. (2017). *Bandwidth recovery: Helping students reclaim cognitive resources lost to poverty, racism, and social marginalization.* Stylus.

Vygotsky, L. S. (1930). *Mind and society.* Harvard University Press. http://www.unilibre.edu.co/bogota/pdfs/2016/mc16.pdf

Vygotsky, L. S. (1978). *Mind in society: The development of higher psychological processes* (M. Cole, V. John-Steiner, S. Scribner, & E. Souberman, Eds.). Harvard University Press.

Walker, T. (2014a, November 2). *NEA survey: Nearly half of teachers consider leaving profession due to standardized testing.* NEAToday. http://neatoday.org/2014/11/02/nea-survey-nearly-half-of-teachers-consider-leaving-profession-due-to-standardized-testing-2/

Walker, T. (2014b, September 2). *The testing obsession and the disappearing curriculum.* NEAToday. http://neatoday.org/2014/09/02/the-testing-obsession-and-the-disappearing-curriculum-2/

Walsh, M. E., Madaus, G. F., Raczek, A. E., Dearing, E., Foley, C., An, C., Lee-St. John, T. J., & Beaton, A. (2014). A new model for student support in high-poverty urban elementary schools: Effects on elementary and middle school academic outcomes. *American Educational Research Journal, 51*(4), 704–737. https://doi.org/10.3102/0002831214541669

Welcoming Schools. (n.d.). *Definitions to help understand gender and sexual orientation for educators and parents/guardians.* Human Rights Campaign Foundation. https://static1.squarespace.com/static/5beb22573917ee0ad11974b0/t/5d9cf48e 1bb19027b0196bc4/1570567311051/GlossaryForGradeSchoolers2018.pdf

White, A. (2019, January 23). *Inclusion: Helping all students belong in your classroom.* https://go.magoosh.com/schools-blog/inclusion-helping-all-students-belong-in-your-classroom

Whitehouse, E., & Shafer, M. (2017, March 9). *State policies on physical activity in schools.* The Council of State Governments. http://knowledgecenter.csg.org/kc/content/state-policies-physical-activity-schools

Wilkinson, R., & Pickett, K. (2010). *The spirit level: Why greater equality makes societies stronger.* Bloomsbury Press.

Williams, J. J., Paunesku, D., Haley, B., & Sohl-Dickstein, J. (2013). Measurably increasing motivation in MOOCs. *Proceedings of the First Workshop on Massive Open Online Courses* (16th Annual Conference on Artificial Intelligence in Education, Memphis, TN).

Wilson, C. (2011, May 6). The reluctant transgender role model. *New York Times.* https://www.nytimes.com/2011/05/08/fashion/08CHAZ.html

Winn, M. T. (2018). *Justice on both sides: Transforming education through restorative justice.* Harvard Education Press.

Witnessing violence can change a kid's mind. (n.d.). Childhood Trauma: Changing Minds. U.S. Department of Justice, Office of Justice Programs. https://changingmindsnow.org/

Witt, H. (2007, July 29). In minority neighborhood, kids' risk of cancer soars. *Chicago Tribune.* http://www.chicagotribune.com/chi-072907shipchannel-story-story.html

Wyles, L. (2017, May 24). *8 microaggressions your kid could be experiencing at school, but doesn't know how to talk about.* Romper. https://www.romper.com/p/8-microaggressions-your-kid-could-be-experiencing-at-school-but-doesnt-know-how-to-talk-about-59994

Zayas, L. (2015). *Forgotten citizens: Deportation, children, and the making of American exiles and orphans.* Oxford University Press.

Zero to Three. (2017). The basics of infant and early childhood mental health: A briefing paper. https://www.pafec.org/wp-content/uploads/2019/02/The-Basics-of-Infant-and-Early-Childhood-Mental-Health_-A-Briefing-Paper.pdf

Zong, J., Batalova, J., & Hallock, J. (2018, February 8). *Frequently requested statistics on immigrants and immigration in the United States.* Migration Policy Institute. https://www.migrationpolicy.org/article/frequently-requested-statistics-immigrants-and-immigration-united-states-7

ABOUT THE AUTHOR

Cia Verschelden has worked in higher education for more than 3 decades. A residence hall director during her doctoral research, Verschelden also served as a faculty member in social work, sociology, women's studies, American ethnic studies, and nonviolence studies. She was most recently the vice president of academic and student affairs at Malcolm X College in Chicago, Illinois. Her research and writing related to equity in educational opportunity led to publication of her bestselling book directed at faculty, student affairs, and administrators in higher education, *Bandwidth Recovery: Helping Students Reclaim Cognitive Resources Lost to Poverty, Racism, and Social Marginalization* (Stylus, 2017). She has applied the same concept to the pre-K–12 context in this volume. Verschelden holds a BS in psychology from Kansas State University, an MSW from the University of Connecticut, and an EdD from Harvard University.

Race & Diversity books from Stylus Publishing

Building on Resilience
Models and Frameworks of Black Male Success Across the P-20 Pipeline
Edited by Fred A. Bonner II
Foreword by Tim King

Diverse Millennial Students in College
Implications for Faculty and Student Affairs
Edited by Fred A. Bonner II, Aretha F. Marbley, and Mary F. Howard-Hamilton

Answering the Call
African American Women in Higher Education Leadership
Beverly L. Bower and Mimi Wolverton

The Department Chair as Transformative Diversity Leader
Building Inclusive Learning Environments in Higher Education
Edna Chun and Alvin Evans
Foreword by Walter H. Gmelch

Multiculturalism on Campus
Theory, Models, and Practices for Understanding Diversity and Creating Inclusion
Edited by Michael J. Cuyjet, Chris Linder, Mary F. Howard-Hamilton, and Diane L. Cooper

Creating the Path to Success in the Classroom
Teaching to Close the Graduation Gap for Minority, First-Generation, and Academically Unprepared Students
Kathleen F. Gabriel
Foreword by Stephen Carroll

Race & Diversity books from Stylus Publishing

Advancing Black Male Student Success From Preschool Through Ph.D.
Edited by Shaun R. Harper and J. Luke Wood

Contested Issues in Troubled Times
Student Affairs Dialogues on Equity, Civility, and Safety
Edited by Peter M. Magolda, Marcia B. Baxter Magolda and Rozana Carducci
Foreword by Lori Patton Davis

Critical Race Spatial Analysis
Mapping to Understand and Address Educational Inequity
Edited by Deb Morrison, Subini Ancy Annamma, and Darrell D. Jackson

Closing the Opportunity Gap
Identity-Conscious Strategies for Retention and Student Success
Edited by Vijay Pendakur
Foreword by Shaun R. Harper

Beyond Access
Indigenizing Programs for Native American Student Success
Edited by Stephanie J. Waterman, Shelly C. Lowe, and Heather J. Shotton
Foreword by George S. McClellan

Critical Mentoring
A Practical Guide
Torie Weiston-Serdan
Foreword by Bernadette Sánchez

Teaching and Learning books from Stylus Publishing

Of Education, Fishbowls, and Rabbit Holes
Rethinking Teaching and Liberal Education for an Interconnected World
Jane Fried With Peter Troiano
Foreword by Dawn R. Person

Creating Wicked Students
Designing Courses for a Complex World
Paul Hanstedt

Dynamic Lecturing
Research-Based Strategies to Enhance Lecture Effectiveness
Christine Harrington and Todd Zakrajsek
Foreword by José Antonio Bowen

Designing a Motivational Syllabus
Creating a Learning Path for Student Engagement
Christine Harrington and Melissa Thomas
Foreword by Kathleen F. Gabriel

Course-Based Undergraduate Research
Educational Equity and High-Impact Practice
Edited by Nancy H. Hensel
Foreword by Cathy N. Davidson

Creating Engaging Discussions
Strategies for "Avoiding Crickets" in Any Size Classroom and Online
Jennifer H. Herman and Linda B. Nilson
Foreword by Stephen D. Brookfield

Teaching and Learning books from Stylus Publishing

A Concise Guide to Teaching With Desirable Difficulties
Diane Cummings Persellin and Mary Blythe Daniels
Foreword by Mary-Ann Winkelmes

Hitting Pause
65 Lecture Breaks to Refresh and Reinforce Learning
Gail Taylor Rice
Foreword by Kevin Barry

Connected Teaching
Relationships, Power, and Mattering in Higher Education
Harriet L. Schwartz
Foreword by Laurent A. Daloz
Afterword by Judith V. Jordan

POGIL
*An Introduction to Process Oriented Guided Inquiry Learning
for Those Who Wish to Empower Learners*
Edited by Shawn R. Simonson

Teaching as the Art of Staging
A Scenario-Based College Pedagogy in Action
Anthony Weston
Foreword by Peter Felten

Project-Based Learning in the First Year
Beyond All Expectations
Edited by Kristin K. Wobbe and Elisabeth A. Stoddard
Foreword by Randall Bass

Advancing Black Male Student Success From Preschool Through Ph.D.

Edited by Shaun R. Harper and J. Luke Wood

"Harper and Wood have provided a timely and definitive text that offers rich conceptual, empirical, and practical analysis on Black males and education. This book explains the challenges Black boys and men encounter in pursuit of education and offers meaningful ways to disrupt these troubling trends. It is mandatory reading for scholars, practitioners, and policymakers."—*Tyrone C. Howard*, *Professor and Director, UCLA Black Male Institute*

White Teachers/Diverse Classrooms, Second Edition

Creating Inclusive Schools, Building on Students' Diversity, and Providing True Educational Equity

Edited by Julie G. Landsman and Chance W. Lewis

"The second edition of *White Teachers / Diverse Classrooms* adds seven essays to 14 of the original chapters. In the first edition, the editors selected essays about pedagogical methods that might close the achievement gap between white and African American students. The new edition contains seven articles describing approaches for teachers working with Latino, Asian, or Native American students. Summing Up: Recommended."—**Choice**

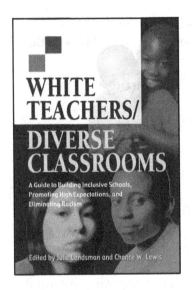

White Teachers/Diverse Classrooms, DVD-ROM

Teachers and Students of Color Talk Candidly about Connecting with Black Students and Transforming Educational Outcomes

Edited by Julie G. Landsman and Chance W. Lewis

The Poverty and Education Reader

A Call for Equity in Many Voices

Edited by Paul C. Gorski and Julie Landsman

"*The Poverty and Education Reader* is a top pick for teachers and educators, as well as social issues readers, and packs in essays, memoirs and poetry with the idea of analyzing the schooling experience of poor and working-class students. Low-income family experiences are targeted with the idea of profiling proven strategies teachers and schools have used for closing educational gaps, and contributions come from a range of writers, from teachers and students to parents and scholars, discussing views of poor students and their families and approaches that have made a difference. Don't consider this a 'fix' for poor students: look at it as a series of articles on ways youth is alienated by education practices—and

how to overcome this with new school and classroom routines."—**Midwest Book Review**

Critical Mentoring

A Practical Guide

Torie Weiston-Serdan

Foreword by Bernadette Sánchez

"*Critical Mentoring* is a savory blend of theories, thoughtful concepts, and evidence. Perhaps its practical utility is the book's most praiseworthy feature. Readers learn not only what this unique brand of mentoring is but also how to more effectively develop and support youth, particularly those who are often pushed to the margins." —**Shaun R. Harper,** *Professor and Executive Director, University of Pennsylvania Center for the Study of Race & Equity in Education*

22883 Quicksilver Drive
Sterling, VA 20166-2019   Subscribe to our e-mail alerts: www.Styluspub.com